Picking Up the Linen Threads

Picking Up the Linen Threads

A Study in Industrial Folklore

by Betty Messenger

Blackstaff Press

Published by Blackstaff Press Limited, 3 Galway Park, Dundonald, Belfast BT 16 BT16 OAN.

First published in 1978 by the University of Texas Press, with the assistance of the Andrew W. Mellon Foundation.

ISBN 0 85640 210 9
Printed in the United States of America

Grateful acknowledgment is made to the following for permission to use material as specified:

David W. Bleakley, for material from his M.A. thesis, "Trade Union Beginnings in Belfast and District with Special Reference to the Period 1881–1900, and to the Work of the Belfast and District United Trades' Council during That Period" (Queen's University, Belfast, 1955).

David Hammond of the British Broadcasting Corporation in Belfast, for eight lines of a song beginning "Hold her on," from a recording in the BBC files; and for five verses of a song beginning "Oh, do you know her," from Hugh Quinn, "Notes to Children's Street Tunes and Games of Old Belfast," typescript at the BBC in Belfast.

Mourne Observer Press, for four lines of a song beginning "Och it's aisy knowin' the flowerers," from W. J. Fitzpatrick, *An Old-Timer Talking*, 2d ed. rev. (Newcastle, Co. Down: Mourne Observer Press, 1963).

Nora Connolly O'Brien, for four lines of a song beginning "Cheer up, Connolly," from her book *Portrait of a Rebel Father* (Dublin: Talbot Press, 1935).

Public Record Office of Northern Ireland, for the contract of work between employees and management (D.1882/2/1), by permission of the Deputy Keeper.

Textile Times International, Belfast, Northern Ireland, for four lines of a song beginning "My love, she is a doffer," from the *Linen Trade Circular*, 13 November 1965.

Dorothy M. Wadsworth, for material from a letter to the author, 9 January 1975.

To William McKee of Killyleagh,
a linen worker, historian, and friend;
the late Dr. James Ryan,
who knew so well the workers he served;
and James Vitty,
a very special kind of librarian

Contents

Illustrations

PHOTOS

FIGURES

Acknowledgments

I wish to express my deep appreciation, first and foremost, to the many men and women at operative and management levels, mostly retired, who by relating their experiences to me made this study a fruitful one.

I am also indebted to the individuals still engaged in making linen who were willing to discuss with me special facets of production; to those who, though not directly connected with the industry, supplied me with contacts and leads; to members of the teaching staff at The Queen's University of Belfast who arranged gatherings, the purpose of which was to enable me to converse with scholars with related interests; and to the "backbenchers" with whom I frequently drank coffee and who provided me with the opportunity to discuss my research problems in a relaxed fashion. Of the scores of persons who so kindly responded to my call for photographs, I can mention here by name only those who, acting in a private capacity, supplied the pictures I was actually able to use in this book, namely: Mrs. Sarah Dixon, Mrs. Ethel Dodds, Mrs. Theresa Grimley, Mrs. Mary Johnston, Mrs. Agnes E. McAuley, Mrs. Fred Morrison, Mrs. Margaret Smyth, Mr. and Mrs. William Topping, Mr. Charles Morrison, and Mr. John Weatherup.

During the course of my study, I toured Killyleagh Flax Spinning Company Ltd., The Ulster Weaving Company Ltd., The New Northern Spinning and Weaving Company Ltd., William Ewart & Son Ltd., and Hilden Mill of Barbour Threads Ltd., and I wish to thank the persons who gave me permission to do so and others in those firms who took time away from their own work to answer my questions and to guide me through the mills and factories. Miss Dorothy Wadsworth and Mr. Alexander Finlay were particularly giving of their time. I am grateful, also, for the resource materials supplied me by interested individuals in still other firms, namely, John Andrews & Company Ltd., Bessbrook Spinning Company Ltd., Edenderry Spinning Company Ltd., and Spence Bryson and Company Ltd.

I was extended every courtesy by numerous institutions in Northern Ireland, and I am extremely thankful for the offers of help and for assistance provided by concerned persons at the Linen Hall Library, the Belfast Charitable Society, the Belfast Public Library, the library and other units of The Queen's University of Belfast, the Lambeg Industrial Research Association, The National Trust, the British Broadcasting Corporation, the Ministry of Commerce, the Linen Export Board, the Ulster Folk and Transport Museum, and the Ulster Museum. In Dublin, I was accorded every politeness at the Irish Folklore Commission and the National Library.

Finally, and very importantly, I wish to thank my husband, who shared this undertaking, as everything else, with me enthusiastically.

Introduction

Wonderful times then in the mill.
You got a wee drink, got a join, done your work,
and you had your company, and you got peace to do it.
It didn't matter whether you were up at six o'clock
in the mornin' or not. You got through. (#53)[1]

Fifty years ago the production of linen was the principal industry of Northern Ireland. Today, although it is a vital part of the economy, the industry is marked by mergings, diversification of efforts, and the closing down of many mills and factories, and one can rarely, if ever, see in the countryside fields of ripening flax or distinguish on the streets of cities and towns the linen workers from those laboring at other jobs.

Many of the structures in which yarn was spun and cloth was woven may now be abandoned or diverted to other industrial purposes, but the tall chimneys, so much a feature of flax spinning mills, and the saw-tooth roofs that were characteristic of weaving sheds in linen factories identify the sites where the manufacturing activities once flourished. The buildings themselves remain cold and formidable and help to perpetuate the image of the "dark, Satanic mill" which, it is said, has dominated the visual reconstruction of the industrial revolution.[2] Although the image is based in large measure on transformations noted in the cotton industry in England, it could well have emerged from close observation of changes in the manufacture of linen in Northern Ireland, where conditions and developments were similar in many ways.

Earlier "catastrophic" views of the effects of the industrial revolution on the lives of those most directly involved have, since Victorian times, been disputed, debated, and modified to a degree, but in Ireland, at least, their lasting influence has been to direct attention of most observers of the linen scene toward the negative features of the industry. There, the biases and values of legislators, government officials, and those who, in their capacities as labor leaders, doctors, and reformers, came in contact with the industry only tangentially permeate the writings and tend to set the dominant gloomy tone so pervasive of the literature. There is no need to question the zeal or direction of their endeavors or certain positive achievements that resulted from their dedicated efforts. But it should be pointed out that what is missing from their reports and other accounts hitherto presented is the overall perspective of the men and women who did the bulk of the work in transforming flax into linen cloth.

Lengthy narrations purporting to be reflections of workers about numerous facets of their laboring days, similar to that made in England in the 1860s by the Journeyman Engineer,[3] do not exist for the linen industry, and scattered brief reminiscences, found in various trade journals and newspaper feature articles over the years, do not yield all the missing portions of the picture of life in flax spinning mills and linen weaving factories. A rounded reconstruction of what it was like to be a linen worker in Northern Ireland during most of the nineteenth century is, of course, unattainable, for the people who could best tell the story are now deceased. But it is possible to speak with numerous persons who labored in the early decades of this century and to recover a wide range of reactions to their work experiences. My own quest not only led to the discovery of additional examples of objectionable aspects of the factory system everywhere during this era but also revealed a new and brighter dimension to the usual picture. The harsh conditions in mills and factories, stressed so often in the past as well as today by outsiders or those with a reformist bent, are not the only features of the work experience remembered by the operatives themselves. What the men and women who were employed in the linen industry in Northern Ireland often focused upon in their conversations with me—and, important to note, what industrial workers in certain other eras and places may also have deemed to be of importance to their working lives—provides the framework upon which this book is built.

I have written the book primarily to document the folklore of an industry. Its form and contents serve best the interests of folklorists. Nevertheless, it contains themes, sometimes only implied, which are relevant to the concerns of at least two other groups of scholars—historians and students of industrial relations. To each group, in turn, I pointedly address a few remarks before I take up my main thesis.

"All historians look at the past through the spectacles of the present; those who believe themselves to be totally 'objective' are often the most naïve in their acceptance of the values of the world in which they live."[4] Until recently, historians who have attempted to assess the effects of industrialism on the lives of ordinary working-class people, both inside the industrial plant and at home, have, typically, relied on quantitative evidence or that obtained from more subjective written sources (novels, travelers' accounts, official reports relating conditions, and the like), supplied by persons who neither participated fully in the work experience—or, if they did, appear to have been somewhat atypical of those they described—nor inquired into more than a limited aspect of it. They have interpreted their data (already filtered through the minds of outsiders looking in) from the perspective of people living, for the most part, in both another age and another social milieu and, thus, in an even more disadvantageous position to empathize with the workers whose lives they seek to understand. Then they have made judgments about the relative well-being of those individuals during the years under scrutiny.

Much of what has been written on this subject pertains to occurrences in England between 1790 and 1840. In his excellent review of the literature, E. P. Thompson makes it quite clear that, if it has been difficult for historians to agree about the exact nature of changes in the "standard-of-life" of laborers who joined the industrial work force during those years, it has been even more difficult for them to arrive at a consensus regarding alterations in the "way-of-life" of the same workers in that era.[5] The specific topics explored and the arguments advanced by scholars investigating the concomitants of industrialization in succeeding decades up to the present are not precisely those over which historians writing about the years immediately following the industrial revolution have deliberated, but they touch upon the same basic issues; similarly, the question of whether people have found adequate satisfactions as a result of their employment under the factory system of production remains a thorny one. My own study was not designed to furnish information that might be of use to researchers who have assumed opposing intellectual stances in the matter. It was undertaken with little more in mind, initially, than to learn about an industry through its folklore. Despite this fact, I feel that a number of my findings, derived from hundreds of interviews with men and women who were allowed to associate freely about numerous facets of their working lives, have a bearing on the broad topic which has engaged the attention of those scholars. To be more specific, my data seem to cast a shadow over the validity of some of the more pessimistic statements that have been made regarding the overall quality of life of many workers. In particular, they suggest that certain features, characteristic of most textile industries until relatively recently and consistently viewed as highly reprehensible by outside observers, were not regarded in quite such a negative light by many linen workers in the first decades of this century and were not as detrimental to their "happiness" (that elusive quality) on the job as most critics of the industrial system have assumed. I am thinking now especially of such things as child labor and the fact of men, women, and children working in a far from ideal environment.

In the pages that follow, I do not intend to argue the point directly. Readers who are so inclined can evaluate what is reported and draw their own conclusions as to whether the claim I have just made is a plausible one, both as it pertains to the workers I discuss and as it may apply to textile workers elsewhere and at other times. I hasten to add, however, that, while seeming to place myself on the side of those who have interpreted the effects of the industrial factory system in a somewhat more positive way than have certain of their fellow researchers, I am not denying the facts (judged by today's standards) of long hours, low wages, unhealthy work areas, inadequate safeguards on machinery, authoritarian foremen, autocratic management, and highly restrictive regulations governing behavior on the job, all of which smack of "exploitation" and "slave labor" to most outsiders.[6] Both male and female employees themselves recognized the imperfect conditions under which they labored. I am asserting that, imbued with an ethic which exalted work well done and comparing their lot with that of their predecessors and of persons employed at certain other jobs, the linen workers, by and large, did not feel completely oppressed by those conditions. If they could not physically avoid the harsh realities of mill and factory life, they could and did find ways to mitigate their damaging effects.

I am well aware that the degree to which workers responded affirmatively and found satisfactions in their daily routines varied according to whether they were male or female and according to the type of job at which they labored. Simply stated, women (and children), in general, appear to have been happier at their work than men, and, among the former, those in the wet-spinning rooms were the happiest. The reasons for the diverse reactions are numerous and complex. Some of them are stated explicitly in the chapters of this book which deal specifically with the lore of spinners, hacklers, and weavers. Others are only implied, especially in comments I make when trying to account for differences in the amount and kind of folklore that characterized each work area. All of them were suggested to me by the statements of those I interviewed and should be of interest to the second group of researchers, namely certain sociologists and other students of industrial relations who have also delved into the matter of worker satisfaction, although for different reasons.

In their search for factors making for satisfaction on the job and, consequently, industrial peace, such researchers have been led to investigate, among other things, the status hierarchy among workers and prestige symbols attached to each job in an industrial plant, the effects on an individual of repetitive and monotonous labor, worker solidarity, and interactions between foremen and their subordinates. In trying to understand the full significance of their traditions to each group of linen workers I studied, I had cause to reflect upon the same topics. Out of my reflections came a realization that there was a direct connection between the industrial folklore I was collecting and job satisfaction.

Everett Hughes some years back set forth as an aim of industrial sociologists "to penetrate more deeply into the personal and social drama of work, to understand the social and social psychological arrangements by which men make their work tolerable or even make it glorious to themselves and others."[7] Viewing my data in the light of his remark, one can see that the folklore of an industry both reflects some of those arrangements and is itself one such device. To illustrate: the words to the song on page 65 reveal that there were friendly competitions between spinners in different rooms which helped to make the performance of specific tasks less distasteful; the actual singing of the verse served to lighten the load of any chore which it accompanied. As well, "joins" (pp. 184–185) seemed to shorten a working day, particularly a Monday, and the use of nicknames (Figure 1) helped to enforce a satisfying camaraderie among the hacklers.

Anthropologists and anthropologically trained folklorists, expressing it in a slightly different way, have long held what I have just pointed out: that folklore (1) mirrors the culture of which it is a part and (2) serves a vital function in helping to maintain that culture. In their research they have used folklore as a tool in both senses. Students of industrial relations have discovered that the creation of opportunities for pleasing social relationships does as much to allay worker discontent as does the bringing about of other types of reform in the industrial milieu, but they have given little indication that they recognize the role played by the folklore in helping to build that satisfying social environment. I have tried in these introductory remarks to alert them to the possible value of combining folkloristic evidence with other types of supportive data in their studies. I will not, however, in succeeding chapters develop arguments that relate specifically to their work.

I began the research which has led to the writing of this book abruptly, without an opportunity to acquire prior information about technical aspects of the industry or to acquaint myself beforehand with any part of its long history. The usual kind of difficulties I had anticipated having while trying to assemble a body of lore completely unfamiliar to me and then present it in a meaningful way—some of which are recounted in Chapter 1, in which I state my intentions and outline the methods I used to collect my material—were compounded by those basic gaps in my knowledge. I hope to spare readers the same experience; Chapter 2 provides the means. In it, I present a brief historical overview of the industry and a description of the processing of flax as it passes through a variety of industrial firms. The subcultures of the spinners, hacklers, and weavers, revealed through an analysis of the folklore transmitted in their respective work areas, are, in turn, depicted in the next three chapters, while folklore less definitely bound to a particular place is described in the one which follows; those four chapters form the core of this volume. Although, for illustrative purposes, I have sometimes had to draw upon material relating to the production of textiles in England, rather than in Ireland, I have done so in order to indicate what I consider to be the long-standing nature of certain attitudes and practices prevalent in the linen industry of Northern Ireland in the early 1900s. The fact of that persistence is of interest in itself, but, in addition and by implication, and if the parallels I perceive between the experiences of workers in England and Ireland are valid ones, it suggests—brashly, given the numerous variables that would have to be taken into account— that roughly similar conditions may well have provoked roughly similar responses on the part of textile workers elsewhere, past and present. I have also made reference in Chapters 3 through 6 to analogues for some of the lore of the linen workers. For example, in a note, I point to a close resemblance between the words to the song which appears on page 106 and those which have been reported as having been sung elsewhere. Omissions in this regard can be attributed in part to my inability to find suitable analogues but in larger measure to my feeling that, too often, those that are presented in folklore studies are more imagined than real.

Much more solid research is required before meaningful generalizations can be made about the relationship between folklore and industry. The final chapter of this volume includes a few guidelines for those who, stimulated by my work or for other reasons, attempt to provide the necessary comparative data.

Picking Up the Linen Threads

ONE
Research Context

Over twenty years ago, Peter Opie expressed a wish "that someone would study the lore of industrial Britain."[1] Ten years ago,
A. L. Lloyd in *Folk Song in England* repeated the call, asking for
systematic research

> [in order that] a rich store of folklore native to the industrial
> proletariat, including material being created in our own
> time, may be brought to light. The matter concerns not only
> songs, in fact, but also tales, proverbs, customs, beliefs,
> craft-slang, and other speechways, and oral history in the
> form of personal reminiscences of great or lesser events of
> working class life. Properly organized and carried out, such
> an enterprise could produce valuable materials for histori-
> ans, social scientists, writers, musicians, and the like, clearly
> enough, but its supreme importance is in its service to the
> working class itself, in drawing together the scattered and
> hidden bits of the industrial community's heritage, and in
> stimulating the continuation of workers' creative traditions.
> As yet, the working class itself is only dimly aware of the ex-
> tent and value of its own home-made culture, because the
> thing has never been properly looked into and publicized.[2]

In response, I undertook to assemble such a body of lore in a part
of the world which, over the years, I had come to know well. By so
doing, I hoped to show that industrialization does not necessarily
cause the disappearance of oral and material folklore but may actually provide the climate in which lore of various kinds may
flourish.

American folklorists are no longer bound by narrow concep-
tions of who and what constitute "folk" and "folklore." But if
many of them now recognize the possibility of collecting lore in
an urban milieu, few have actually extended the locus of their re-

search to the city. And the work of those who have is still characterized by a tendency on the part of the researcher to think in
terms of retentions or to emphasize the continuity of traditions of
city folk with their rural and ethnic backgrounds. Adopting what
is considered to be a somewhat newer approach, I concentrate on
folklore arising from the experiences of people laboring in an
environment associated with the urban scene and only incidentally explore rural antecedents; most transfer of culture that I
explore is that from street to industrial plant.

The modern linen industry in Northern Ireland is largely an
urban phenomenon, and so the oral and material traditions with
which I deal fall within the rubric of urban folklore. Because,
however, some production of linen was carried on outside of
cities and, more important, my major contextual concern is not
the centers in which spinning mills and weaving factories were
located but, instead, the places of work themselves, my study is
more accurately described as an investigation of industrial
folklore.

Archie Green in *Only a Miner* has grappled ably with the problem of appropriate terminology for this kind of study, made some
useful distinctions, and provided some workable definitions.[3]
Here, it is sufficient to point out that I reserve the term *industrial
folklore* for those traditions—the conventional genres of the
folklorist plus personal narratives—directly associated, in both a
formative and a performative way, with an economic enterprise
that is characterized by large-scale production of goods, extensive mechanization of the production system, and, often, large
factory organization. Lore connected mainly with domestic production or that reflecting facets of workers' lives other than their
jobs does not fall within the category as I conceptualize it.
Moreover, in agreement with Green, I do not consider most oc-
cupational lore—that of cowboys, sailors, farmers, lumberjacks,
tailors, and the like—to be industrial folklore.

If industrial folklore is thus narrowly defined, there can be said
to be almost no full-scale studies by American folklorists which
examine in depth a variety of traditions linked to a single industry. Obvious exceptions are the highly regarded volumes of
George Korson and Mody Boatright,[4] who, however, did not attempt to tie the traditional material they collected so firmly and
closely to the daily routine of its bearers as I do. Nor have they

dealt with industries whose lore invites really meaningful comparisons with that relating to the production of linen under the factory system.

In fact, when one examines the literature for studies concerned with industrial developments in textiles of any kind, it soon becomes apparent that folklorists have closely scrutinized only one genre—folksong. So I must restrict myself here to commenting on a few of the more relevant statements that have been made in some of the major works about "labor songs" and "industrial songs"—in the sense in which Green employs those terms[5]—even though the lore of the linen workers, reported on in pages that follow, is far more inclusive.

John Greenway, for instance, considers the songs of laborers in cotton mills and factories in his somewhat specialized study, *American Folksongs of Protest*, and notes the large number of excellent songs which emanated from groups of organized workers in that textile industry. In Northern Ireland, where unionization in most segments of the linen industry came about relatively late and where religious differences often prevented workers from uniting against management, there are found few songs reflecting labor unrest and strike activity among linen workers. But at least one of the principal factors that Greenway cites as contributing to the abundance and quality of such songs of protest in America—the type of strong singing tradition which existed among the people who furnished much of the labor force[6]—probably helps explain the number, if not the type, of industrial songs in Northern Ireland. What he considers a lesser cause, but one which I examine in depth, is the nature of the work itself: "The textile worker is properly a machine tender whose duties are mechanical and monotonous; such work has already been conducive to singing simple, rhythmic, inconsequential songs. Fitting union words to these songs is almost a subconscious process. As the worker sings or hums a well-integrated melody, the tune is acted upon by the force uppermost in his mind . . ." [7] One who knows the textile industry well would not agree that the duties of all those who labor within it are completely mechanical. The degree to which they are does have some bearing on the varying quantity of lore, including songs, which is found among different groups of workers, however, and is a point I will enlarge upon later.

Greenway treats only one kind of folksong. Lloyd discusses several varieties of industrial work songs—that is, "the kind of vernacular songs made by workers themselves directly out of their own experiences, expressing their own interests and aspirations, and incidentally passed on among themselves mainly by oral means"[8]—a category of song that he feels has been little explored in England.

His own work centers on the musical compositions of miners, but he comments at length upon the singing traditions of workers in the cotton industry as well. Although he analyzes songs recovered from numerous sources other than informants with whom he dealt personally and songs related to both craft and industrial aspects of cotton production, the fact that he describes lore from Yorkshire and from the Northwest of England makes much of what he says particularly relevant to the situation in Northern Ireland.

To illustrate: one can find parallels in Belfast and elsewhere with the singing of hymns by women at their looms, the relatively small amount of singing by men in weaving factories, and the influence of music halls on the songs of English industrial workers in the early 1900s.[9] In fact, David Hammond, well known in the field of Irish folksong, is said to have described the following song (air: "McNamara's Band"), one he had recently heard and then sung at a ballad competition in the 1960s, as being "in the tradition of Belfast mill songs where the makers of the songs borrowed freely from the music hall and the hymn book for their musical sources":

> My love, she is a doffer, she works among the flax,
> And every time I think on her, so help me, God, I'm vexed;
> You know I'm only a tenter, my true love she knows it not;
> And I hope she never hears of it, for I love her a hell of a lot.[10]
> (*Reprinted by permission of Textile Times International,*
> *Belfast, Northern Ireland.*)

It is certainly in the same style as one I encountered, also of obvious music-hall derivation:[11]

> Sorting together up in Greeves',
> Pulling your flax out all day,
> Stand and you talk of your colors so gay,

There you're working there all day.
You call on the fellows; you call him a doll,
You talk of the boys that bring you to the hall,
He holds your hand; gee, isn't love grand?
Sorting together up in Greeves'. (#31)

The reasons advanced by Lloyd for the dearth of tunes accompanying industrial songs in England in the mold of an older folk tradition—a greater urge to make comments in verse than to create melodies, and the employment of well-known airs to speed the circulation of the message contained in the songs[12]—can probably be applied to spinning-mill and linen-factory context as well. I shall not, however, have much to say about the melodies of the songs I introduce in the body of this work, being mainly concerned with the texts as they reveal and explain the subcultures of the workers.

There are differences in length and style between the songs I collected and those that have been reported as originating with textile workers elsewhere; I shall account for some of these later. But I do not intend to consider the artistic merits of the items I include, although Lloyd has done so and has given several reasons for dissimilarities between songs of his workers and those which originated in preindustrial days.[13] His final statements on the subject have some bearing on corresponding lore of the men and women in the linen industry: "For all that, clumsiness and cliché are not the significant marks of industrial folklore. The point of the songs lies in their appropriateness as lyrical statements of the emotional and practical problems of the bearers. In that, many of them are singularly successful."[14]

The implication of his remarks, that by using a socio-historical approach one can arrive at the most meaningful evaluation and interpretation of industrial folksongs, is a point of view with which I agree. The idea is not a novel one. Greenway long ago stressed, in connection with folksong scholarship, the value of studies with social and historical context and emphasis "in man rather than works,"[15] and Green's *Only a Miner* provides one example of the way in which this can be done successfully. The contextual and functional (in the sense of the interrelationship between parts) approach of the work of many folklorists with an anthropological background, regardless of the genre they study, is another, and it has determined the way in which the materials on the following pages are presented. That is, my concern is to describe the settings in which not only songs but the whole corpus of folklore of three groups of linen workers circulated and to relate the traditional materials with these and other aspects of mill and factory subcultures.

The time period encompassed is, roughly speaking, the first three decades of this century, selected because by 1935 technological and social changes had considerably modified the industrial climate that nurtured the kinds of lore which had come to interest me most and because most of the men and women who could provide information about their working lives before 1935 had been initially employed after 1900.

The fact that the texts collected belonged to an era that had passed presented me with certain difficulties. First, most of the details of the context in which the lore circulated had to be reconstructed and could not be observed, although the validity of recollections was increased by questioning numerous people about the same topics. Second, the mills and factories I visited, in order to better acquaint myself with the processing of flax and yarn, and the pieces of equipment I saw in them had been changed in layout or modernized so that they no longer corresponded in many respects to descriptions which had been provided of them, a hindrance to accuracy lessened through my being able to view various photographic collections and machinery exhibited in museums.[16] Third, because I was seeking workers of a certain age, often out of touch with their former workmates, it was the more difficult to acquire an adequate sample.

The problem of locating likely sources of information is, of course, a major hurdle to be overcome by any folklorist. Limited space prevents me from describing in detail the ways in which I solved it and carried out my research. Here, I can point out that, despite a reluctance to work from the top of the linen-manufacturing hierarchy down, for fear of being put in contact only with those sharing management biases, I received invaluable aid from several such individuals, as well as from managers and personnel directors in several mills and factories. Other leads were provided by persons with such diverse occupations as the consulting physician in a home for the elderly, trade-union officials, the owner of a record shop, a former headmistress of a mill school, a doctor who counted large numbers of linen workers among his patients, university professors with relatives in the industry, professional folk singers, shop employees in the neighborhood of mills and factories, a folklorist in touch with mill workers in his church, and reporters who publicized my work.

Compounding the difficulties of finding people to talk to in the first place were those inherent in trying to acquire information from people scattered all over Northern Ireland, in sampling each time new material was obtained, and in working with persons still leading busy lives or whose time was restricted because of institutional rules. I was also hampered by the absence of telephones in many homes, making it difficult for me to arrange or cancel appointments, and by the unsettled nature of the province at the time.[17] The use of postcards to communicate, an acceptance of leisurely Irish attitudes toward time, and spreading my research over several years helped mitigate some of the problems.

Having encountered certain difficulties in establishing rapport when my husband and I studied a peasant community in the Irish Republic, I was somewhat unprepared for, but delighted at, the rapid welcome I was accorded by the people with whom I had chosen to work in Northern Ireland. This, despite my expectation of suspicion on their part, given the state of affairs there. It may well be that the contrast in ease of interaction which I experienced is an indication of a fundamental dissimilarity in attitude and behavior between rural and urban/town dwellers anywhere. In that, there would seem to be certain implications for folklorists as to the desirability of conducting research in one type of community or another. But, having also spent a considerable amount of time visiting and observing in all sections of both parts of the island, I am inclined to believe that the greater candor and sincerity exhibited by those who have dwelt most of their lives in the North may very well reflect a basic difference between them and the Irish in the South, so typically reluctant to share information freely and openly about themselves and many facets of their culture. Whatever the reason, once I established contact, interviews proceeded in an unhampered way.

By the time I finished, I had conducted extensive interviews with eighty-four persons—twenty-four of them males—who had worked in spinning mills and weaving factories, and most of whom came from families of which other members had also been employed in various jobs within the industry. (Scutchers [who worked elsewhere], handloom weavers, persons tangential to the industry, etc., also contacted, are not included in this figure.) Their combined work experience had been in at least thirty-two mills, sixteen of them outside of Belfast, and sixteen factories, of which seven were away from the city. Regrettably, although I ranged as far as places along the southern, western, and eastern boundaries of the province, I could not include all centers of weaving and spinning in the sample. Nor did I find it possible to collect the lore of the bleaching and finishing and the making-up branches of the industry.

Working methods were much the same from the beginning. A first visit, often unannounced, during which I explained myself and my project and assessed the quality of the information which a man or woman could supply, was followed by other visits, during which I employed the tape recorder. Infrequently, conditions were such as to allow recordings to be made during the initial interview.

My most valuable recording sessions resulted when a group of people gathered, usually by chance, and the participants, stimulated by the presence of others who had undergone similar experiences, were able to reconstruct situations from an era which they usually took no pride in recalling on their own. I was helped as well by transcribing interviews as quickly as possible and then carrying around with me in small notebooks, for sampling purposes, new material jotted down in summary form. When I finally reached the stage where I knew more about the industry and its folklore as a whole than did most of the individuals with whom I spoke, I was able to get down to essentials quickly, particularly with new informants. And it was then that I had the added satisfaction of seeing the positive response to me, an outsider, using "their" jargon and singing "their" songs, most of which they had put out of their minds and had not seen fit to share with those outside the trade. This despite the fact that those men and women are part of a broader culture where pride is usually taken in verbal skills and in which there is a strong singing tradition. Still, as Lloyd said, "The working class is only dimly aware of the extent and value of its own home-made culture."[18]

Because it was my desire to let the linen workers reveal what was of importance to them, I began most interviews by directing all with whom I spoke to tell me what it was like to work in mills and factories or to recall as much as they could about any facet of their work experience. I provided leads, initially, only when there was a lull in the train of recollections and, in subsequent interviews, when I wished to determine whether specific practices, learned about elsewhere, existed in their places of work. Repeatedly, certain topics were brought up by particular groups of workers, and it is those concerns that are emphasized here and around which additional explanatory materials are built. The organization imposed upon the data is, of course, my own. It has been necessary to generalize, and what follows is not an exhaustive account of the variations for any one category of behavior. It is, however, unlikely that the average mill or factory employee will be unable to identify in most respects with my portrayal of his or her job.

As for the specific recollections that are quoted at length, they were chosen both because they are typical of attitudes and ideas expressed and because they make the points particularly well or in colorful fashion. It is possible to glean from them some idea of the vocabulary and idiomatic speech employed by numerous persons in Northern Ireland, but I have not tried to reproduce dialect in a way that would be of use to the specialist. Nor have I hesitated to make deletions—often of repetitious speech mannerisms —where I felt the rambling in speech served no purpose essential to this type of study. Furthermore, in a desire not to draw special attention to specific individuals and firms but rather to use the experiences of many persons in such a way as to make them representative of those who labored at similar jobs in mills and factories, I frequently have omitted proper names or have introduced pseudonyms.

Finally, each photograph that appears in this book was selected for one or more of the following reasons: because it illustrates technical features of the industry for which verbal descriptions may prove inadequate; because it captures the essence, if not all the details said to have been typical, of a situation; because it seems to reveal particularly well the personality of a group of workers; because it helps to show either continuities or changes in dress or physical environment in various work areas over the decades covered in this study; because, having been provided by a worker, it very likely mirrors a conception of people or of a job that he or she felt to be accurate; or because, as far as I can determine, it has not been used in other publications.

TWO

Historical & Processing Overview

There is general agreement that little of importance occurred in the areas of linen manufacture or trade in Ireland until the closing decade of the seventeenth century. However, the flax plant and its cultivation had been known since the arrival of the Celts in the first millennium B.C.[1] Suitable conditions for the growing of the crop were present, and it was eventually cultivated throughout the island. From early times there was widespread spinning of yarn—probably by simple distaff and spindle—but relatively little cloth was woven, and most of that was of narrow measure, coarse, and primarily for home consumption.

Although there were efforts made to stimulate the growth of the industry all over the island, steady progress took place only in the North,[2] particularly in the counties of Antrim, Armagh, and Down. By the late 1700s, the linen trade had become concentrated there. The development cannot be attributed to deliberate action on the part of government officials in Ireland and England but resulted from a complex set of circumstances, described ably elsewhere.[3] Because most stages in the production of linen eventually faded away in the South but flourished in the North, it is sufficient to confine a discussion of advances in the industry mainly to the latter area.

Commenting on the situation there—although his remarks are, in general, true of Ireland as a whole at the time—E. R. R. Green says: "Until the eighteenth century the making of linen cloth was still little more than a supplement to the main business of farming. The farmers grew their own flax, and their wives and daughters and servant girls spun it into yarn. And when the men were not busy in the fields they wove the yarn into cloth on the hand-loom. The cloth was bleached at home by slow traditional methods. What the people did not need for themselves was sold to merchants at fairs."[4] In the next 150 years this domestic system, unique to neither Ireland nor linen, was to evolve into a factory mode of production.

Historians have summarized well the economic changes that took place until about 1850; they have detailed social ones less adequately.[5] All the literature—and this holds true for almost everything that has been written about textile industries elsewhere —has certain limitations. Authors too often employ indiscriminately the words *mill*, where spinning takes place, and *factory*, where weaving is done, making it difficult for one to follow development in the separate ends of the industry. And even social historians have not clearly differentiated between men and women when they have noted the numbers of and roles played by workers as they moved from their homes into those mills and factories. Certain omissions in my own brief review of the period can be attributed, in part, to these things.

The first three quarters of the eighteenth century were marked by the growing use of the spinning wheel, the growth in number of markets where flax and yarn could be obtained to meet increasing demands, and the weaving of wider measures, better grades, and greater variety of cloth. Some farmer/weavers acquired the means to invest in surplus yarn and looms and hired others to weave for or in conjunction with them. In certain instances, the work was done on the premises of the, at first, very small "manufacturers"; more often, under the *putting-out system*, the weavers wove yarn, received from the entrepreneurs, in their own homes. Some persons in this period also undertook to specialize in bleaching, using machines for several operations. Obviously, these and subsequent changes occurred at different rates in various parts of the province.

> The rise of the cotton industry [introduced into Ireland in the 1780s to help alleviate the effects of a major depression in the linen trade] combined with the effects of changes in bleaching methods marked the beginning of the transformation of the Irish linen trade. The superior organization and equipment of the cotton industry had a decisive influence.

The spinning mills familiarized themselves with power-driven machinery and factory systems of production. The cotton manufacturers also demonstrated the possibilities of direct employment of hand-loom labour on a large scale as a consequence of millspun yarn.[6]

The new industry was accompanied by a trend toward urbanization, especially in towns along Belfast Lough. In those centers, mills were built, close to supplies of imported raw cotton. Simultaneously, manufacturers who supplied weavers with yarn, imported in large quantities or provided by local spinning concerns, tended to settle in port towns and a few other places. There, the production of cotton almost displaced that of linen, attracting to it spinners and weavers who came for higher wages, among other reasons, but it never gained much headway further inland except where there were adequate systems of communication to connect the hinterland with the ports. Nor did it seriously disrupt the coarse and very fine branches of linen production anywhere.[7]

In the nineteenth century, when linen made a strong comeback, the influence of the interim industry could be observed. In the early years of the century, there were to be found mills in which flax was spun by machines. At first these were small, few in number, utilized dry-spinning processes which yielded only coarse yarn, and relied on water power. A rapid increase in their number was delayed by the presence of women who could spin higher (finer) counts of yarn by hand at home and settled for a small remuneration. It was the application around 1828[8] of the wet-spinning method, developed three years earlier in England and necessary for the production of fine yarn by machine, which hastened the substitution of machine for hand labor and brought about revolutionary changes in the linen industry as a whole.

Another major advance was the introduction of steam power in the production of linen yarn in 1829. Now, the number of mills proliferated. Many women, finding it no longer worth their while to spin by hand, went to work in the newly established plants; some turned to hand embroidery and the making-up side of the trade; and others, along with young boys, turned to handloom weaving, competing with male weavers, already economically depressed.

The new spinning firms tended to distribute their product in bulk to large-scale manufacturers or, like the latter, to hand it out directly to individual weavers. In either case, the handloom weavers—for all the weaving was still done on handlooms—whether working on factory premises (early recognized by employers as being the most efficient way to get the job done properly) or, to escape such confinement, in their own homes, became more and more employees working for wages. Those who resisted doing so turned almost solely to farming or emigrated.

Some production of damask was organized as early as 1766[9] on a fairly large factory scale; that of other fine cloth, such as cambric and diaper, in the early years of the next century. Improvements in machine spinning and increasing supplies of capital helped to bring about the establishment of still more factories in which plain, coarser cloth was woven. But the real advance in factory production was made with the application of steam power to weaving around 1850. The delay in the utilization of power looms may be attributed in part to certain technical difficulties in weaving fine linen yarn but mainly to the continued willingness of handloom weavers to work for low wages. Manufacturers, desirous of holding down their expenses, were reluctant to interfere with the prevailing methods of production. Between 1845 and 1850, the weaving population declined as a result of famine and emigration. The consequent shortage of qualified craftsmen caused wages of those who remained to rise, and this led to the installation of power looms which could turn out most kinds of cloth—to weave the very finest threads, the handloom was still considered best—in a more economically efficient manner as well as help manufacturers meet demands which were stimulated by a growing market.

With the adoption of power looms on a wide scale and the subsequent inability of the majority of handloom weavers to compete, the transition from a domestic system of production to one utilizing complicated and power-driven machinery in mills and factories was complete. Often reluctantly and despite outcries that family life would be weakened or that moral corruption would result from placing comparative strangers of both sexes and all ages into close daily contact with one another, large numbers of men, women, and children, out of economic necessity, had moved from their homes into the new working environment. "About the middle of the nineteenth century, linen was undoubtedly the staple industry of Ulster, and fifty years later, its importance had in no wise declined."[10]

An increase in the production of linen yarn and cloth took place in many parts of the province. But industrialization, stemming from the time of the rise of the cotton industry, was most rapid, obvious, and concentrated in Belfast, which by 1800 had also become a focal point for overseas trade in the textile. For one thing, it was advantageous to build new mills near the major supply center for imported coal and flax, now in increased demand. As machine spinning proliferated, many spinners went to the city, and to smaller towns, continuing a process begun when cotton spinning was at its peak. Weavers, too, poured into the places where yarn was in abundant supply and were soon working in factories or at home, employees of large-scale manufacturers.

By 1850, power-loom weaving was only beginning in Belfast, as elsewhere in the province, but one-third of the total flax spinning mills with over half the output in the entire country were found in or close to the city,[11] and the community had grown from 20,000 persons in 1803 to over 100,000 in 1851.

Although there have been a few investigations of selective aspects of the linen industry after 1850, there has been no comprehensive research which covers events from then through the years encompassed in this book. And, as regards social history in the early decades of the twentieth century, one finds for Ireland the same glaring gaps in the literature—of special relevance here is the lack of studies on the work experience—that are noted by Paul Thompson in his recent book on Edwardian England.[12] Nevertheless, it is possible to bring the linen workers into somewhat sharper focus.

Expansion, especially in the 1860s, was mainly an urban phenomenon, with much of it taking place in Belfast. In fact, by the beginning of the next century, the population of that center had grown to 350,000. Residential segregation, characteristic of earlier working-class settlement there, continued, as newcomers flocked into those districts already occupied by Catholics or Protestants like themselves. To accommodate the influx, houses were built—one thousand a year at mid-century but increasing to four times that figure, yearly, by 1900[13]—usually within walking distance of mills, factories, and shipyards where workers would labor.

Much of the construction was ordered by the firms which needed housing for their employees. Although small and crowded together on narrow streets, the buildings, with dry toilets and gas lighting, were constructed according to specifications set forth in city bylaws and were, for the standards of the day, quite satisfactory. Their physical qualities and proximity to places of work were certainly much appreciated, if one may generalize from the pleas for similar arrangements made much earlier by one member of the working class in England.[14] Some, with water-borne sanitation and electricity installed in the early decades of the present century, are still being used and are even now occupied by men and women helping to produce textiles. Similar housing patterns prevailed in other large towns, but where a factory, or more often a mill, was somewhat isolated in a rural area, crowding and segregation were not so obvious.

As production became industrialized, female labor was used predominantly. In flax spinning mills, women had always held the majority of jobs, although some types of work remained the exclusive province of men. With the increasing use of power looms, women weavers came to replace men at that type of work in factories, and they labored there at other processes as well. The making-up branches of the industry—hemstitching of handkerchiefs, for example, or shirtmaking—were also carried on mainly by women.

The transition from handloom weaving to power-loom weaving was, as has been noted, a striking feature of the late nineteenth century. But the rate of changeover was not the same in all districts. Retired linen workers of today, living in several parts of the province, tell of grandparents working for very low wages in the 1880s. And the weaving of fine linen on the handloom continued in centers both inside and away from Belfast until very recently. As late as 1946, a handloom factory was opened about twenty-one miles outside of Belfast and, before the death of its owner sixteen years later, the enterprise had grown to include over sixty looms.[15] At present, some of the men and women who brought years of experience to bear on the weaving of that linen survive to carry the memories of their craft, but today only one person, much younger than they, earns his living at the trade.[16]

As had happened elsewhere, in Northern Ireland the industrial revolution in linen brought in its wake a working environment which was unsatisfactory in many ways.[17] Along with technological improvements, it became necessary to effect changes for the better in the social and economic conditions of the men and women who labored in mills and factories. This involved, for one thing, putting into operation various regulations, enacted throughout the century in England but applicable to Ireland. That there was a time lag between the enactment of appropriate legislation and its application, and that there continued to be violations long after some of the more grievous malpractices had disappeared in most places, is not surprising. Still, there was gradual progress, and by 1901, some significant advances—in many respects, ahead of those in other countries[18]—had been made, at least on paper. Thus, in addition to improvements in hours worked and legal starting ages, workers had some hopes of being insured against risks of unemployment, women had joined the ranks of men as factory inspectors, and studies pointing out safety hazards and industrial diseases to which workers were susceptible had brought other undesirable working conditions to the attention of persons who might be in a position to bring about the desired changes.

As for income, most linen workers were considered in 1900 to be poorly paid, although their real wages had increased over 200 percent since 1850 and they were better off than those engaged in agricultural and domestic pursuits.[19] Still, trade unions that aimed at improving the conditions of unskilled workers in linen and other industries were slow to develop, and there was little progress made in that respect until well into the 1900s.

In the first decades of the twentieth century, most of the women, who held the majority of jobs in linen mills and factories, continued to live within walking distance, long or short, of their places of work. Their wages and those of young boys and girls usually supplemented the money brought into homes by their menfolk, large numbers of whom were employed at unskilled jobs, but were sometimes the only source of income for a household. Especially was this true during the 1920s, when the linen

industry was for a time spared from a slump and widespread unemployment found in other industries. When "there was green
grass growing in the shipyards"—an expression used by the
workers to describe the economic climate of the period—the
wages of women "put the bread on the table."

And, although they continued to work long days and under trying conditions, they saw their workweek reduced to forty-eight
hours by 1920. Also, by then, changes in lighting, ventilation,
and general health requirements, while they had not completely
eradicated unsatisfactory aspects of work, had improved the situation substantially. Men, working as general laborers, foremen,
or at various craft jobs in mills and factories, experienced similar
changes. The response of some of the men and women to all that
was going on around them at work in the first decades of the
1900s will be concentrated upon shortly, but they and their jobs
can be appreciated better when seen in relationship to the production process as a whole.

Folklorists have described certain aspects of the planting and
harvesting of flax; they have also written about the *retting*—
soaking of flax in, usually, streams or lakes in order to dissolve
gummy substances and loosen usable fibers from unusable
portions of the stem—and the *scutching*—removal of refuse from
dried, retted flax fibers, in two machine processes, called *breaking* and *scutching*—of the raw material.[20] Others have provided
more technical accounts of those activities and of what happened
to scutched flax, eventually spun into yarn, after it reached the
spinning mill and was weighed, classified, and stored until further disposition.[21]

Usually, the fibers of flax were sent from the Storeroom, in
turn, to the Roughing Shop, Machine Room, and Hackling Shop.
In all three areas, they were cleaned further and straightened.
Long fibers for *line spinning* (as opposed to short fibers, flax fluff,
and refuse used in *tow spinning* of coarse yarn) were conveyed to
a Preparing Room—more often referred to as the Roving Room
by the workers—where they underwent additional processing.
There, *spreading*, *drawing*, and *doubling*, carried out on a series
of machines, produced from the loose fibers a ribbon, or *sliver*, of
even, regular weight. Passing next through a *roving frame*, the
sliver emerged, further elongated, as threadlike *rove* and was
twisted and wound onto bobbins. These were removed from the

machines by female *rovers*, placed in boxes, and transported to the Spinning Room, to be dealt with in detail later.

Sometimes *winding* was carried out in a mill, but most wet-spun yarn, on filled bobbins taken from spinning frames, was passed on to the Reeling Loft. In the skillful hands of *reelers*, all female, it was unwound from the bobbins onto wooden reels and measured, most frequently into *hanks* of 3,600 yards. *Drying* of these hanks of yarn in the Drying Loft and *bundling*, according to the quality of dried yarn, followed. In some instances, the product was boiled or bleached before being distributed to manufacturers of cloth.

A typical mill was four stories high. *Roughing, machine hackling*, and *hand hackling*, as well as the operations carried out in preparing rooms, were done on the ground floor. Spinning rooms generally occupied the next two stories, with one floor devoted mainly to the spinning of fine yarn and the other to the production of coarse yarn. At the top were the reeling and winding areas, equipped with comparatively lighter equipment. After reeling, the yarn was sent down by means of a chute to the drying area, typically located above the boiler room, set apart from the main building.

The ordinary operative referred to work areas in various ways, particularly if there were more than one of a kind. Thus, one spoke of Number Four Spinning Room or Number Two Roving Room, or labeled them with the name of the foreman there—that is, "Billy Kale's" or "Tommy O'Neill's Room."

Writing about 1920, Alfred S. Moore estimated that there were fifty spinning companies in Ireland—seventeen in Belfast, one in the South in Cork, and the rest operating throughout Ulster—at the time. It was customary to talk of mills according to the number of spindles they contained, spindles referring to those found on the numerous frames in the spinning rooms. In 1920, Moore posited an average of twenty thousand spindles per mill, although there was considerable variation if, as he says, there were fifty thousand spindles in the largest firm. Similarly, his figure of 750 employees per mill is only an average.[22]

Of these, females outnumbered males approximately three to one at the general operative level, holding most of the jobs in the preparing, spinning, and reeling rooms.[23] The supervisors of those rooms were men, however, as was the mill manager. Men did the roughing, hackling, bundling, and most of the drying. In addition, they held many types of jobs related to the maintenance of mill and machines. Children and young people of both sexes were employed, the former part-time, at a variety of tasks.

Some mills adjoined factories (as in Photo 1), but the majority of the latter were usually at a distance from the places from which they obtained their yarn. Consequently, the materials required for weaving had to be transported to them.

Once in the factory, the yarn soon went to the Winding Room. In a process which was almost the reverse of reeling, yarn intended for use on a loom as cross threads, or *weft*, was wound onto *pirn* bobbins, in which form the yarn was inserted directly into the weaver's shuttle. Similarly, longitudinal *warp* yarn was wound onto spools, but these were sent to the area where *warping*—which separated and arranged threads from the single spools on a large *warping beam*, or warping roller, in such a way as to allow them later to roll out lengthwise on the loom—took place.

Dressing followed and was carried out in the Dressing Shop. The threads on the filled warping beam were pulled forward and passed through a large container of *size*, the application of which adhesive material laid down loose fibers and added strength to the yarn. Emerging from the dressing, the threads were drawn onto the *weaving beam*, the roller to be used on the loom.

The complicated and tedious tasks of *drawing-in* and *reeding the sley*, performed elsewhere in the factory before the weaving beam was actually attached to a loom in the Weaving Shed, were undertaken only when a new kind of cloth, requiring a beam which contained a different quality of yarn or more or fewer threads, was to be woven. Where it was simply a matter of providing a machine with the additional yarn needed for weaving the same kind of cloth, the ends on the new beam were merely joined to the threads of the old, already firmly fixed in place on the loom.

Like the spinning mills, the more modern factories of the era were four stories tall. The Weaving Shed, containing heavy looms, was always "on the flat." Weft winding was done on the next floor, warp winding above that, and dressing and *slashing*—the term employed in Northern Ireland when yarn of heavier counts is treated—on the top floor. Until the turn of the century, however, the weaving factory had more typically been built as a single-story building. The Weaving Shed, with its characteristic glass roof, comprised one part of the building. Warp preparing and weft preparing were most often carried out in separate rooms, although sometimes a single room was adequate for both. Adjacent to the Dressing, or Sizing, Room was that where drawing-in and other acts essential for the setting up of the loom took place. Cloth inspection, *cropping* (the clipping and smoothing of loose ends), and darning were done elsewhere.

According to Moore, there were 37,292 power looms, located in a hundred factories throughout Ireland, in 1912. In the North, about 22,000 looms were in Belfast, and 13,000 were scattered elsewhere in the province; there were 2,888 in the South.[24] The last factory was built shortly before 1914,[25] but the number of power looms seems to have peaked at 37,789 in 1920.[26]

As in the mill, the supervisors in the factory—the manager and the foremen of the warping, winding, and other departments—were men. *Tenters*, overseeing the operation and maintenance of weaving looms, were also male. Dressing and *cloth passing* were within the province of men as well. Women, in most factories, were the warpers and winders at the general operative level, and women also did most of the weaving. Some men wove on looms which turned out very coarse and heavy cloth and on very wide looms, often used for damask. And, in a few places outside Belfast, they did some warping and large numbers wove.

Cloth emerged from the looms in a brown, unbleached state. Many pieces were sent away to the bleachworks soon afterward. The bleaching operation was a protracted one, utilizing several types of machines and employing methods which differed slightly according to the use for which the cloth was intended. Later, the textile was starched slightly, stretched to its proper width, and passed on damp for *finishing*, the object of which was to close the fibers of the cloth and to impart to it a somewhat glossy surface. *Beetling, calendering,* and *mangling* were processes employed to achieve various desired finishes. Dyeing and printing followed.

It is obvious that all these operations involved large numbers of

Photo 1. York Street Flax Spinning and Weaving Company, Belfast, ca. 1900. From the Welch Collection, by courtesy of the Ulster Museum, Belfast.

workers employed at a variety of tasks. Embroidery and other handwork on fancy linens, which were done in homes on factory order,[27] and making-up, still another branch of the linen industry, utilized many others. To recapture the past through the folklore of such diverse groups in their entirety is beyond the scope of this book. Instead, I have chosen to take a closer look at, mainly, the men and women in the spinning rooms, hackling shops, and weaving sheds.

THREE

"You Will Easy Know a Doffer": The Spinning-Room Workers

*We were happy. You stood all day at your work
and sung them songs. You'd a heard you with the frames on,
singin' then. We had no pay hardly, but we were happy.* (#52)

By far, the spinning end of the linen industry yielded the most lore, and of all the workers in the mill the women and girls in the spinning rooms were the most colorful.

Various methods of producing linen yarn were employed early in this century, but the most common was wet-spinning, generally understood to mean the system whereby rove was moved on a spinning frame through a trough of hot water. This method produced the finest counts—reckoned in terms of *lea* (number of lengths, each 300 yards, which weighed one pound)—of yarn. A typical wet-spinning room, with two machines in each row and a *pass* extending the length of the room between them, is shown in Photo 2. Although a worker might tend three sides, the average spinner stood between two frames and operated one side of each; the area in which she worked was called her *stand*. At each end of the room, operatives moved back and forth across the pass to mind the single remaining sides of the two-sided machines.

Photo 2. Wet-spinning room in Bessbrook Spinning Company, County Armagh, ca. 1900. From the Welch Collection, by courtesy of the Ulster Museum, Belfast.

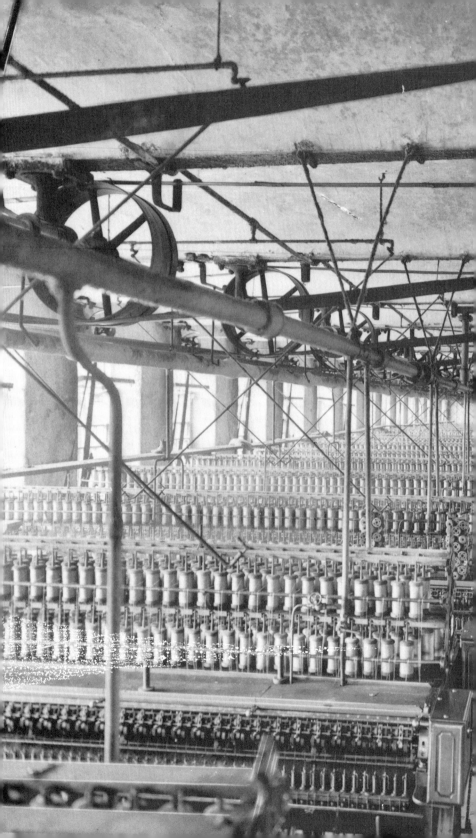

Supervising operations within such a room was a *spinning master*, who spent much of his time walking up and down the pass seeing that all was functioning smoothly. Also acting as supervisors were *doffing mistresses*. They saw to it that full bobbins of spun yarn were *doffed* from each machine and replaced with empty bobbins to be filled. Those who did the actual doffing were children, most of whom began work under the half-time system, dividing the workweek between school and mill. Although this method of employment in textile industries, which persisted until after the First World War, was essentially the same as that legalized by the English Factory Act of 1833 and regularized in 1844, some important modifications had been made through legislation of successive Factory Acts. For example, by 1901, the legal starting age had been raised from eight to twelve years, and, in Ireland, alternate days in school and mill had replaced the practice of having children work half a day and attend school the other half.[1]

The 1892 Education Act made formal education for all children compulsory, but those boys and girls who were employed in mill or factory even before that time were obliged, under terms set forth in the Factory Acts, to attend school as half-timers until they reached the legal age for leaving school. Normally, the school leaving certificate and the opportunity to work full time could be acquired when a child attained the age of thirteen and the status of "young person." The fact that a fairly substantial number of children only a year younger worked in mills as half-timers reflected the impoverished conditions of their families and the necessity for them to help supplement the household income.[2] Indeed, one obtained a child's birth certificate, or "lines," as early as possible so that not a day after the twelfth birthday should elapse before beginning work:

> My grandfather took me away to get my lines to the City
> Hall. It was a union then, they called it. . . . And when he
> came home [having given the wrong date], I wouldn't a
> been startin' till Tuesday. And I cried my eyes out. Oh, I
> wanted in on Monday to work, for my mother needed it. And
> they took me down to church on the Shankill Road where I
> was baptized, and I got my lines. And it [date of birth] was
> the 26th of January, 1902, and that threw me. I was in on a

Monday. When I went down to pass the doctor, he says, "You didn't allow no time," and I said, "No." (#40)

Some children began working when they were even younger. In country areas, inspectors closed their eyes to the practice. In Belfast, families got around the legal starting age in more devious ways:

> I knew a man, and if the children wasn't the age, and their mothers pushed for money, he was a good writer, a good pensman. . . . And he got your baptism lines all right, but he fixed them up, so whatever age that woulda suited your mother—do ya see? You were born maybe two years before you were born atall. You weren't in the world, yet you were two years runnin' about. They forged the lines. And still, it was never catched on. The majority of the people that was in, with forged lines at that time. (#47)

Parents' complicity in such conniving was neither unique to Northern Ireland nor a new practice. It had probably taken place, in England at least, since legal age limits were established in 1819.[3]

A half-timer in Northern Ireland spent Monday, Wednesday, and Friday in the mill and Tuesday and Thursday at school one week; the following week, and succeeding alternate weeks, the arrangement was to work all day Tuesday and Thursday, plus Saturday morning, and to attend school on the weekdays in between. The child kept the same hours on workdays as were kept by those employed full time, the workweek being at that time fifty-five and a half hours.[4]

In those mills which commenced operations at 6:00 A.M. and closed at 6:00 P.M., an hour's break for breakfast and another for midday dinner were allotted on weekdays; where work began a half-hour later or ended a half-hour earlier, one and a half hours were divided up between the two meal breaks. On Saturdays, typical hours were 6:00–12:00, with one-half hour set aside for breakfast. The employment of children on a three-quarter-time basis, a possibly illegal practice, was encountered in only one country mill, although it may have occurred elsewhere. Under it, a child alternated a day at work with one divided between mill and school. On the latter, the young employee went to work at

6:00 and remained until 8:00; the hours between 9:00 and 12:00 and those between 1:00 and 3:00 were spent in school; and one returned to work at 3:30—"I hitched a ride on the bread van to get there on time"(#42)—remaining until 6:00, and also went in on Saturday morning.

Under terms set forth in the Factory and Workshop Act (1901), all half-timers were obliged to attend school during regulation hours. An added incentive to do so arose from the fact that unexcused absences—records of which were kept by the schools and forwarded to the mills—had to be made up on mill days, with a consequent loss in pay. Because there was no general compliance with compulsory school attendance, schooling received during half-time employment was, for some individuals, the only formal education they ever received:[5]

> I was only in the third class when I came from school. That's all the class I was in. I didn't learn anythin' in school. The first time ever I went into school, I was twelve year old. That's the first day I ever had my foot in a school, for I used to work with my father. . . . You got away with it in those days. (#36)

Half-timer regulations were removed from the statute books under the Northern Ireland Education Act of 1930, but the actual hiring of half-timers seems to have been dying out about 1923. Today, the expression "You're nothing but a half-timer," directed at an individual who seemingly has no interest in work, is lazy, or is a bad time keeper (frequently late to work), brings back memories of the now defunct system.

While it was in effect, a number of children attended schools built by, often adjacent to, and partially run by the mills. Technically, the schools were part of the National School system, established in 1831, and they operated under rules set up by the Commissioners of National Education. Although created to educate mill children, often from several mills in the area, who might otherwise find it difficult to reach outlying National Schools and, thus, be unable to work under terms set forth in the Factory Acts, some were attended by any employee's child who wanted a full-time education or even by others in the region—farm children in rural areas, for example. Where a Catholic school was nearby, children of that religion often attended it instead.

Mill administrators helped to appoint the managers of their schools, and often a director of one was a trustee of the other. There were certain advantages to these arrangements. Although most funds for the running of the school were provided by the government, an interested mill owner would see to it that additional money was forthcoming for supplies, upkeep, and supplements to the gratuities and contributions received by teachers.[6] Some of these institutions were, therefore, somewhat better than many in Ireland. Certainly more understanding of half-timers was displayed in such places. In contrast, where a school was not directly associated with the industry, not only might the physical plant be less adequate, but the schoolmaster was apt to give no encouragement to the children who were destined for the mill:

> What a school it was. . . . if you didn't bring coal, my, there was no coals. You just froze away. It was a bad old place. It was only whitewashed but once or twice a year. . . . And the master took nothin' to do in them days. Mind askin' them one time to learn us some more—sums, you know—than what we was gettin'. "Not atall. You fellows only want to learn to count, and read and write, because you're only goin' to K. Mill and S. Mill." Everybody was for the mill. There was nothin' else for you in them days. (#2)

And when the official leaving age came, little attempt was made to retain a child:

> I was only thirteen when I had reached the seventh standard. Well, that was the height you could go. And the schoolmaster came to me and he says, "I canna be bothered with you, a day at the mill, a day at the school. You've reached the high standard. It's no goin' to do you any good if you're goin' to be a mill worker," he says, "so I'll give you a certificate. . . ." I was thirteen and I went into the mill full time. (#23)

The combination of the necessity and desire to supplement the family income, plus the lack of any great love for the kind of learning instilled in them during the years of their formal education, served to provide most children with a somewhat positive attitude toward the work experience. In addition, there was the expectation, created by siblings and other members of their families who had preceded them into mills and factories, that this was the "natural" thing to do. "We were reared up to that" (#52).

It was usually one such family member who "spoke for" the child, i.e., made arrangements with the foreman in a particular room for the youngster to work there. Sometimes this was done before the actual time of employment: "We [five girls and two boys] were all spoken for before we were twelve. . . . There was so little industry then that your mother had spoken for you to get into the mill before you were the age" (#23); likewise, "My second sister—she spoke for me, you see, and then, when there was a vacancy, I got it" (#54). In other instances, the beginner simply appeared with someone, ready to begin.

As well might a child be spoken for by an aunt, a family friend, a schoolmaster, a Sunday School teacher, "Jane Brown, up the street," or, in rare instances, just gather up courage and speak for herself. In outlying places, the demand for spinners was often far greater than the supply. One mill manager, faced with losing the services of seven girls in a family desiring to move to another area, promised, if all would remain, to see that the son in the household learned a trade.

Although many of the children entered the mill with a certain eagerness—"couldn't get into the mill quick enough" (#55)—the first days on the job were not always pleasant ones. Some youngsters were flustered by noise and by the whirling belts driving the spinning frames. Others felt the length of that first day: "When I went home I thought it was dinner, not breakfast time" (#17). But it was the combination of heat, steam, and oil fumes from the machinery which produced "mill fever" in many:[7]

> I'll never forget it [the first day]. I went in, and we were always used—just flying about the country. . . . I lived . . . two or three miles up the road. And . . . I started at the mill that day, and I was all right until I came in after dinner time and something came over me. I think it was want of air—used to fresh air—and thought that the place was all reversed. And I said, "Them windows wasn't on that side of the room when I was in this morning on the other side."
>
> And I felt awful, and my head seemed to be light, spinnin' round and round, you know. . . . So, the next day, I didn't feel too well, and on the third day I went out ill. . . . They said

it was "mill fever" . . . system gettin' accustomed to the mill.
So I laid for about three days and then I went back and I
never looked behind me after that. There was an awful lot of
people took it. (#22)

One of the two songs best known and most widespread in the
industry is the "Doffer Song": [8]

> You will easy know a doffer,
> When she comes into town,
> With her long yeller hair,
> And her ringlets hangin' down,
> And her rubber tied before her,
> And her picker in her hand,
> You will easy know a doffer,
> For she'll always get her man.

> *Chorus:* For she'll always get her man,
>   For she'll always get her man,
>   You will easy know a doffer,
>   For she'll always get her man. (#s 55, 57, 58, 59)

The song is, in a sense, most representative of the learners in a
mill, for many children received their introduction to its subculture while working in spinning rooms as *doffers*, a generic term
encompassing a variety of jobs assigned prior to one's becoming a
full-time spinner and a word which also designates a specific job.
After placement in a particular room, each learner was assigned
by the spinning master to the care of a doffing mistress:

> . . . he [foreman] took my baptism lines . . . he put me in the
> middle "half," Mary Jane Ramsey's half. . . . The Spinning
> Room went in half. . . . One doffing mistress doffed one half,
> and the other did the other. I was in the "middle half" . . . [a
> friend was in] "half the door," and then there was the "top
> half." . . . A wee girl was sent to learn me. I got so long to
> learn. (#39)

To understand what she learned, one must be familiar with the
machine on which her efforts were expended.
  Simply described, each side of a two-sided wet-spinning frame
consists of: an area called the *creel* at the top, along which are

one or two rows of *skewers*, or "skivers"; at the bottom, the *builder*, constantly moving up and down and so-called because the bobbins of yarn are built up in that area; and various parts in between. In the wet-spinning process, spools of *rove*, or loosely twisted flax fibers thicker than the yarn will be in its finished state, are placed by a spinner on the skivers. The rove moves down, passing through shallow troughs of hot water—usually kept at a temperature of 150° to 200°F.—then between a set of rollers, next through openings in the metal thread plate, and finally down into the builder area, where it passes through the eye of the *flyer*, a metal part screwed on to the top of each bobbin spindle, and is twisted and wound onto the yarn bobbin. (See Photo 3.) A pulley belt, connected to the central driving shaft of the room and to a revolving cylinder within each machine, drives the frame.

The doffing mistress usually assessed the proper instant to doff a particular frame, the time taken to fill the bobbins on a machine being dependent upon the quality of yarn being spun, with coarser yarn requiring less time. When the moment arrived, she blew her whistle as a signal for the doffers who were assigned to her to come running and perform their tasks. Each young person went to a designated portion at a frame and prepared to doff a "share" of the approximately 80–120 filled bobbins—to cite representative figures for a machine spinning fine yarn—on each side.

The frame was stopped by moving a handle at the side of the machine, which action shifted the driving belt from the tight to the slack pulley. The subsequent doffing was a complex operation. It involved shifting metal weights, or *drags*, which regulated the tension on yarn bobbins, breaking the lines of fiber coming down from the rove bobbins and throwing the ends up over the rollers, flattening the flyers and pulling the end of yarn from each onto its own yarn bobbin, removing all flyers and then the full bobbins of yarn, and throwing the full bobbins of yarn into nearby boxes. An empty bobbin was then set on each spindle. If necessary, the flyers were oiled, and then they were replaced and tightened. The ends previously thrown up over the rollers were brought down and attached to the flyer eyes. The weights were readjusted, and the frame was ready to be set in motion.

"They could have done that like lightnin', singing all the time.

And it was great" (#4). The speed was important, for almost as soon as one frame had been doffed, the workers moved quickly to another and repeated the process. And so their day was spent, flying from one end of the room to the other in response to the whistle of their doffing mistress.

The former operative, asked to name the steps which had advanced her from doffer to spinner, would usually reply, "Doffing to laying to spinning." In reality, there was a slightly more involved breakdown of duties. She might have *caged* at first. That is, she would have lifted out the full bobbins of yarn thrown hastily into boxes by the doffers and have placed them in orderly fashion in *cages*—wooden containers which were specially constructed with spikes to hold the bobbins and which were used to transport the yarn to reeling rooms for the next stage in processing.

She would most likely have been given a partial share of doffs before a full one. Then, prior to becoming a *layer*, she could have been asked to *lay around*—move from frame to frame assisting those more experienced than she. The trained layers, two or three to a side, came along after the doffers had done their work. One youngster, often a boy and called the *handle-holder*— "hanel-holer" in Belfast parlance—moved the handle at the side of the frame slowly, providing the gradual start which gave the required time for the flyers to pull the yarn around and onto the bobbins. It was the task of the layers at this point to see that all rove ends were securely threaded through the flyer eyes and that, as the large machine came to life, the yarn was wound properly on the bobbins. Any end that was *down*, or broken by the starting motion of the frame, was *laid up*: having stopped the flyer with her left hand, the layer brought up the end of the strand from the yarn bobbin to meet the rove end coming down from the rollers, joined the two between her palms by slapping the hands and flexing the wrists simultaneously (the motion frequently accompanies the singing of verse 3 of "Doffing Mistress," p. 49 below), and guided the thread through the flyer eye and into the thread plate. The frame was then turned on fully.

Photo 3. Details of a wet-spinning frame in the Clonard Mill of Ross Brothers, Belfast, 1960. By permission of Dr. W. A. McCutcheon.

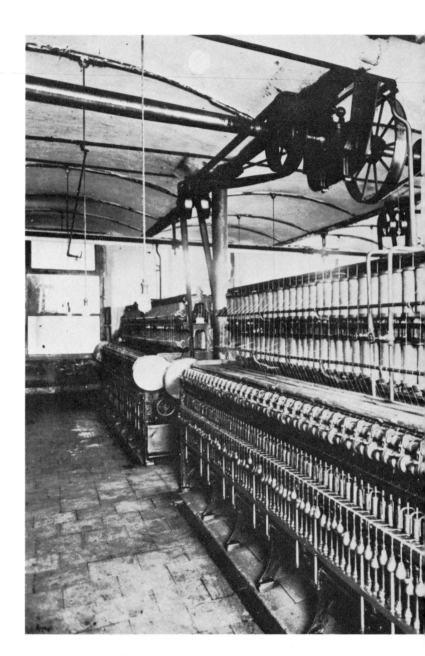

skewer

rove bobbin

rove guide

rove thread

rove bobbin

rove guide

creel

wooden hot water
trough lid

feed roller

drawing roller

thread plate

yarn bobbin

builder

flyer

drag

As a *piecer*, the young operative helped spinners by fixing broken ends and placing rove on the skivers. (Piecers could also be older women hired especially to lend a hand to a spinner who was "in a bog"—behind in her work.) Later, she would have substituted for a spinner when a machine lay idle. Finally, she was given first one side and eventually a stand to herself. It was "just like a trade," taking, on the average, two years to learn.

The *picker*, mentioned in the "Doffer Song," was a tool used for digging out *laps*—portions of rove that lapped around the roller when breaks in the thread occurred. Sometimes the *chopper* with which the doffer loosened the flyers on the spindles was mentioned in the song instead. These tools were worn proudly on a cord, which was made of plaited mill band, tied around the waist, and fastened with a button. (See Photo 5.)

> I couldn't get the pickers and things on me quick
> enough. . . . You thought you were great; you had some wee
> thing hangin' till you. . . . You were so proud it was great. . . .
> You thought it was great comin' out after work with them
> shakin' in front of you—oh, dear . . . like a horse and his bells
> were comin'. (#24)

The picker, so attached, was also a work hazard, for it sometimes became caught between the moving rollers when laps were being extracted and pulled the operative in toward the frame.

At first the youngsters received only learner's pay, characterized by all as being very low. Gradually, in accordance with their acquisition of various skills, the money paid to them increased slightly. It is impossible, however, to posit here a basic starting wage for children, who commenced working in different years during this period and were employed in country areas as well as in different mills in Belfast. There seems to have been no industry-wide starting wage for a particular year. But, in connection with wages, a few points may be made.

The pay, sometimes received weekly but more often fortnightly, consisted of a larger sum earned for the "big week"—Monday, Wednesday, and Friday in the mill—and a smaller amount for the "wee week" when one worked Tuesday, Thursday, and Saturday morning. Thus, one woman, whose employment began in 1914 in Belfast, received three shillings for the former and two shillings nine pence for the latter.[9] Earlier designations, applied in England to non-pay and pay weeks—"blank week" and "Good Friday" (when money was received Friday)[10]—had, in the decades under discussion here, been modified in Northern Ireland to "blind week" and "pay week."

Regardless of the manner in which her wages were distributed at work, the girl eventually turned them over for disposal to the member of her family who kept house. It was not unusual for this to continue until the girl married, or, if she remained single, until she was well along in years. A small sum was returned to her for personal expenditures. Although more substantial purchases were saved for and made as time passed, pocket money received during the early weeks of employment was often splurged on less essential items. A former spinner, who started in a small town in 1917, recalled:

> I remember my first pay. I brought it home to my mother. She spit on it for luck. . . . All our mothers done it, when we were all young . . . spit on your first pay for luck. . . . Out of seven and six, I got the sixpence. Well, we went to a dance, and that left fourpence. Well, then . . . bought a tuppence worth of cherry lips. They were a wee scenty smell, so that when you danced with a fella and leaned up to talk with him, there was a lovely smell. . . . and then, the other tuppence done you for Wednesday night, for the barn dance. (#23)

Another girl, given threepence out of three shillings ninepence earned for a week in 1908, lost the entire amount in a "ha-penny a pull" pinball machine, found at McGee's, a confectioners' shop on the Falls Road in Belfast.

Lying week was another feature of the pay system. The first week's wages were withheld until one's employment with a firm ceased. This ensured that a bookkeeper had time to ascertain wages, but it also served to compel workers to give adequate notice of leaving or to relinquish the lying-week money.[11]

The *rubber*, mentioned in the "Doffer Song," was a waist apron, often made from hessian sacks that had been used to hold meal, or from potato bags, or from "fine baggin'"—flour sacks that were bleached to resemble coarse linen. The apron was gathered and tied on at the waist with a white band, and it was usually worn over a longer one. Its protective function—to keep oil and water, sprayed from the spinning frames, off the clothes of the worker—seems to have given it its name. A large oilcloth *glazer* with a bib front and a skirt extending almost to the floor (see Photo 9), introduced during this period and made a mandatory article of clothing for operatives in the wet-spinning room, came to replace it. At first, glazers were black, but yellow and red ones appeared in some places as time passed.

A rubber (later, a glazer), an apron, sometimes removed during work hours when a glazer was worn, a Newtownards "strip petticoat," and a blouse, called by them a "jumper," constituted a kind of costume worn throughout the various mills by many wet-spinners and female doffers. The heavy petticoats were dark and full and were made of a thick fabric manufactured in Newtownards,[12] with thin stripes of varying hues—black and red or light blue and dark blue, for example—running through the material. Spinners vied to see who could have the loveliest colors. Although an overskirt, which was removed and hung on a wall peg, was added by some, the petticoat was made of "fittin' material," and it could be worn outside without being covered further. "We were very tidy going to work" (#52).

One's mother asked the grocer or baker to save flour sacks for her and, when they were available, purchased them for sixpence. The bags were bleached to remove printed labels, sometimes not completely: "One of mine had a steam roller on it" (#7), and from them a shift, a kind of undergarment, was fashioned. An entire shift might be made from such bags, although sometimes only a top was constructed from one and to it was added a crocheted skirt. Knickers, or drawers, with a flap at the back and a slit up the middle, were also made from the sacks, or from red flannelette. In addition:

> My sister and me wore one shawl . . . cut in two, and we were bare feet—winter and summer, bare feet. I never knowed what it was to wear a shoe, only on Sunday, goin' to church. . . . But the rest of the whole winter around . . . you went to work in your bare feet. In the winter time, I used to take big hacks on my feet, and my father would have to put cobblers' wax on them. With frost, don't you know? (#41)

The barefooted doffer was a familiar sight on the streets of Belfast and country towns, and "hacks," or coarse, split places on the skin, which were aggravated by exposure to the combination of the outside cold and pools of warm water in the spinning rooms, were endured by many.

Boys could cage and doff and advance to be handle-holders and layers. Like their female counterparts, each carried a chopper and picker and wore a rubber. Beyond that, shirts and knee-length pants constituted their only "uniform." Not destined to be spinners (although a few did spin in rural areas), they progressed to be *rove drawers*, transporting rove from the preparing rooms to the spinners and empty rove bobbins back, or *yarn hawkers*— "We called him a 'yarn boy' even if he was 100 years old" (#68)—carting filled cages to the reelers and bringing back empty ones. When a lad worked full time, he could also be a *band-tier*, whose main responsibility it was to replace the waxed bands running from the central drum of a spinning frame to individual yarn spindles, and then an *oiler*, who lubricated the moving parts of the machines. Generally, older lads, if they remained in the mill, moved on to jobs in the Mechanic Shop or other rooms, became foremen in one of the processing rooms, or served time as apprentices for the roughing and hackling trades.

The only male job associated with the Spinning Room which seems to have become immortalized in songs was that of the band-tier:

> A for Barney,
> B for Ross,
> Oh, but I love Barney Ross.
> All the world will never, never know,
> The love I have for the band-tier-o.
>
> *Chorus:* The band-tier-o,
>   The band-tier-o,
>   The love I have for the band-tier-o. (#53)

Sung in this form, it was intended by the doffers to tease the lads in their room.[13] However, circulated for years among children as they played on the streets, a variant went as follows:

> A for Apple,
> P for Pear,
> I love the girl with the long, yellow hair.
> All the world will never, never know,
> The love I have for my Ethel-o. (#53)

"You could have sung any name" (#53).

It is not necessary here to ascertain the original version of the song. What is important to point out is the interrelationship between a children's street song and one encountered in the mill, not surprising when it is known that doffers, youngsters all, had leading roles in each scene. Most likely, this is one of the instances, frequently encountered, where a song originally a part of the larger culture was adapted to a mill situation or person. Indeed, some persons who recalled this being sung on the streets were not sure whether they had encountered it elsewhere.

One thing was stated with certainty: "Oh, the lovely band-tier. We were all in love with the band-tier. . . . He woulda give us a ball of band cord, or whatever we wanted—for wee lines—put up a line for your clothes [laundered in the mill and hung to dry there]" (#42); he also provided extra oil for lubricating the frames. The band-tier, as the object of all affections and, frequently, the cause of jealousies, was also the subject of another verse, the words of which passed not only from one end of a Spinning Room to another but from mill to mill. Its tune is thought to be derived from a hymn:

> Didn't I give you half a crown,
> Didn't I give you silver,
> Didn't I give you a two-shilling piece,
> For to stay away from the band-tier-o?

> *Chorus:* The band-tier-o,
> The band-tier-o,
> She's away with Tommy, the band-tier-o. (#67)

A medley points to a possible connection between the two band-tier songs:

> Fan a win o, win o, win o,
> Fan a win o, daisy,
> Fan a win o, a hi ti adle,
> Away with Tommy, the band-tier-o.

> *Chorus:* The band-tier-o,
> The band-tier-o,
> The lovely blue-eyed band-tier-o.

A for apple,
P for pear,
She is the girl with the long, yellow hair.
All the world will never, never know,
The love I have for the band-tier-o.

Chorus

Fan a win o, win o, win o, *etc.*

Chorus

There were three doffers in a room,
Oh, but they were posies,
They sang so sweet, so very, very sweet,
To charm the heart of the band-tier-o.

Chorus

Fan a win o, win o, win o, *etc.* (#30)

In a large firm which produced thread as well as yarn, young girls engaged in a variety of tasks connected with that production selected a tune with an obvious music-hall background and sang the praises of lads working in other parts of the mill:

My boy works in the Dye House,
My boy's a toff [dandy],
My boy works in the Dye House,
And he knows how to walk.
He's well educated,
And he knows how to talk.
My boy works in the Dye House. (#14)

When her turn came, a girl substituted the place where her boy worked—Tar Shed, Mechanic Shop, etc.—but those employed outside the spinning rooms would not choose a lad from there; that was "not swanky enough." Their young men, during the dinner hour "when you'd be out in the yard, getting a boy and that type of thing," responded with "My girl's a doffer/She knows how to walk," and concluded with "My girl's a doffer girl" (#44).

And when the boys had gone to war, the girls used the dinner hour to write to them. The letters received by the soldiers contained sentiments not always unique:

> There's a soldier on yon hill,
> Watching a girl in Ewart's mill.
> Although she's a doffer,
> And her wages is small,
> He'll marry that doffer,
> In spite of them all. (#40)

The rhymes were composed as they sat writing: "If one woulda got one, they'd a told it to another. Somebody else woulda told them, and afore you knowed, the whole room knowed it" (#54). As the verse, and ones similar to it, spread, the names of other Belfast mills where siblings or friends worked—"Craig's, Ross's" —were substituted, and somewhere in transit "She's the tidiest wee doffer of all" (#38) replaced the last two lines.

A short tape recording, made in 1970 by the BBC in Belfast and kindly lent to me, was recognized by only one person, a woman who worked both in that city and in mills in small towns:[14]

> Hold her on,
> For we've no fear,
> We're all good doffers,
> Doffs round here.
> They're all oul' coalies,
> Doffs round there,
> Especially the doffer
> On the handle share.

However, numerous persons thought it most likely that the doffers or, more specifically, the layers, were addressing themselves to the handle-holder, though not mentioning the individual by name. While they professed no fear, the "coalies," or cowards, working elsewhere were afraid to stop the moving flyers to lay up any ends not being wound properly onto the bobbins. Positions along a frame were designated in various ways—"head share, middle share, low share" or "head share, second doffer, third doffer, end doffer," etc. Here, the child on the "handle share," being closest to the source of fear—the lever which set the huge machine in motion—was the greatest coalie.

Stopping the flyer to repair a broken end was, for the beginner, a somewhat traumatic experience, but the mastery of it gave great satisfaction:

> The first day I put my hand on it to stop the flyer . . . I thought I was a woman because I was able to put my hand on it, you see. But then, through time, there was a hard skin formed on your hand. And then, when we were young and went out to dances with the fellows, we always made sure we gave them a finger, for fear they'd see the hard skin—and that we worked in the mill. . . . they would have said to us, "Where do you work?" and we said we worked in an office. . . . We didn't want to say we worked in the mill for fear the boys wouldn't even want to come out with us again. (#23)

The hard skin referred to was the "spinner's welt" which formed on the left hand. To provide partial protection for the hand, many spinners wore a patch of leather—perhaps a heel from shoe—perforated with four holes and placed over the palm of the hand. It was held on with two pieces of cord, drawn through the holes and tied, one over the back of the middle fingers and one around the wrist.

When all frames were doffed, the doffing mistress would say, "Stands," and each youngster moved to the side of a spinner to whom she was assigned, there to make herself useful and to pick up further "tricks of the trade." One helpful category of information acquired was that relating to "signs." One learned that an empty rove bobbin placed upright on top of the creel signified to the band-tier that a new band was needed on a yarn spindle. Laid sideways at the top of the frame, the empty bobbin meant that one needed assistance in removing a lap from the back roller. A full bobbin set on the trough lid near the end of the frame was a signal to the *roller boy*, who passed periodically through the room distributing and replacing rollers, that a new one was sought. It was essential that the need of a replacement be drawn to his attention quickly, because worn rollers would not properly draw the rove thread out of the trough and down toward the builder area.

If most of the half-timers grew to tolerate the dampness and heat and smell of the rooms in which they worked and mastered with satisfaction the techniques of spinning, they never fully overcame their distaste for *wiping down*. Approximately twice a month, the frames—half of them on one day and half on another—were doffed as they became full and brought to a halt. Troughs were emptied and thoroughly scoured out with a wide brush; any accumulated waste in the bottom, which might dirty rove as it passed through the water, was pulled out with bare hands. Doffers assisted in the operation, using their *scrapers* to dig away stubborn muck. The builders were removed, and they and the *shores*, or drains, behind them were scraped free of gummy substances that had been squeezed out of the rove. Special cleaners, older women, were usually employed for the wiping down, but, where they were not available, spinners were given extra money, perhaps threepence, and did the job. They carried buckets of water, which was dashed over machines and onto the stone tile floors, splashing all around them. Shouts of "Hurry up! There's another frame off. How many for wipe down?" resounded through the room. "It was slavery right enough" (#39).

Afterward, spinners and doffers wiped down the entire frame, scrubbed below it, and dried the pass. "Muck-up day," it was called, and appropriately enough, given the nature of the work. Not on this occasion did one wear a clean rubber or petticoat. But it could well have been on one such day, while the workers, who had remained at the mill during the dinner hour in order to lay up ends in readiness for an afternoon of spinning, were singing and relaxing for a few moments, that this verse originated:

> The yellow belly doffers,
> Dirty wipers down,
> The nasty, stinking spinning room,
> The stink will knock you down. (#4)

"Terrible smell, you know. . . . They used to say that all the time. They rhymed everything—rhythm all the time. You see, they were all goin' that quick, you know" (#4).

"Yellow belly," referring to the color of the glazer worn in some mills during these years, was echoed on the streets. In Belfast, as children ran around playing, boys might shout, "Oh, don't have anything to do with her. She's an old yellow belly" (#40). Elsewhere one heard:

> Sion Mills is a nice wee place,
> It's surrounded by a hill,

And if you want a yellow girl,
You'll get her in the mill. (#84)[15]

Maximum spinning-room efficiency was largely dependent upon the spinning frames being doffed at the proper moment. The responsibility for seeing that, ideally, none ever lay waiting and idle, fell to the doffing mistress. Selected from among experienced spinners in a room, she was a person who not only had a fairly high degree of intelligence and had shown herself to be a good time keeper—to be able to arrive at her job promptly—but also, and most important, was able to judge when a frame was full and ready for doffing. Although she most likely was in early or late adulthood, she might be as young as fourteen, as one woman declared herself to have been when selected for the position.

It was also important that she be able to get along with the doffers, whom she instructed and with whom she worked so closely. She might have "boxed your ears if you didn't hurry" (#6), or "If you wouldn't come, she'd get you by the hair and pull you up the pass" (#20). But the doffers recognized that, while she had to be strict and often cross, she was usually kind to them. Indeed, a close bond often grew up between them and the older woman. A former doffing mistress speaks:

> I had my workers spoiled . . . because . . . I wouldn't a said a cross word for them. And the spinning master . . . used to say . . . "I would like you to talk a wee bit more strict to these ones here because . . . they're just gettin' . . . too much of their own way. . . ." Twice a year they used to . . . buy me a new whistle—whenever the pea in it went. . . . Now, can I mind the wee song they used to sing? And they used to come and say, "There's a wee present for you." (#33)

Once the working relationship had been achieved, it was very difficult to accept gracefully a new doffing mistress, and, for a time, she was on trial. Such is the theme of "Doffing Mistress," as well known in the mill as the "Doffer Song" previously commented upon:[16]

> Oh, do you know her, or do you not,
> This new doffin' mistress we have got?
> Ann Jane Brady, it is her name,
> And she hangs her clothes up on the highest frame.

Chorus: Raddy rightful rah, raddy rightful ree.
On Monday morning when she comes in,
She hangs her clothes on the highest pin.
She turns around for to view her girls,
Saying, "Dang, you doffers, lay up your ends."

Chorus

Lay up our ends, we will surely do,
Our hands are steady, and our touch is true,
Lay up our ends, we will surely do,
All for Lizzie Murphy, and not for you.

Chorus

Oh, Lizzie Murphy, are you going away?
Is it tomorrow, or is it today?
You'll leave us then with a broken heart,
For there's no one left that now will take our part.

Chorus

Oh, Lizzie Murphy, when you've gone away,
Every night, it's for you we'll pray,
We'll send for you when you're far away,
And we'll bring you back, and we'll make you stay.

Chorus

Numerous respondents sang the song, and never was it presented the same way twice. Verses were omitted or sung in a different order, and within the stanzas phrases and words were altered constantly. The version above is taken from an unpublished typescript of Belfast street songs and rhymes, gathered together by a schoolmaster over fifty years ago.[17] Although it has possibly been tampered with in an effort to improve its metric and literary qualities, I use it here not only because it was collected relatively early but also because, being complete, seemingly, it provides a good comparison with later variants.

It is not surprising that a frequent alteration is the substitution of different names. For, whatever the origin of the song,[18] it came to be applied to many individuals—most often a doffing mistress,

occasionally a spinning master, infrequently some other person.
That the words in some stanzas of variants do not quite make
sense when given in conjunction with those in others—as I often
heard them—can be understood when one realizes that individual verses were often sung by themselves, as demanded by the
occasion, and with varying meanings associated with them.
Here, the first two verses merely describe the newcomer—"That
was the new doffing mistress comin' up"—although some variants evaluate her as well. As for the third verse, "Maybe that she
was the doffin' mistress that they didn't like, you see, and the
other doffin' mistress, she left or went back to spinnin' or the
spinnin' master fell out with her" (#30). Such words were also
sung to a disliked spinner who had asked for assistance with the
laying up of a number of fallen ends.
    The fourth and fifth stanzas express grief at losing an old
friend:

> She'd be goin' away. Maybe she got a better job and—she'd a
> give in her notice. . . . And then, when she was goin' away,
> they woulda bunched up and bought her a wee present . . .
> these doffers. . . . the last night she'd be in that, they woulda
> all gathered in a bunch and give her the wee present, and
> they woulda sung that. . . . Many's the time I was among
> them when we done it . . . maybe sixpence each, and you
> hadn't it. . . . She was good to them, you see. (#52)

    The reluctance to break the bond perpetuated the custom, ex-
tended, as here, to a spinning master, of following home the ones
whom they liked:

> I mind one night . . . our spinning master [Sammy] was
> leaving and we folleed after him, singin' "Lay up our ends,"
> and all like that. . . . We sung that the whole road to his
> house . . . he was goin' to another job . . . and then sang
> round the door for about ten minutes:

> > Lay up our ends, we will surely do,
> > Lay up our ends, we will surely do,
> > Lay up our ends, we will surely do,
> > All for Sammy Acheson and not for you.

Chorus: Raddy rightful ah, raddy rightful ay.

On Monday morning when he comes in,
He hangs his coat on the highest pin,
He turned around sayin', "How do youse do?"
And sayin', "Hi, you doffers, lay up your ends."

Chorus (#47)

These verses have a slightly different connotation—the expression of loyalty to Sammy and then a recollection of what it was like when he was in the mill.

At times, work became unbearable for a doffing mistress. The spinning master might "get on her back" over the frames not being doffed promptly enough, and she would leave. The doffers, sensing injustice in the situation, would huff and "lie behind"—not do their work. They might even strike. One such act of rebellion lasted a day or two, the doffers hanging around the gates of the country mill until their doffing mistress was reinstated. If the spinning master managed to arrange her return, she would be warmly welcomed. At least, such was the hypothetical situation posited to explain this widespread song:

Hi, Nelly Jones, you're welcome back again,
Welcome back again,
Welcome back again,
Hi, Nelly Jones, you're welcome back again,
For we are all behind you. (#33)

One can, as well, imagine it as a musical tribute to a doffing mistress or spinner who had returned after an illness or absence of any sort.

It did not always require a special occasion to evoke a song: "They [doffers] just sung all day, and they were crucified with sweat runnin' out of them" (#4). In one, references to some person, and to the parts of a spinning frame (see Photo 3), seem to serve no other purpose than to provide background for an expression of exuberance:

Up comes Henry Hanna,
With the whistle in his hand,
And he said, "Doffers, doff no longer,

For the flyers they go round,
And the builders up and down,
And the rollers they are watered in the morning." (#7)

The words spring from a Protestant song—or a Catholic counterpart—to the tune "The Boyne Water," to which this is set. The Protestant words:

Up comes a man,
With a shovel in his hand,
For he says, "Boys, go no farther,
For we'll tighten up the rope,
And we'll make them curse the Pope,
On the Twelfth of July in the morning."

A Catholic variant:

Up comes the Pope,
With a shovel up his coat,
And he says, "Boys, go no farther,
For we'll tighten up the rope,
And we'll cut King William's throat,
On the Twelfth of July in the morning." [19]

And sometimes, imitating fife and drum bands which march and play the melody on the Twelfth of July, a day commemorating the Battle of the Boyne in 1690, a singer added appropriate gestures: "An old spinner taught me that. She drummed on her glazer with two pickers as she sang" (#51).

Although no one positively identified Henry Hanna as a spinning master replacing an absent doffing mistress, there were those who recalled actual doffing mistresses named in the song. Sometimes, as in one mill, it was "Up jumps Tilly Coats/with a whistle in her coat" or "Up jumps Sara Ann/with a chopper in her hand"; it didn't matter, for "The rhyme comes in to suit the person" (#2). For variation, one might conclude with "And the troughs are filled with water every morning" (#2) or "So we're all goin' to Bangor in the morning" (on a mill trip) (#41); or, even, "And we'll all get our lines in the morning" (#s 55, 57, 58, 59)— get fired for singing so loudly. The song was most likely adapted to the mill quite some time ago, for it was said by one woman, herself in her seventies, that "Older women sang this . . . if you

Photo 4. Doffers, spinners, oiler, and doffing mistresses in a wet-spinning room in the Linfield Mill of the Ulster Spinning Company, Belfast, ca. 1915. By courtesy of Mrs. Sarah Dixon.

know what I mean. . . . women older than me, and the younger ones picked it up from them" (#33). The words "Boys, doff no longer" (#41) in one variant help recall the fact that in some places and in some rooms boys were employed in large numbers.

Boys were, however, mainly passive bearers of the musical traditions in the earlier part of this century. The majority left the spinning rooms after a few years, and those who remained had less and less contact with the female doffers and spinners as they moved up the job ladder. In addition, "You never got the boys singin'. . . . They used to play more pranks than anything else" (#45). Boys seem to have whistled, rather than sung, while they doffed. And, when the girls were having a "bit of a sing-song" during the day, the lads preferred to fight with one another or rest on the stands. They teased the girls, stole one another's flyers as they doffed, and threw cold water on the feet of the spinners. Small wonder that the doffing mistress became cross with some of her charges. When she did, her reactions were noted in a song, or verse:

> Tilly is our doffing mistress,
> She is very cross,
> And if you break a spindle,
> She will tell the boss.
> And when you get your wages,
> You'll find they will be short,
> For they fine you on a shilling,
> For the spindle you have lost. (#45)

An unintentional lewd remark could arouse merriment, as did that of one doffing mistress who, never satisfied on wipe-down day with the way in which the pass along the outer sides of the frames was being cleaned, repeatedly issued the order to "Do your back passage" (#39).

Although the doffing mistress might be an object of amusement, it was the spinning master toward whom jibes were more often directed. The doffers were fond of many of the men, as they demonstrated by providing a traditional sendoff for the ones whom they liked when such individuals left the mill. But, while a man might conceive of himself as a kind of surrogate father— "Our spinning master used to say, 'Sure, he reared us'" (#55)— he remained, in general, a more stern and threatening figure than the doffing mistress, who, in a sense, acted as a buffer between him and the youngsters. He had to be authoritarian, because the overall responsibility for production in a room was his. An experienced spinner could be sympathetic to his reactions to frustrations on days when all the ends seemed to be down and too much waste was being made. But the doffers saw mostly a man with "a look as good as a summons." They "used to call him everythin'" (#39), and behind his back they ridiculed him in song. This one, sung to the same melody as "Doffing Mistress" (see note 16), demonstrates a common assessment of foremen:

> Johnny Larkin comes up the pass,
> He spreads his feet like an old jackass,
> He turns around for to view the frames,
> Saying, "Damn you, Doffers, get up them ends."

Chorus: Raddy rightful, *etc.* (#41)

A slightly more derisive variant is:

> Billy Gillespie goes down the pass,
> He spreads his wings like an old jackass,
> He opens his mouth like an elephant's trunk,
> Saying, "All you doffers, you think I'm drunk."

Chorus: Raddy, *etc.* (#42)

Billy Gillespie was identified as a *winding master*, the person responsible for overlooking another process in some mills. If, indeed, he was—other people tagged him differently—the variant illustrates how the song was attached to numerous foremen, regardless of where they worked.

However much they may have chafed at the actions of those supervising them, the youngsters, in retrospect, viewed them more tolerantly:

> The belts are broke,
> And the frames are stopped,
> And no one here for to put them on,
> But we'll send for Ritchie,
> When he's far away,
> And we'll bring him back,
> And we'll raise his pay.

Chorus: Raddy rightful, *etc.* (#4)

The tune of "Doffing Mistress" is again employed, and the last four lines are but a rearranging of the words in stanza 5 of that song (see p. 50). As for Ritchie, he was a spinning master, later a manager, who had moved to a mill elsewhere.

In the minds of the doffers, probably the most formidable person with whom they had to deal was the gateman. Almost everyone could recall a time when someone, young or old, had been shut out of the mill because of arriving late, perhaps by only a few minutes. An employee in a weaving factory—for the practice prevailed there also—describes what could have happened:

> An alarm clock at that time cost two and six to three and six. Not many homes had an alarm clock. So the horn screeched at half-past five in the morning. You could have heard that for miles away. . . . At ten to six, that was the time you must be near the gate. And if you didn't get in for six o'clock, you were shut out, and you were fined threepence . . . "out fines." . . . Now, an old man that I worked with. . . . he lived about four or five hundred yards from the factory, and he ran with his shoes not laced. And he got about forty yards from the gate, and the old man on the gate . . . says, "You missed it." And he shut him out. (#28)

The amount of fine and the period of time one was actually kept off the job varied from place to place.[20]

Where the horn was not sufficient as a wakening device, people relied on the "knocker-up," or "rapper-up," in their area to give them a morning call. The custom was an old one.[21] In one neighborhood in Belfast, it was a sailor with one arm who walked the streets, rapping on doors with a stick. Not until someone in a household answered, "Right," did he move on. From each residence where he stopped, he collected three or four pence for the week's alarm service. An old woman called Sally knocked up the residents in another neighborhood. With a long cane she tapped on windows and called, "Are you up there?" The sixpence she received weekly from each customer was considered by them to be her "gold mine." Some, like "Maggie Smash-the-Lamp," acquired their nicknames from their work.

Even with this assistance, the fear of being late remained, as it

had for those almost a hundred years earlier,[22] a shared experience for the workers, and the names of the men who could shut
them out survive in still another mill song:

> At half-past five, the horn will blow,
> Six o'clock we all must go,
> And if you be a minute late,
> Robert McCabe will shut the gate.

> *Chorus:* So early in the morning,
> So early in the morning,
> So early in the morning,
> Before the break of day. (#52)

When the starting hour was moved to eight o'clock, the
gatekeeper remained an object of dread. Doffers in one mill,
where the change occurred in 1917, recalled "a big, big, tall man
with a heavy black mustache. We were terrified of him" (#14). At
this later date, they continued to sing the song but altered the
words to reflect the new time:

> At quarter to eight, the horn will blow,
> At eight o'clock we all must go,
> And if we be a minute late,
> Jimmy McIlhenny will shut the gate.

> *Chorus:* So early in the morning,
> So early in the morning,
> So early in the morning,
> Before we get our tay. (#14)

"Some sang 'Before the break of day,' but we always said 'Before
we get our tay.' . . . We always said 'tay,' not 'tea'" (#14). In the
chorus of the well-known traditional Irish children's song, to the
tune of which the doffers fitted their verse, the former words are
sung, however.[23]

It seems likely that another source, the hymnbook, provided
the musical and poetic inspiration for a slightly different rendi-
tion of the same theme:

> Be in time,
> Be in time,
> When old Matt Church calls you,

Be in time.
If you are a minute late,
Matt Church will shut the gate,
And his cry will be, "Too late,"
Come in time. (#s 55, 57, 58, 59)

The admonitions of Matt Church echo those directed at Protestant workers by their ministers, in an anecdote, told by a Catholic, which illustrates some commonly held ideas about various segments of the working class:

> In the Presbyterian Church, the man who went in heard the preacher preaching at them about the virtues of punctuality —"to be in time for your work in the morning; that's the way to get on in life; be there on time, on the dot; don't miss a second; be there when the gates are opening, and walk in. . . ."—and all that. Well, the next thing that happened to him, he went to a Catholic Church. Well . . . a preacher there. . . . preached at them and he said, "There are too many in this congregation who are late for Mass. Now it's— ah—it's very wrong to be late for Mass. . . . You must all promise to be on time for Mass every Sunday morning." (#74)

Usually by the age of fourteen, those girls who chose to remain in the mill became full-time spinners. Most of them continued to wear small black "clouds"—referred to as "wraps" in some areas—over their shoulders in warm weather, but within a year or two many had saved enough money to purchase their own larger black shawl, covering them to the knees (see Photo 10), and a few had accumulated the funds needed for a more expensive, but lighter, hip-length variety. Of those fortunate enough to be able to purchase a Paisley shawl, it was said, "They have hens in the bank" (#64). They frequently added to their wardrobes black shoes and stockings, at least to be worn outside the mill. The oilskin glazer, often worn over a white apron, was, of course, mandatory at work, but some spinners, desirous of appearing as attractive as possible, removed the bib and took tucks in the skirt portion in order to show off their waists. Persuading the hacklers to "turn a pin" for them, they generally accumulated sets of hackle pins (used to dig out broken ends from the bobbins), deco-

Photo 5. Tools of a doffing mistress in a wet-spinning room: left to right, *whistle, scraper, picker, hackle pins. Photo by author.*

rated with brass tops. These were attached, along with their other tools and sometimes with metal chains, to cords tied around their waists (see Photo 5). Some went on to compile excellent attendance records, and the hardships they endured, while often traveling long distances to work, particularly to country mills, were commented upon frequently by their former coworkers.

In attempting a reconstruction of the working life of the spinner, one finds that the outsider stresses facts of that existence quite distinct from those emphasized by the former operative. The difference in emphasis and the reasons for it bear closer scrutiny.

The wet-spinning process, in the "old days" before there were proper ventilation and drainage in the rooms, before splash boards were installed to help prevent water from being sprayed on the spinners and the floor, before rings replaced whirling flyers, and when lubricating oil was thrown off from rapidly moving parts of the frames, was, in the words of the operatives, "a dirty one." Water collected on the stone tile floors; steam rising from hot water in the troughs kept the rooms hot and moist; and the workers labored in clammy, often greasy, clothes and in their bare feet. By the early years of this century, the physical conditions reported by C. D. Purdon in the 1870s[24] had improved, but the life of the spinner was far from ideal. For some, it was more difficult than for others:

Every room was different . . . coarser yarn on . . . filled up the bobbin more, quicker. . . . The thicker the yarn was, the more work there was to be done, because them all had to be emptied in a half hour or a quarter of an hour. . . . They would get the same pay, but they were murdered for it . . . overworked for it . . . very, very heavy work for them, and the sweat never dried on them. . . . We were what they called the clean room. . . . The other rooms was very unhealthy. Soon as you went in, you'd a smelled oil, and you'd a smelled everything. . . . It was terrible. I don't know how they stuck it, to tell you the truth . . . it would have sucked the whole system with the heat and that. . . . They got used to that, just like us. (#33)

Most spinners mentioned but did not stress those unpleasant conditions, and they spoke frequently of what they considered to be the positive aspects of their jobs. To them, the steam made the rooms pleasant and warm, and it was considered to be beneficial to those with bad chests. The moisture kept their skin clear and gave them healthy "big heads of hair." Warm water on the floor, although contributing to wrinkling and flabbiness of the skin on the feet and to "toe rot" (defined by a nurse as athlete's foot), was soothing to the feet of many. And most observed that the rooms were, at least, comparatively healthy:

> The more it's dirty and wet, the Spinnin' Room is about the healthiest part of the mill you can work in. I think the Reelin' Room, and where the piecer-outs is among the flax and stuff, and the Machine Room where the wee lads works . . . makin' the flax, and the Rovin' Rooms and the Cardin' Rooms—I think, everybody in . . . that part of the firm has always bad chests. They seem to take asthma or somethin' wrong with their chests, go bad with their lungs and things . . . but you'd hardly ever hear tell of a Spinnin' Room girl goin' that way. (#41)

"Clocks," or cockroaches—attracted by water, muck in the troughs, and food brought in for dinner—were ubiquitous, but they were more of a nuisance than a hazard to one's health.

It was their appearance as they left the mill each day, created largely by the conditions under which they worked, that helped to shape and confirm the impression, shared by most outsiders and other employees, that the spinners were, indeed, "the lowliest form of life." They may have managed occasionally to scrub their hands, legs, and feet before leaving work, but more often they did not find the time to do so, and, furthermore, nothing could remove stubborn grease marks or the "rotten, stinkin'" oil smell from their clothes. The picture they presented as they walked home, wrapped in their large shawls and often in their bare feet, or in shoes without socks, was not a flattering one. In a country town, "the shopkeepers used to say, 'Here's the oul' spinners comin'. Get off the footpath,' and let you by. In them days, the spinners looked poorly, because they had nothin' but shawls on . . . all huddled up, you know" (#2). Even farm laborers, themselves very badly paid, felt superior and obliged to call out, "Lift the hens, mates. Here's the spinners comin'" (#7).

An anecdote, amusing and meaningful in Dublin, although

apparently originating in Belfast, one hundred miles to the north, demonstrates how widespread were the deprecatory impressions of the mill girls:

> I had a great friend in Belfast one time . . . whom all Republicans . . . still know about and remember. . . . He told me of the annual excursion of the mill girls in Belfast, out to the seaside. . . . Was it to Bangor or one of those other places where they go into the sea? Well, all the girls, when they got there, on their annual excursion, they went into the water and were flopping around in the water and enjoying themselves. And one girl said to the other, "Maggie, your belly's very dirty. You mustn't have been on the excursion last year." (#74)

The unflattering remarks directed their way could not be totally ignored. But the spinners learned to live with them, and, in the end, they served to reinforce an in-group solidarity, almost unique to this class of workers. The esteem that many spinners had for themselves and their attire is suggested by Photo 6. Less easy to disregard was the reality of their unpleasant working conditions. Still, if those could not be completely eradicated, they could be improved. A Belfast man, working out of the mechanic shop in a number of firms, could comment with a high degree of certainty:

> You know, the amusin' part about it—the spinners—this is really amusin'. Lookin' at them in the streets, comin' to their work, and goin' from their work—now I'm talkin' about the old days before they started to wear coats and dress themselves up, you see—those days, used to say, "Dirty old bitch," or somethin' like that. And the majority of their stands—you coulda lift—me lift their trough lids—they were scrubbed pure white, and their stand was as clean as could be possible. And the brasses along their frames was glitterin'. (#38)

Thus, if she could not keep herself spotless, each spinner could endeavor to maintain a work area as free from grime as possible. Indeed, it was almost as if the "dirtier" the room the more the workers there tried to compensate. Many came to think of their machines as their own, rather than belonging to the firm, and exhibited pride in keeping them clean. A kind of informal compe-

Photo 6. Studio photograph: wet-spinner and doffing mistress, 1917. By courtesy of Mrs. Theresa Grimley.

tition developed between the women, with each attempting to outdo the others in cleanliness, a rivalry encouraged by managers who recognized that cleaner yarn resulted when parts of the spinning frames were kept immaculate. Only rarely, however, was encouragement translated into prizes for the best-kept stands, as was the case at Christmas and the Twelfth of July, for a period of time, in one mill. But it was well known which workers were fastidious and which places were kept the tidiest. The operatives boasted about their rooms:

Number Four's a dirty old room,
Number Two's no better,
If you want a tidy wee girl,
Number Three, you'll get her. (#s 55, 57, 58, 59)

That was sung "any time atall, when we were havin' wee parties and all, we used to sing them in the mill" (#58).

They were cleaner in the Spinning Room than they were in anywhere. . . . Everybody was boot clean, everybody. If they'd a seen anybody doin' that [scratching] in their head, the spinnin' master would have . . . said, "There's a wee tick. Away and see the nurse." And you had to go or you'd lost your work. Right enough, the Spinnin' Room workers was all really clean. Well, any dust that was on you, it was out of there, through the work. . . . My mother . . . used to say, "There's 'clean' dirt and 'dirty' dirt." Well, that was clean dirt that we worked among, you know—in our bare feet and that.
And then, when we were doin' the pass you . . . coulda slid from here to Amerikay on to the black soap. Everybody was scrubbin' with the big brushes . . . and they'd nearly a fought—who would have their half the cleanest. . . . And everybody would love to have her stand nice and clean, and you kept brushin' it when there was any of the laps . . . on the ground. (#47)

More a task assigned by the mill manager than a personal attempt at cleanliness was the scrubbing down of the "lobbies"— landings outside the rooms on each floor—and stairs leading to them. Special personnel were usually engaged for this, but workers from the spinning rooms might assist. A song, probably of music-hall derivation and possibly originating in the years of unemployment immediately following the First World War when returning servicemen sought work, came to be associated with the process:[25]

> Do you want your old lobby washed down, Mrs. Brown?
> Do you want your old lobby washed down?
> For I'm healthy and strong,
> And it won't take me long,
> Do you want your old lobby washed down? (#s 55, 57, 58, 59)

Frequently sung by everyone in the Spinning Room—"I was tired of listening to it" (#4)—it had highly suggestive overtones. A spinner revealed that "You'd get a crack on the back for singin' that, for it wasn't a good song" (#67). Good or bad, it is still sung today in public houses, with, perhaps, only its bawdier connotation.

During most of the day, the conscientious spinner walked up and down her stand, checking constantly to see whether all of her ends were up, gauging the proper moments to replace a rove bobbin, noting whether yarn bobbins were being properly filled, and shifting the drags, which served as weights, from nick to nick along the front rail of the builder. The secret of good spinning was said to lie in the ability to regulate these weights so as to provide the correct amount of tension on the yarn bobbins and, thus, minimize broken ends, a constant source of frustration to the spinner. The drags themselves were a kind of hazard for the women. As cords supporting them rotted, they often broke, causing the weights to fall on the bare toes of the spinners. The strain induced by constant surveillance of the numerous ends on the frames—one machine was dubbed "Royal Avenue," after a long street in the heart of Belfast, because it had 158 ends—probably provoked this rhyme:[26]

> My two frames go like a train
> From breakfast time to dinner;
> I'll give a curse to any girl
> Who wants to be a spinner. (#4)

"I shouldn't say that, 'cuz I loved the spinnin'. . . . But they said everything in the mill" (#4).

Management frowned upon operatives who left their work area in order to go to the toilet or for a drink of water; in one country mill, a fine of one penny was levied upon the person who did so without first obtaining permission. Also, the women were not supposed to sit down during working hours. And "you were sometimes too busy to look out of your eyes" (#52). Snuff, at such moments, was a consolation for some:

> I know all the old spinners did take snuff for you see there was no smoking allowed in the Mill so a Lot of them did snuff when their work was Bad many a time I heared them say give me a Pinch and it will keep my heart up.[27]

Spinners were not alone in this practice. A woman, now over one hundred years old, was told that she would "never be a reeler until I could take a pinch of snuff," which she carried in a "tupenny Colman's mustard box" tucked into her blouse (#82). Elsewhere, the habit caused the women to be spoken of as "snuffy reelers." But the spinners seemed to have been the only ones who noted their usage of it in a song—the "Snuff Box Song":

> I give my heart to any wee girl
> What lives to be a spinner,
> That has a discontented mind,
> From breakfast time to dinner.
>
> When I go in, the mill is on,
> The belts are always shakin',
> I turn on the spinning frame,
> And the ends are all a breakin'.
>
> Johnny Larkin comes down to me,
> And his tongue goes clitter, clatter.
> Sez I, "Come here, upon my soul,
> Will you tell me what's the matter?
>
> "My work is bad, and, when I go home,
> I cannot take me dinner.
> Unless you damn near change it, Johnny,
> Look out for another spinner."
>
> And when the work is good again,
> I'm in a better temper.

Bring out your box; we'll have a snuff,
For I'm the girl who'll venture. (#s 55, 57, 58, 59)

I first heard the song in Belfast. A year later, a variant was sung for me in a small town twenty miles southeast of the city. Most likely, the origin of the song will never be reliably ascertained. But, thirty miles southwest of Belfast, a former spinner told me that her version, to the air of "The Girl I Left Behind Me," was "composed" and sent during the time of the First World War by a British soldier to his girl friend, her aunt. Workers in that area are said to have learned it and to have sung it repeatedly as they traveled on the tramways to and from their jobs:

I give my curse to any girl
Who learns to be a spinner,
For brokcn-hcarted she will be
From breakfast time to dinner.

When the mill, it goes on,
The belts is all a crakin' [creaking],
The frames goes like the railway train,
And the ends is always breakin'.

When the gaffer [spinning master] he goes by,
His tongue goes clitter, clatter.
He rares and tears, and he curses and swears,
And says, "What is the matter?"

My frames are workin' very bad,
And I can't take no dinner.
I took out my box and take a pinch,
And perhaps I'll spin the better. (#81)

Despite pressures, there were moments when machines were going well and all ends were up. At such times, operatives might do laundry in hot water drawn from the pipes (see Photo 2) which led to the troughs on each frame, sometimes drying the washing on lines attached from the ends of their machines to a window molding. Those obliged to eat at the mill and to whom food could not be brought prepared a meal. A spinner filled a can with water, added tea and perhaps some cloves, and brewed the mixture in the trough of her spinning frame, maybe for hours. Often this provided the only accompaniment for the usual "piece" (of bread) carried to work in a paper or bit of cloth. But occasionally eggs were boiled in cans of water or were tied in cloth, to the corner of which a string was attached, and dangled in the trough. Or soup or stew, left over from Sunday's dinner, was warmed up. By turning the steam on full and heating them all morning, one could even cook sausages on the trough lid.

During a meal break, and in the morning before the starting horn blew, workers found additional opportunities to perpetuate their traditions: "We used to all sit, before 'she' started; we'd a got down on our—behind—and there was a sing-song. And maybe there'd a been a day you didn't want to come out. You'd a got your lunch sent in to you—you'd been all sittin', eatin'. . . and singin'" (#24). Even in mills with a reputation for strictness during work hours, or in rooms where the nature of the job was such that no frivolity prevailed, the workers could "carry on" during the dinner hour. Those so inclined and willing to risk slipping on oil-spotted floors were able to engage in an activity usually possible only then:

> I learned to dance in the mill. . . . We'd go down during the dinner hour, and we learned to dance then, up and down . . . the stands . . . "The Pride of Erin" and the "Arabian Waltz" and "The Lancers." . . . a girl . . . a great dancer, and took us in turn . . . and she taught us all that. . . . It is really happy memories of the mill. (#23)

The spinners on each side of a frame spun for a particular reeler, who, in turn, minded one side of a two-sided reel. The cage into which doffers placed full bobbins of yarn bore the number of the frame from which the doffs were made, and this corresponded with that on the side of a reel. Filled cages of yarn were transported to the reeler for whom they were intended. Placing the bobbins upon individual sockets of the *bobbin carrier* across the top of her machine, the reeler attached an end from each to the circular *swift* at the bottom, usually two and a half yards in circumference. (See Photo 7.) She then set the machine in motion. After 120 turns of the swift had reeled a *cut* of 300 yards of yarn, a bell rang, signaling the fact. Around each cut, a *leasing* was tied to separate it from succeeding ones. When the twelve

shifter, or
bobbin-carrier

swift

*Photo 7. A reeler and her reel in the Owen O'Cork Mills of Belfast Flax and Jute
Company, Belfast, ca. 1918. By courtesy of Mrs. Agnes E. McAuley.*

cuts which formed a *hank* had been reeled, the swift was col-
lapsed and all hanks stripped from the machine.

No single bobbin of yarn contained the 3,600 yards required to
complete the reeling of one hank, and so the reeler was obliged to
replace bobbins frequently. When this was done, the new ends
had to be *tied-in* to the loose ones already on the swift. It follows
that the fuller the bobbins sent up by her spinner, the less was
the tying-in required of a reeler. In addition, the more the yarn on
each bobbin was in a continuous thread, the fewer were the ends
she had to tie-in. A reeler, on piecework, who had to "make her
pay," sought to reel with the minimum number of stops for these
tyings-in. She was aided or hindered in the process by her spinner.

Friction occurred between the two women when a spinner, for
various reasons, sent up inadequately filled bobbins—the constant plea of the reelers to the spinners was, "For God's sake,
send us up big, fat doffs" (#47). The reeler could also be held
back by a spinner who did not piece together properly any broken
ends, thus forcing the reeler to pause in her work to rectify the
error.

If the two were "pally," the spinner made a special effort to spin
well and make big doffs. The reeler occasionally responded with
gifts of chocolate and the like. But it was asserted by a spinner
that a situation more likely developed whereby the reelers, constantly under pressure and seldom pleased, "would have took the
feet from us when comin' down the stairs" (#33).

The reeler who received "bad doffs" and "bad spinnin'" could
make known her displeasure with the operative and simultaneously draw the attention of the spinning master to the fact by
sending back empty cages with large X's marked upon them. The
spinner, upon receiving these, would mutter, "That bloody well
rotten reeler up there got my spinnin' sent down" (#53). However much the marking of the cages momentarily relieved the
frustrations of the reeler, she ran a calculated risk, for "If you
tramped on her [spinner's] toes . . . she'd a give you double work,
and double tyin'-in. She got her own back" (#23).

In fact, it was said, "You never got anything like a bad spinner
and a good reeler for to fight their way through" (#53). Reflecting, although very mildly, antagonisms between the two is this
song:

Never marry a reeler,
For you wouldn't know her pay,
But marry a good old spinner,
With her belly wet all day. (#22)

The verse can also be viewed as a compensating response to a social distinction deliberately fostered by the reelers: "The reelers wouldn't a touched clothes with ye" (#47). They considered themselves to be "aristocrats," "toffs," "the ladies of the mills," better than all the others: "We thought we were cleaner anyway" (#87). To flaunt their social superiority, many appeared at their reels "dressed up terrible," in blouses made of satin and crêpe de Chine (these worn only in later years), and they made sure that others knew they not only could buy shoes and stockings but could keep them on all day while at work. Early, in one mill, it was a reeler who first wore a coat to her job, and she was made fun of for "dressing up," but eventually it was common practice for most of the reelers to wear coats, not shawls. They did continue to wear the "patch," a coarse canvas apron (see Photo 7), which for many years had protected the reeler's skirt from wear and tear when she stopped her reel with her knee.

If reelers were at the top of the mill female social hierarchy, they were also very "hard wrought." It was not unusual for a reeler to remain at her reel through the dinner hour in order to make her pay. Some went with candles to be used to illuminate their work long before starting time in the morning and, with the steam power shut off, turned their reels by hand. The underlying significance of the remark "The reelers are going up with candles" (#68), made by those who observed the women walking to the mills in darkness, was understood by most linen workers. And at the end of a day, it was common practice for a zealous worker to carry home bobbins of spun yarn in order to right the ends there, so that she might not be held back on the following morning. Their seemingly insatiable desire for material to work with led the spinners to conclude that "they would eat the yarn" (#68).

The necessity to maintain strict count as to the number of yards reeled—monetary penalties were levied for high or low yardage counts—increased the pressure under which reelers worked, and this, combined with their being on piecework, almost precluded any opportunity for frivolity and displays of camaraderie on the part of this group of workers. However, this lack was more than compensated for—to their way of thinking—by the opportunity to earn higher wages and to work in cleaner surroundings.

With the spinners, motivations seem to have been different. It is true that jobs in spinning rooms were easier to come by than were the others, but an important factor keeping most of them at spinning, even when encouraged by relatives and friends to seek other employment and when substitute jobs were available, was the good times they had at their work in the mill. Such statements as "At that time it was great in the mill. . . . I would go back in the morning if I wasn't the age I was [seventy-six]" (#53) express far more than blurred recollections by elderly people of a past that never was. Repeatedly, along with statements of their harsh working conditions, comments were volunteered as to "happiest days of my life" (#23), "never wanted to leave" (#4), and "all the fun we had in those days" (#40). In some cases, it was mainly a matter of the job's having suited the personality of the worker. A woman with five sisters employed at various processes in the weaving factory preferred her own work:

> I liked the mill all right, because I was a bit devilish, and my pay was goin' on like, whether I worked or not, do ya understand? When we got our spinnin' master out of our room, we could have carried on like anything. Well, then, somebody would have shouted, "Whoo-oo! Oul' lad!" . . . that meant he was comin'. And when he comes, everybody was workin' as hard as niggers. . . . That's why I liked the mill. You got a good laugh. (#47)

A new spinning master who tried to reform things pitted his will against his subordinates, and the nature of the contest was appropriately verbalized in a mill version of a well-known football song:[28]

> It's a rare old room to work for,
> It's a rare old room to spin;
> When you read the history,
> It's enough to make your heart grow sa-a-ad.
> For we don't care what Johnny Larkin says,

Photo 8. Wet-spinners outside of Castle Gardens Mill of George Walker and Company, Newtownards, County Down, ca. 1930. By courtesy of Mrs. Ethel Dodds.

> Damn the hair we care,
> For we only know there's going to be a fight,
> And Number Three workers will be there. (#41)

The "fight" here was but another term for "carrying on" among themselves, the choice of words being a flexible one:

> Everybody puts their own words till it. . . . We'd a sung them at parties and one thing and another. And there would have been—gettin' a new spinnin' master—would have made up a

song about him. Them was all made up, you know. They weren't in print. They were all made-up songs then, that you made up out of your own minds. (#41)

Sometimes "fight" implied opposition of a stronger kind, when the women vowed not to work for the man with whom they disagreed, and the song then ended, "And the Number Five spinners won't be there" (#33).

Words more closely reflecting a mill setting appear in a set of mill variants:

> It's a rare old room to spin in,
> It's a rare old room to spin,
> For when the rove is comin' down,
> It's enough to make your hair grow thin.
> We don't care if the ends are up or down,
> Not a hair we care,

(A) For we only know that there's going to be a trip,
    And the Number Five spinners will be there. (#7)

        or

(B) For we only know there's going to be a march,
    And Shrigley spinners will be there. (#52)

Whether the emotion being registered is that of a carefree holiday spirit because of an impending mill outing (A) or militant discontent forecasting a strike (B), the choosing of a football song around which to build the words again seems apt.

A remark, "Anywhere you didn't make your own money, you carried on like the devil" (#47), must be qualified. For one thing, the amount of tomfoolery that actually transpired varied from mill to mill. A spinner employed in a town outside Belfast explained the lack of opportunity for such behavior where she worked:

> Maybe you wouldn't believe me, but when we were young, the mill was nearly like a concentration camp. You daren't look up. You daren't sit down. You couldn't a spoke to the girl that was beside ye. . . . There was so little industry then [in her town]. . . . They would think you couldn't work and sing. If you were concentratin' on your work, why you wouldn't be singin'. (#23)

For another thing, not all workers engaged at tasks for which they were given a set pay regardless of output sang and carried on equally. The doffers in the preparing rooms, for example, who removed from the roving frames there full bobbins of rove that were sent to the spinners, were described by the latter as being "just much the same as us" (#47). The rovers had opportunities to sing and sometimes modified songs from the spinning rooms: "They put Spinning Room in; we put Roving Room in" (#54). But, in general, the spinners noted, "They [rovers] never bothered, you see. They were more refined. We were called the roughs" (#47). If a desire to appear more ladylike was not a sufficient restraining device, the choking dust raised in the preparing process acted as a further deterrent.

In addition, it must be realized that there were always individual workers who expressed themselves in song or devilish behavior, regardless of the general tendency in the room where they labored. There were other spinners who were not particularly outgoing, who preferred the Spinning Room for different reasons. For them, there prevailed in that place a spirit of equality, manifested partially in the fact that no one dressed better than anyone else. Also, one's coworkers were described as being more friendly than elsewhere and willing to lend a hand when needed. The spinner with many ends down, who needed the assistance of a layer or piecer to help "square her up" or who, wishing to leave the room for a minute, called upon a "mate" to watch her frames for her, may not actually have made her request in the form of the following song, but the words do suggest the cooperative effort which many felt to have been a positive aspect of their work experience:

Hi, Mary Dougherty, will you lay me up an end,
Lay me up an end,
Lay me up an end?
Hi, Mary Dougherty, will you lay me up an end,
For we are all behind. (#53)

The verse has the same tune as "Hi, Nelly Jones," on page 52, not an unusual thing, because "there were loads of different words to them [tunes]. You might go somewhere else and you'll get different words to them" (#30).

Sometimes a request for help evoked a reply. One such (to the

Photo 9. Wet-spinners in Milewater Mill of York Street Flax Spinning Company, Belfast, ca. 1943. By courtesy of Mrs. Fred Morrison.

same tune), offered by a particularly spirited woman, can be looked upon more as good-natured bantering than as a pointed expression of ill-will:

> Hi, such and a one, you may go to hell,
> You may go to hell,
> You may go to hell.
> Hi, such and a one, you may go to hell,
> For we don't want you here. (#53)

That there was friction, as well as amiability, at certain times is not surprising, given the conditions under which the spinners operated. A feeling that preferential treatment had been meted out by an overlooker, or foreman, could provoke some outbursts against a fellow worker, as could remarks carelessly made. Often, antagonisms which arose outside the mill were continued during mill hours. However, the room at one mill labeled the "tight end" because a fight seemed to occur there every day was more likely the exception than the rule. Word of such incidents probably spread, and they may have been exaggerated in the telling. As a result: "You see, the mill girls got an awful bad name and that—the name of rowdies and fighters and one thing and another. But they weren't, just a name they got" (#41).

The mill girls, from Belfast especially, also acquired the reputation for colorful language. A favorite anecdote about William Conor, who painted, among other things, the industrial life of the city,[29] has as its theme the so-called coarseness of their speech. It relates how he used to dress himself in working man's clothing and hide his sketch pad behind a newspaper as he roamed the streets, hoping to catch his subjects in natural poses:

> He saw two young mill girls in shawls . . . walking at their lunch break. He was charmed with the grace and poetry of their motion and he said, "They walked like princesses." So, he was following them and wondering how to catch this in a sketch book. Suddenly they stopped and looked into a small shop window. He then had to pass them in case they'd notice what he was after. When passing them one girl said to the other, "What did I tell ya? Buns as big as your arse for a 'make' [ha'penny]." (#70)

In all fairness, it must be emphasized that their talk was equally characteristic of a multitude of other persons from the same socioeconomic background. Attributing rough language— or so it was deemed at the time—solely to mill girls, which usually implied the spinners, was part of the long-standing negative stereotyping of that class of workers.[30]

Disregarding the fact that they might be creating additional unfavorable impressions by their boisterous behavior, the girls, released from a hard day's work, continued to sing mill songs, and others, as they spilled out of the buildings. "Many's the time they'd a come down out of Wolf Hill and you'd a wondered what was wrong . . . singin', linked arm in arm and comin' down, many in fours and fives" (#42). Not everyone looked down upon them for this, and, apparently, one person was even a little envious:

> There used to be a man. . . . he was very wealthy, and he was visiting Belfast here. . . . but he had no health. And they were all comin' down out of Wolf Hill one night, and everyone singin' like Billy-o. And he stood and watched. And he says, "I'd give all the money in the land," he says, "if I could only come down like them workers." (#42)

The singing continued until the workers reached the mill gates or their street corners and parted to go their respective ways, or, in the country, until they came to a bridge or crossroads and set off in different directions.

Their songs and other traditions accompanied them wherever they went. In the case of some, it was from one mill to another in Belfast. A few moved between mills, close to each other, in outlying districts, and still others traveled from the city to rural areas. Between one mill in the country and Belfast, there was a considerable amount of traffic. The spinners who left the city—running away from debts, having had rows with their men, in trouble for fighting and drinking, or simply to escape to a more pleasant environment—responded to advertisements placed in newspapers and were provided with free transportation to the new place of work and lodgings when they arrived. A number married and settled in the area. Many drifted back to Belfast, carrying newly acquired traditions with them.

I cannot go into details about their lives while they were away

Photo 10. A painting of mill girls by William Conor (1881–1968). By courtesy of Mr. James Vitty, Linen Hall Library, Belfast.

from the city. But the stories which circulated widely about the behavior of some gave the mill town in which they worked temporarily a reputation in Belfast that was not really deserved. And the actions of certain of these women helped to reinforce in the country the stereotyped negative notions held about mill girls everywhere.

However, like Conor, who saw so much to admire in the dress and form of the "shawlies" (see Photo 10), still another individual, a discerning person, was able to view the women as the majority preferred to think of themselves:

> There used to be a man who lived across the street, and he was—like, he never worked in public much in his life—he was always a farmer. And he used to say—ah, "They must be queer and happy in the mill, because the mill girls is always smilin'." (#55)

Today, there are doffers and doffing mistresses and spinners at work. They are, though, all grown women. Some recall the songs and other traditional aspects of mill life, just described, but they say these are no longer part of their working lives. Pressed for reasons, they cite the introduction of new machines and time-motion studies which have changed in large measure the working environment. Certainly, however, the cessation of the hiring of the very young, which had ensured a supply of enthusiastic youngsters, full of song and sport, has been an important contributing factor as well.

FOUR

"But the Hacklers...
Are of the Best Class"

You couldn't get a hackler now at all.
They're all dead practically. They've all lived their
life and have gone on. . . . They were craftsmen. (#1)

If I cultivated the spinners, among the numerous females in the mill, for the richest yield of lore, I turned to the hacklers, among the male employees, for material of most interest to the folklorist. In this endeavor, I was faced with a scarcity of available informants.

Hand hackling, as a process, was dying out in Belfast around 1920 and continued only until the late 1930s in some of the more remote areas of the province. Therefore, while I could rely upon the testimonies of numerous persons to verify the specifics of material relating to the spinning rooms, I am forced to generalize about the experiences of those known most commonly as hacklers on the basis of a very small sample. Still, I did talk with enough people to allow me to infer with a high degree of certainty that the kinds of traditions shown clearly to have existed in one mill were most likely widespread throughout the industry. What follows is, essentially, a picture of the hackling shop in one country mill, supplemented with reminiscences obtained from persons elsewhere.

Hackling, as a general system of operations, consists of drawing conveniently sized *pieces*, or handfuls, of previously scutched flax fibers through a series of *hackles*—tools consisting mainly of rows of sharp, pointed pins set into a board—with the goal of cleaning and squaring up the pieces and splitting the fibers within them into finer filaments of an even size, ready for further

processing. During the period under investigation, this was usually accomplished in a series of three major actions, occurring in
this order: roughing, machine hackling, and flax dressing and
sorting. It is with the last step that the term *hackling* came to be
associated in informal mill parlance; its practitioners were known
as *hacklers* or *flax dressers* or *sorters*.

Roughing, a hand process like hackling, differs from it in several respects. Suffice it to say here that it was the rougher who
prepared pieces for the first hackling they were to undergo and
subjected them to an initial combing over a rough hackle (see
Photo 15), one on which the pins were spaced farther apart than
those on the tools employed by the flax dresser. From the
rougher, parcels of squared-up pieces of fiber were passed on to
the Machine Room, where individual pieces were fed into a machine designed to subject them to further treatment by a number
of hackles, graduated in size. The flax dresser gave the pieces intended for fine yarn additional combing and, finally, sorted them
out into bunches, according to the overall quality of the fiber.

The areas in which roughers and hacklers labored frequently
adjoined one another (see Figure 1), and the craftsmen in each,
as well as sharing certain modes of behavior, usually knew what
went on in the other place of work. For this reason, although it is
the lore of the Hackling Shop with which this account is primarily concerned, I have considered it appropriate to include materials relating to both groups.

Apprentices to the hackling trade were usually selected from
the supply of boys found in the Machine Room, working at several jobs connected with the tending of each hackling machine
found there. (See Photo 11.) Although a lad might commence
work when he was only twelve, as a half-timer, he became eligi-
ble to begin serving his time in the trade only when he neared the
age of sixteen, and even then he was not assured of being chosen
to learn the work. There could be only one apprentice to every
seven flax dressers, the eldest hand in the Machine Room usually
being taken on first. It follows that a boy's chances depended

*Photo 11. Young boys at hackling machines in York Street Flax Spinning and
Weaving Company, Belfast, ca. 1900. From the Welch Collection, by courtesy of
the Ulster Museum, Belfast.*

MACHINE HACKLING

PATENT BELFAST.

TREET MILL.

R.W. 1221.

largely upon the number of hacklers working in a mill and how long he was able to wait for his opportunity to advance.

The fortunate individual began his apprenticeship, which lasted seven years before 1920 and five years after that, by being assigned to a *berth* which happened to be vacant at the time, and by being given the coarsest grades of flax with which to work. At first, he had only to pull the fibers through one hackle —"touch-'em," as it was termed—and was not expected to know how to break off ends. After working with several parcels and getting "on to the run of it," he was provided with flax of a better quality and gradually refined his techniques of handling it. By the end of a year, it was known if a lad could "make a shape of it." If it appeared that he could not and if he was to remain in the mill, he was sent to work as a rougher or back to the machines.

His pay at the beginning was what he had been receiving in the Machine Room and continued at that rate until a designated period of time—three weeks in one mill, six months in another—had elapsed, after which he was told, "You're on your own hook. What you make you get, and what you don't make you don't get" (#2). The money earned by the apprentice for this piecework was less than fellow hacklers received for the same output, but it increased a specified amount every six months or year while he served his time.[1]

Berths were positioned in a Hackling Shop in different ways. In some mills they were located side by side along the walls of a room; in others, they formed two rows, facing and adjoining one another, down the center; and, in very large shops, a combination of the two placements was used. Hackles and a *touch pin* upon which he squared up the ends of dressed flax were screwed into a wooden ledge before each man, and alongside him was a shelf upon which he laid the pieces of fiber with which he was working. (See Photo 13.)

Hackling was considered to be a highly skilled trade, requiring the ability to dress flax properly and, as well, an eye for determining the quality of yarn into which it would eventually be spun. The flax dresser did his work using two or three hackles instead of the one used by the rougher. One of the hackles employed was known as a *ten*, a wooden block into which were inserted up to 468 pins; the *switch*, used next, contained, roughly speaking, anywhere from 2,000 to 8,000 shorter pins. "They

Photo 12. A "blow through the ten hackle": left to right, sorter's switch, ten, touch pin. Posed for author at Killyleagh Flax Spinning Company, Killyleagh, County Down.

called it [the Hackling Shop] Spike Island, so many pins about the place" (#2).

After being brought from the Machine Room, parcels of flax of appropriate quality were apportioned to each flax dresser. From them, he drew out individual pieces, of which there were about ten to a parcel. Grasping the root end of each handful in turn, he subjected it to a *blow* through the ten hackle (see Photo 12), broke off short fibers and coarse ends, which formed part of what was known as *sorter's tow*, on his touch pin, gave it one or more additional pulls through the ten, and then combed the top and bottom sides of the piece several times through the switch to *finish* it. Next, he seized the handful of fibers by the other end and repeated his actions. To catch bits of dirt which clung to the fibers, a *nap extractor*, located to one side or in front of the switch, was utilized. Familiarity with the hackler's motions allows one to get the point of this joke:

> A hackler met a foreman on the train and asked him if there were any jobs available in his parts. The foreman said, "What sort of a hackler are you?" Then the oul' boy took his muffler off and gave it a bit of a blow over the carriage door. Then he said to the foreman, "How's that?" The foreman replied, "You wouldn't do atall." Then the hackler said, "What's wrong?" The foreman again: "You're taking off too much tow." (#2)

Before he completed his work the hackler made his own characteristic *lap*, or fold, in each piece and built the dressed flax into one of several stacks, being careful to sort it into a bunch with others of the same quality.

Each hackler had to meet his quota of dressed flax daily—at one period of time, at the coarse end of the shop, fifty-seven pounds of flax destined to become warp yarn or fifty-four pounds for weft yarn, but, at the fine end, only forty-five pounds of fibers to be spun into weft. The man who dressed very fine grades of flax, those which necessitated his combing the fibers through three hackles, was allowed to produce a smaller amount of weft flax than his fellow workman who could do his work in only two steps, on that number of tools. Those who dressed coarser and, therefore, heavier flax, earmarked for warp, turned in the heaviest bundles. In general, it may be said that a beginning hackler worked with coarser grades of flax—perhaps only 3s, 4s, and 5s—and progressed to fine and then the finest qualities of raw materials—"16s in them days"—as he acquired more precise skills and as older men who had handled these sorts vacated their berths. Physically, he moved up the line of berths to the top end where the finer work was done.

While spinners were at the low end of the mill status hierarchy, flax dressers were considered by all to be "the elite." Some persons attributed the high prestige accorded them primarily to the belief that they were the mainstay of the industry, inasmuch as

Photo 13. A "gentleman of the mill" at fine hand hackling and sorting (probably at Doagh Flax Spinning Company, Doagh, County Antrim), ca. 1919. From the Green Collection, by courtesy of the Trustees of the Ulster Folk and Transport Museum, Holywood, County Down.

"it was up to the hackler—the way he done his work—and his stuff was hackled—made the stuff" (#38). Others explained the fact that they were considered to be the "cream of the trade" in monetary terms; although foremen and skilled mechanics often earned more than they, the hacklers did receive wages considerably higher than those of most of their coworkers.[3]

The clothing that they wore may have contributed to their being designated the "gentlemen of the mill." At one time, it had been considered elegant enough to be mentioned in a song:

Hi ho, the hacklers-o,
Hi ho, the hacklers-o,
Hi ho, the hacklers-o,
On a Monday morning.

There they go,
With their long-tailed coats,
Silken hats and dandy cuffs,
Their apron shines like powder puffs,
All on a Monday morning. (#7)

"Billy Mason wore a long-tailed coat" (#7). But such a garment and the high hats fashionable at the turn of the century eventually disappeared. So did the white linen waistcoats and white linen hats worn at one time by many of the craftsmen. The hacklers continued wearing collars and ties to work, but these they removed and hung on a small bench while hand dressing and sorting the flax; they hackled in their vests and shirt sleeves (see Photos 13 and 14). In the evening, they set up pieces of broken mirrors at their berths and fixed their ties and smoothed their hair before venturing out.

It was the white apron which persisted as a characteristic part of their garb and an item of clothing always mentioned in connection with them. An apprentice was told to acquire one when he went on piecework:

> You must have a linen apron, you see. But some of them hadn't the money, and maybe their wives had bleached a flour bag. And the flour bags in them days was decorated with big ships sailin' across. So, an old fella had a flour bag on, and the ship was sailin' across. It wasn't bleached out properly. And all the boys got up on the other side of the boards and looked over, and made comments on the ship— draw his attention to it: "Oh, she's sailin' well. Do you think she's in a head wind?" Or he says, "I think she's in a tack." . . . He had to get hisself a linen apron after that. (#2)

Dust, raised while flax was being combed, often settled in the hair. The white linen hat, used earlier to prevent this, was replaced in winter by the everyday woolen, peaked variety. When warmer weather arrived, the hacklers switched to paper hats (see Photo 14). These were blue in some mills but more usually white and are remembered as being characteristic of the men. In one country mill, they were constructed from the *Belfast Telegraph* and were "the shape of a bag of sweets."

Their relatively high status made flax dressers desirable as husbands: "You were counted grand if you got a hackler" (#26). The girl fortunate enough to be married to one shared some of his prestige in the community and obtained the satisfaction of being called, in some areas, a "hackler's lady." She, more than most, could expect a degree of monetary security. There was, for example, the hackler's comparatively high pay. At one time, when a farm laborer was earning ten or twelve shillings weekly, her husband could be making fifty. In addition, many such men, with adequate resources and ability, became the shop owners in a town, leaving the operation of the business in the hands of family members while they continued on in the mill. When machine hackling replaced the hand operations entirely, the hackler fortunate enough to own a shop "retired" to it. Many others merely became redundant.

One man, only an apprentice at the time of the transition, did not leave the mill. Instead he was advanced through the years to the position of foreman in the Machine Hackling Shop, a job from which he had recently retired at the time of this study. And, although the nature of his work had changed, he still remembered earlier days. Imbued with an intense curiosity about happenings in the past—in the mill and outside—and well able to characterize events and people as he witnessed and heard about them, he was an excellent source of information about life in the shop where the flax dressers worked during the first decades of this century. As an apprentice, though, he was more observer than participant in the conversation of his coworkers, and he played the same passive role even in the company of his father, who had himself been a hackler for fifty years:

> I never talked in the hacklin' shop. . . . I just listened to all, cocked my ears, laughed . . . listened all the time. . . . [My father] he gabbled from mornin' till night, you know—the yarns he could spin. (#2)

Although flax dressers were among those whose pay was dependent upon output, they were able, nevertheless, to talk and hackle simultaneously. In fact, conversation helped to relieve the

Photo 14. Flax dressers in their summer hats (mill unidentified), ca. 1926. Photograph by Alexander R. Hogg, by courtesy of the Ulster Museum, Belfast.

monotony of repetitive motions and to reduce tensions generated in the men as they worked, always under pressure to produce each day a specified amount of properly dressed and sorted flax. Contributing to the ease with which words could be exchanged were the physical arrangement of the work areas and the absence of noisy machinery. A single fan helped to draw away *stir*—dust raised in the hackling process—by sucking it in through small vents located in front of each man behind the hackles (see Photo 13). Although "two butterflies could have created more ventilation by flapping their wings" (#2), at least its low hum was not a distracting feature. So a man, four feet away from the hacklers in the berths on either side, could converse with them, and with the men opposite (where the berths were so positioned), in an ordinary speaking voice; those at a distance from one another could communicate by shouting back and forth.

"The 'crack' in the Hackling Shop was good" (#2). Throughout the mills, it usually began with a discussion instigated by the "reader." While others in the room continued at their work and took turns doing some of his, it was customary for one man, chosen because of his ability to read exceptionally well, to transmit in a loud voice selected portions of the daily newspaper. The ensuing commentary on events of the day could last several hours, and often great arguments followed reports of speeches made by politicians or editorials commenting upon them. Particularly were the issues of a National Health Scheme and Home Rule hotly debated in the mill during that era. Possibly an extension into the workplace of the activities carried on in extracurricular Reading Rooms, so prominent a feature in the lives of working men in early nineteenth-century England,[4] the morning news sessions were a welcome part of each day. It was to the hacklers, considered by all to be well informed, that others in the mill came in order to find out about current happenings.

Later the talk was extended to other topics:

> You would listen to all the chat. You'd be, maybe at an end where it was all horse racin', football, and such like. And then you were prickin' your ears up to hear the conversation farther up the shop. . . . you missed a terrible lot of good yarns. . . . You'd advance up the shop to the older hands . . .

they were the ones who were steady . . . and they told all
those tales, kept one another goin' all day. (#2)

Sometimes the conversation centered on personalities of the
past. One such was a hackling master who had died shortly after
the turn of the century. Apprentices to the trade, hearing the
virtues of this "grandfather of the Hackling Shop" frequently
cited, had their curiosity aroused:

> I asked one old hackler if he minded William John. "I think I
> mind him," he says. "I no worked with him, but I can tell you
> a very rare tale about him. I don't believe in ghosts. But, he
> was out bad. And I thought he was gonna die. And then
> again I thought he was gonna get better. But, he had a habit
> of standing at the tow store door . . . in the morn when peo-
> ple was comin' to work. And I was comin' down this day, and
> I seen William John Moore, standing at the door and I says,
> 'That's queer. Why didn't he speak to me?'
>
> "So I went into the Hacklin' Shop, and another one or two
> come in, and I says, 'Joe, I was speakin' to William John this
> morning. I see he's doing rightly.' And they started to laugh.
> I says, 'What are you laughing about?' 'Where did you speak
> to him?' 'Well, he was standin' at the tow store door there,
> and I says, "Good morning," and he never spoke to me.' And
> one says to the other, 'Your granny! William John died at ten
> minutes to eight.'" . . . He says, "There you are now. I've
> seen a ghost, but I still don't believe it." (#2)

The extent to which the supernatural was discussed in the
Hackling Shop cannot be ascertained from the preceding, but
that the room served on occasion as a kind of forum for the airing
of old and new attitudes toward certain elements of it is suggested by another anecdote, recalled as having been related
there. An elderly hackler's activities are described:

> He used to go up to these farms at night . . . for buttermilk
> and the like. And I said, "Well, Willy, where were you last
> night?" "I was over at the forth." That's two rings up on the
> hill, called Castle William, but he called them the forth. "Ah,
> seen any fairies?" Willy said, "I was comin' by along the bot-
> tom of the forth, and I heared the loveliest music." And Willy

says, "I went in to see, and there they were," he says, "all sittin' on the stinkin' weeds [ragweed], playin' their violins." And there was a great laugh. (#2)

The oft-repeated "yarns" which centered on the activities of former hacklers revealed a lighter side of the working day, not always obvious to the outsider, and recalled certain aspects of small-town life which were no longer in existence:

> They used to tell me about . . . Fair Day. . . . And the apple stalls were always close to the gates. And the boys woulda stood with their legs just beside the tables, held up. And when the last horn blew, they went, and down went the apples, and they all pounced. And through the gates, and the gates was closed. . . .
>
> You see, there was one day . . . an old fella, had spectacles —there were all kinds of spectacles. And when the horn blew, they run with the spectacles on—the hacklers, without gettin' honest specs on—and they were all tryin' them on. (#2)

Working all day over the pins in the glare of the sunlight was a strain on the men and resulted in bad eyesight for many.[5] It was hoped that the glasses absconded with on Fair Day would provide relief and enable the men to see more clearly when writing out tickets which stated the date and the bale and sort numbers:

> The hacklers were all adjustin' specs all evenin', tryin' 'em on. "Let me see yours." . . . They were takin' eyes out of 'em, you see. "That's a good eyepiece for the left. Change it for the other." "Lend me your pane. That's a good one for the right." Everyone was changin' with one another. (#2)

The men at the stalls were not the only ones to fall victim to the pranks of the flax dressers:

> It woulda been peddlers come to the mill lane—Plantation Lane—you see, you looked in. And always wagged them over. "Come over till we see your wares." And the top half of the windows bent down. You put a bucket of water on it. And the blinds was on. And some of the boys—had to take your turn—"You pull the blinds down, and I'll pull the water. . . ."

So, opened the bag up to show you your wares. And then threw the water down, come down on the back of his head. . . . Hackler's joke! (#2)

A different kind of "hackler's joke" was regularly played on the unsuspecting until hand hackling died out:

The hackle is along here in the front. In the back of the hackle is a hole where you push your tow—the short fibers from off the flax—you kept pushin' 'em down in this hole. Well . . . what's called hackler's joke, when you went out in the yard or somewhere, they took the tow off and sent a bucket in. The bucket didn't pass through; they just stuck it in tight. And they put a slim layer over the top of this—it was full of water. And maybe you'd a hackled . . . maybe another eight or ten pieces, and then you'd pushed your hand down in the water. And then, you'd jumped back with a shock and somebody would shout, "Hackler's joke!" (#2)

The joke was known in Belfast, as was the following:

And then there was . . . the touch pin. . . . on the other side of the hackle. And . . . some old fella was very vigorous breakin' 'em. It took a good big breakin' off. And there's a wee screw on the side. You removed the screw, for to take the pin out and steal it, and you put a wooden one in its place, dipped in ink so he wouldn't catch it on. And he'd come sailin' in. He'd put the flax around and pulled, broke . . . and he'd a cursed. Another hackler's joke. . . . Them was the value in them days. (#2)

The hackles were similarly loosened:

I seen them—I seen them doin' it—it was a dangerous thing—takin' the screw out of the hackles. . . . And as soon as you woulda put a piece in, you woulda pulled. It just went beside your feet. Sometimes it—danger—took your feet off you, you know. (#2)

However therapeutic—in the sense of diverting the men's attention for a few moments from the task at hand—these antics may have been, there was little respite from the stir, which filled

Photo 15. Roughers in the Barn Mills of James Taylor and Sons, Carrickfergus, County Antrim, ca. 1916. By courtesy of Mr. John Weatherup.

the air and settled in the throats and lungs of the workers. (The roughers, shown in Photo 15, who dealt with dirtier flax, were troubled even more.) In this respect, Monday posed special problems for them. Having been away from the mill part of Saturday and all of Sunday, the men were acutely aware on the following day of the contrast between conditions in the shop and the fresh air outside. "You'd come in on Monday morning, and it just catched ye. You'd be sittin', pantin', you see, there, maybe for hours, and some had to go home early" (#2).

That the constant assault of the stir might be the cause of serious discomfort for the remainder of their lives was not uppermost in their minds then; their immediate concern was to alleviate the "Mondayish" feelings which they were all experiencing. As their distress eased off later in the week, tobacco might be sufficient to keep their mouths and throats moist:

I'll tell you one thing. I never knew a hackler who didn't
chaw tobacco. . . . When we went to take the berths down,
when they . . . made the Preparin' Room over the Mechanic
Shop there, we took the old hacklers' berths down. . . . we
had to use our chisels to cut the nuts away, because there
were at least three-quarters of an inch of tobacco on them.
(#38)

But on Monday a stronger remedy was often required:

Anyone that was chesty, the only freedom they had was a
drink. It cleared the pipes, you see. That's the only thing that
helped them. . . . Sometimes they'd a got someone to bring it
out for them—someone that had an excuse out. That was for
some of the older men that were really bad. (#8)

A man greatly in need of relief had only to remark that he was
going out for a "penneth of nails," or the like. In the days when a
public house was often combined with a shop selling other articles, he walked through the front portion of the premises and secured his glass of whiskey at the back.

Those chronically afflicted sought professional advice, in addition. Monday morning, for the workers in the country mill, was
also dispensary day. Seeking relief from their poucey feelings,
caused by *pouce*, or flax dust, in the air, or from other ailments
which were often by-products of their work, the hacklers,
granted passes to leave the shop, made their way to the physician. There was not much that even a sympathetic medical man
could do for them.

. . . they went up the lane there . . . running along by the
mill. And old Dr. Sproule—he was a bit of a wit, too, and he
used to say, "What brings you fellas here? Sure there's no
cure for youse fellas. Go way up to the other end of the lane."
And . . . up at the other end of the lane was the cemetery.
And he says, "The only cure up there is Tommy Young."
Well, Tommy Young was the gravedigger [and a rougher
himself]. (#2)

It is, in a way, surprising that all flax dressers did not become
heavy drinkers and dependent on spirits. Instead, many confined

their imbibing to the evenings on which they were paid. A woman, speaking of her father, recalled:

> And he wouldn't a took no drink, only every fortnight. He woulda said, "Well, I'm poucey, and" . . . it was fortnightly pay—"I'm goin' in for a good pumper of whiskey to get all that flax away." (#26)

When the hacklers did imbibe, "they all drank the hard stuff," as opposed to porter and soft drinks such as bottled lemonade and fruit squashes. In Belfast, the best rum was obtained at John McConville's, located in the midst of numerous mills. Although payday brought many workers—men, and women "who took a half one"—into the place, the hacklers and roughers were sure to be there on a Monday evening, obtaining the best available relief for the distress in their throats and chests.

Some of the older men found continuity between their plight and that of unfortunates from a distant past in words from the Old Testament:

> The men at the top, the intellectuals . . . used to do a lot of debating. It was all debated on a verse in the Bible. I think it's in Isaiah, and it says, "Woe unto them that worketh and weaveth fine flax." [6] One of them used to say, "That's damnation to us." And, of course, the other'd say, "No, maybe it means the extraction of the pouce and stir, the way it affects your lungs." (#2)

Other portions of the Bible, brought out and read by the revered hackling master William John Moore when there was a lull in the conversation, also provoked animated discourse.

Many foremen recognized, as did William John, that continuing discussions helped to pass time for the flax dressers and, like him, they initiated the talk. Others, less attuned to the needs of the workers, "kept the hacklers down"—would not allow them to speak above a whisper or to whistle—and spent the day circulating through the shop seeing that their strictures were observed. To one such individual was applied the epithet "head beetler," a term reminiscent of the pounding action of the machine employed formerly in a finishing process for cloth. About another, who not only was strict but whose abilities were not respected by his subordinates, it was said, "He couldn't clean dung out of a pig shed" (#2).

"It was a hiss in the Hacklin' Shop" which signaled the approach of a foreman or manager. One man who objected to having his appearance noted in such a way was told, "Look, did you ever see a blackbird down in the hedge when it sees a hawk comin'? It squeals like the devil. Well, the same thing's happenin' now." After the hiss, it was "Heads down. Asses up" (#2).

Word of these and other overlookers was carried about the industry by "tramp hacklers." Usually unmarried men, with a propensity for drink and a seeming disinclination to settle down to steady work, they moved from mill to mill:

> In my time, they woulda come . . . to the back gate mostly, and you always had a few berths empty. . . . I worked beside an old fella from County Cork. In County Cork there was an old spinnin' mill at one time, too. And them fellas woulda tramped to Sion Mills and maybe stayed there a month. And then they woulda come to Milewater. Milewater was York Road Spinning Company, Belfast. And then there was another old spinning company, the Owen O'Cork.
>
> And then, maybe, they'd come down to Shrigley. Maybe to Killyleagh. Maybe some of them woulda spent years there; others maybe spent two or three weeks—got tired of it— went on maybe to Castlewellan, or Annsborough, and so on, across to Kilburney, Scotland, and Clitermore in England. They just kept movin' around. They never had a penny, you see. They all went through it. (#2)

Some elderly men have objected to the use of the term *tramp*. But, long before their time, it bore no negative connotation to the insider, meaning simply "a working man 'on the road' in quest of work."[7] It may be that by the early 1900s the word had come to be applied only to a less respectable breed of artisans.

In instances where there were no available berths, the traveling craftsmen would not depart empty-handed. Instead—in an old custom among working men[8]—someone in the shop "lifted a turn," took up a collection from those at work, that was "enough to put the man on the road to the next place" (#49) or to pay his fare home. The donors usually contributed willingly, knowing they could expect similar treatment if they moved on, as did some, who were lured away by the itinerants.

For those who did secure employment, it was necessary that they locate lodgings. These might be provided by a fellow workman with whom one had become friendly during a previous work stint in a mill. There were, furthermore, always a few boarding houses where they might be accommodated.

In the main, these men were capable and were employed under the same conditions as those who worked more permanently in a place, with one difference. They received equal wages, but, whereas the other men were paid fortnightly, the tramp hackler was given his money weekly, the hope being that he would use it to pay for his "digs," rented under those terms. The remainder of his pay seemingly went for drink. Not for him was there motivation to provide himself with the dress appropriate to the flax dresser. If he even had an apron, it was not of fine white linen but was made of any easily acquired material and was always torn and soiled. A hole was disguised by making a knot in that portion of the cloth: "Put another reef in her" or "more tits on her" (#2).

It was sometimes maintained that the personal prejudices of those in charge of hiring determined where the men would finally land a job. A racist anecdote exaggerating the bias of one individual is built upon that theme:

> The man in charge of the Hackling Shop, he came from a small village here, called Doagh. And . . . it was said if you went there and applied for a job—if you said that you came from Doagh, there were no further questions asked. You just got a job. So, one day a large Negro came up, and he said, "Me Doagh, too." (#62)

It is more likely that, as long as available berths exceeded the supply of skilled hacklers, the foreman of a shop, always intent upon increasing the production of properly dressed flax, welcomed the appearance of such men. As workmen had done in earlier times,[9] fellow hacklers looked forward to their coming for another reason. The wanderers carried with them all the "scandal of the trade" and songs they had heard along the way:

The spinners and reelers of sweet Killyleagh,
Are good at their job, we all must say,
But the hacklers and roughers are of the best class,
From old Dido Kennedy to Jimmy McMath. (#2)

"The verse after that is 'Tra la la, tra la la'. . . . One person [said that] and then another one'd make up another verse, you see" (#2). Whether the same was done in all mills and where the song originated cannot be ascertained. But at least this stanza was known in other places:

I think that come from Tandragee, too. . . . because there is one of the old hacklers that come that way, and he said, "We have one the same." And it was "The spinners and reelers of Tandragee"—here it was "sweet Killyleagh." . . . The same . . . tune from Tandragee. . . . Them old hacklers come from one place to the other and gave these songs and one thing and another. (#2)

A rhyme, or perhaps song, must have been carried in the same way to Belfast, where it was heard fifty years ago in the Hackling Shop of a mill by a man who served time there while training for a managerial position:

Do you ken James McGarry,
Who works on the Braid?
He's a face like a crow,
And a sorter to trade.
Sure I ken James McGarry,
And his brother Jock, twa,
It's strange that I wouldn'ta,
When I come from Buckna. (#62)

"The Braid was a linen mill, Ballymena. [See Photo 16.] The Braid River runs through Ballymena, and this mill was on the River Braid. . . . Buckna was a small town; it was very small. . . . There were quite a lot of other verses [recited about different people]" (#62).[10]

If tramp hacklers were at times bearers of certain kinds of lore, they often became, after their departure, the subjects of anec-

Photo 16. Braid Water Spinning Mill, Ballymena, County Antrim, ca. 1910. From the Lawrence Collection, by courtesy of the National Library of Ireland, Dublin.

dotes, frequently repeated, which related their idiosyncracies. A number of these concern their experiences with landladies:

> I mind laughin'. One time an old fella . . . says to me, "All the landladies in this island, they all cry about me." And I says, "I don't think the old lady in Shrigley would cry about you." "Oh, indeed, she'll cry about me." So, a month or two after he left, I said to some of the boys, "Did so-and-so cry about him?" "Yes, she did." And I says, "Forever, why?" "Because he left with two weeks he didn't pay her." . . . She had good reason to cry about him. . . . He never come back again because once done him in that part. (#2)

There was an old hackler here, through the country. And he was a terrible big man, a great eater, you know. They used to tell about him. He went to different houses. Some didn't feed too well. And one day he got a plate . . . not very much on it. And on the plate was a boat. And he would lift this plate, and he'd look at it, and the old lady would say to him, "Well, Henry, what's wrong with that plate?" "Nothin', no wrong with the plate," he says. "But I'm just lookin' at this boat, and mind you," he says, "the cargo she's carrying today," he says, "will not sink her."

Then, at night, maybe, the old lady would say, "Henry, will you take an egg?" "Well," he says, "I hear two wouldn't do you a bit of harm." (#2)

They also frequently became the butt of jokes, as did the traveling hackler from Cork, a man whose habit of bringing in bicarbonate of soda to ease his bad stomach provided an opportunity for merriment:

Frankie and me were out huntin' one night. And I don't know if you know rabbits or not. They make burrows in the ground. And around the front of the burrow there's rabbit manure—rabbit dung, as we call it. They're wee, round pickles. So Frankie collected four or five of these one night and rolled them in his hand in flour, put them in a little box. . . . I had written on the box "Two tablets to be taken after meals. Vegetable tablets." And Old Mick took these and gurgled his neck and down goes two of them. I could hardly keep a straight face. And around four o'clock in the evening, I said, "Well, Mick, how about your stomach?" "Much better," he says. (#2)[11]

Many of the younger tramp hacklers—twenty to thirty years of age and "too fidgety to settle down"—were good Irish step dancers. By using the mills as a performing arena, they not only kept in practice but also helped to perpetuate the dancing tradition in many areas. On Friday evening, in some firms, while the men were cleaning up, the foreman, desiring to escape from the heavy stir being raised during the operation, left and went about mill business elsewhere. "That was the time the value started." One of the young men placed a piece of hard board on the stone tiles at one end of the shop. "Someone played, maybe a tin flute or a 'French fiddle'—a French fiddle is a mouth organ. . . . And he woulda played a bit of a jig, and this boy woulda step danced in good style." (A good dancer was said to have been one who "did good tappin' with his feet.") (#2)

The fact that the weekend was at hand was certainly cause for merriment, but, in fact, any time a foreman absented himself could be an occasion for dancing; the more spirited tapped their heels rhythmically on the tiles as they worked.

Mobility among the flax dressers was not confined to those specifically referred to in this period as tramp hacklers. "There were that many hacklers movin', goin' back and forth, you never knew who'd be workin' next to you" (#49). The factors which motivated the others were not necessarily related to sheer wanderlust and often indicated simply a desire to secure optimal working conditions. All the itinerants seemed to have shared certain personality traits, however—an unwillingness to yield easily to authority and rather quick tempers—and, since the demand for their labor was fairly constant, they could afford to give in to their frustrations.

Sometimes a hackler, after receiving a "bad parcel"—flax to be hackled which, improperly scutched, was full of foreign particles and "like a hen's nest"—would become angry at not being able to make his pay that day and would be away. Rows with a foreman could easily result in a hackler moving on: "You had no call to be abused or anything—talkin' to you the same as if you were a dog" (#49). Those who shared with a relative a house owned and rented to them by a firm, or perhaps by a foreman in the company, were sometimes more restricted in their movements; an unsympathetic landlord could use the threat of eviction for the individuals left behind, it was felt.

Whether the predicament described in the following mill version of a well-known song could have stirred a flax dresser to move on is not certain:

A foolish young girl was I,
For to fall in love with a hackler boy,
A hackler boy of low degree;
He was in love when he courted me.

There is a black bird on yon tree,
Some say it's blind and cannot see,

But I wish, I wish that it had a been me,
When I fell in with bad company.

I wish my baby it was born,
And smiling on a summer's morn,
And I, poor girl, both dead and gone,
And the green grass growing over me.

Oh, when my apron it hung low,
He followed me through frost and snow,
But now my apron is to my chin,
And he passes my door, and he never looks in.

A foolish young girl was I,
For to fall in love with a hackler boy,
A hackler boy of low degree;
He was in love when he courted me. (#67)[12]

The woman, seventy-nine years old and residing in the country, who sang about the hackler boy, recalled having learned the words from "the old hands," older women, in the mill. There is, thus, the indication that the song in that form is of considerable age. Today, when it is sung, however, the first and last stanzas are usually omitted, and, indeed, those to whom this fact was pointed out confessed to never having heard them. Perhaps the verses faded away as the trade itself disappeared, both more slowly in outlying districts. Lending some support to such a contention is the comment made by a very astute man, a former linen worker in Belfast, after listening to the song for the first time:

That would strike me as bein' from a country mill. . . . In some way, the tone of it to me, and the words of it, would be more like a folk-known one from the country. To me, I can't see the town spinners or mill ones singin' anything like that. . . . You see, why I say that, why it seems to be country —in the town . . . if you asked the ordinary spinner what the hackler was, she probably couldn't tell you. But in the country village, it would be a different thing. (#38)

In other words, he was suggesting that the town spinners, deprived of everyday contact with the hacklers and reminders of their work, would by now be less likely than women in the country to recall and, thus, sing about those men.

The man who was free to move generally continued to do so until he secured a berth to his liking, and when he found a spot where the work was good he often sent word to mates left behind, telling them how many jobs were available. In making a decision to remain in a place, he was strongly influenced by several factors other than pay. One was the quality of flax consistently purchased by a firm and passed on to him to dress. Another was the cleanliness—a concept which included the relative lack of stir in a shop—of the mill itself. In this respect, one Belfast firm was repeatedly mentioned as being outstanding. It was claimed that the worker who was fortunate enough to gain employment there never left. It was also said of the place that "if any old hackler died, there was someone in there before he was in the coffin" (#49). The fact that another mill had proper toilets, hand basins, and towels was considered important enough to be mentioned by other flax dressers. In addition, some men were very much impressed by the presence in a Hackling Shop of a foreman with whom they could work amicably.

Despite a considerable amount of mobility among some of their number, the majority of hacklers were men who had served their time in a particular mill, who were married and had families in the immediate area, and who tended to remain in that one spot. They accepted the fact that work was a necessity, recognized that jobs were hard to come by, took comfort in knowing that "everyone was in the same boat," and were dedicated to their labor, achieving satisfaction in a job well done. For them there were certain psychological advantages. Especially was this so of those who worked in smaller firms where there were, perhaps, only thirty flax dressers, as contrasted with those companies which employed a far larger number. They enjoyed a special kind of camaraderie, over and above that generated by an awareness of sharing the fruits, good and bad, of similar labor. One manifestation of this was the use of nicknames, mainly in reference, among all those employed in a shop over an extended period of time. The knowledge of these was shared with one's coworkers with the understanding that they were not to be readily volunteered to outsiders: "They used to say they didn't tell any tales out of school, as it were. When you got out at night, you didn't talk about it at the corner, you know" (#2).

A delineation of nicknames in common use among the hacklers—and roughers, with whom they were so closely associated—during one period of time in one mill serves to verify the existence of the practice (Figure 1). Accompanying explanations for them reveal their origins, give insights into values and practices of the wider culture from which these men sprang, and provide a more personal image of the craftsmen.

In the country mill, the nicknames were carved on the doors of wooden boxes where bundles of dressed flax were put or on small boards at the back of the hackles. Also inscribed were dates of important events which had taken place in the area—births, deaths, weddings, drownings, conscriptions into the army, and football scores—and when arguments arose as to the time of past occurrences, it was to the inscriptions that the men turned for verification of their points of view. Nicknames are, of course, a common phenomenon in Ireland. But those which circulated among the settled flax dressers constituted a part of the lore of their own mills, and those assigned to tramp hacklers seem to have been transmitted, along with stories about them, throughout the industry. I could not learn whether the carving of names and dates existed elsewhere.

Not investigated in any depth, because they relate mostly to a mechanical process in which the hand hacklers were not directly involved and because they were first mentioned to me at a time when I had no opportunity to conduct research on the topic, were special names for parts of the older-style hackling machine. The few examples that were collected and that are dealt with here briefly demonstrate the existence of such terminology and, furthermore, suggest the possibility of a fruitful area for more concentrated study.

Knowledge of the specialized vocabulary was acquired by the men who served as machine boys prior to becoming apprentices to the hackling trade and by those who worked in proximity to the machines. The response to a query about who would use the terms was: "The people who works it more or less. They hadn't the technical terms for them. They just used these" (#2). Thus, the appellation for the hackling machine which eventually re-

FIGURE I. Nicknames of hacklers and roughers in a country mill

	HACKLING SHOP	
	Ape	
	Smidge	
	Toye King	Tar Pot
	Nell	Darkie
		Wee Man
		Blower
	Larkie	
	Pat	
	Buckie Briar	Cuckle Eye
	Blinkie	Ditto
	Black Bob	Monkey
	Jew	Two Ticks
	Dr. Watson	Dates
	Colby	Rum Hot
	Milk	1. Pinto 2. Harkaway
ROUGHING SHOP	Skart	Travers
		Dido John
	Dido Jack	
		Shoit
		Soup
	Surface Brush	Tut
	Mickie	Waxey

Ape: He could make people laugh. "Thirty-two men gabblin' all day—the shop now and again went dead. You wouldn't a heared a pin drop, only for the sound of the fan hummin'. And maybe it went on for five minutes, and then Ape woulda brightened up and let out one great big Gulliver laugh and brought them all back to life again."

Smidge: "He was always . . . sniffin' about."

Toye King: "He lived out in the Toye [a townland], in a wee thatched cottage. And he was all be hisself, and there was a clutch of houses around him, and he was called the Toye King."

Nell: "Every weekend, when he got out of the mill, some of the grocers here woulda took his horse . . . called Nell. He got that nickname from Old Nell."

Larkie: "Because he was always doin' jokes. . . . He was a Roman Catholic. And I mind one time he was laughin' away to hisself. I said, 'What are you doin'?' 'I'm learnin' this for tonight.' It was 'The Old Orange Flute' [a well-known Protestant song]."

Pat: "That's a middle name. He never used it. We just called him Pat. He didn't like it."

Buckie Briar: "That's a big, long, tall briar, all bent over. . . . this fella looked up at me and said, 'Buckie Briar.' . . . Not now [nicknames], for that generation has all passed away."

Blinkie: "He had a habit of blinkin' his eyes all the time."

Black Bob: ". . . black as the hobs of hell."

Jew: "Every time he was comin' around to collect for a wreath for somebody dead . . . and they called him the Irish Jew."

Dr. Watson: "A great intellect, you know. . . . He one time read Darwin's theory. And I says to him one day in the hacklin' shop, 'What about Darwin's theory?' And he says, 'Do you think we've been bluffed all these years?' "

Colby: "His father was called that."

Milk: "Never took tea, always milk."

Skart: "He was a great swimmer. And there's a bird [which skims over the water]. We call this . . . what's the proper name for it? We call it, nickname, Skart."

Dido Jack: All Kennedys called Dido. "There was a potato come into this country one time, and they were great boys for advertising the Didos. And I think it stuck to them that way. . . . They were big feedin' potatoes for pigs."

Surface Brush: "He married the surface man's daughter, who cleans the roads."

Mickie: "His father was a machine master, and they used to call [it] Hell's Island at one time, as it were, Hell's Kitchen, and then Eddie got the name of Mickie— Mickie, the Devil."

Tar Pot: "He was so black. . . . And the old boys used to say, 'It's gettin' very dark in here,' when he went by. . . . black hair and black skin."

Darkie: ". . . dark, very dark skin."

Wee Man: "He was a wee, small man. They tell me that his father was a hackler before him, and he wore a wee tailed coat."

Blower: "In the evenin', the wind— his chest give up. There was somethin' in it—[sound of strained breathing]. They used to say to me, 'Now, look over there. That's what's goin' to happen to you. Get out.' "

Cuckle Eye: "He had a bad eye—his two eyes in close together. And you wouldn't know if he was lookin' cross-eyed or not at you."

Ditto: "Ditto couldn't read too well. And the passbooks in those days— passbooks was what you got your goods for the week, the groceries, butter, for instance, one and six. . . . the shopkeeper—maybe she got butter, say Tuesday, and she went back Thursday, and she says, 'Give me another pound a butter'— he woulda put it down, 'One pound ditto.' Meaning butter. But Billy would read it, and say, 'What the hell you doin' with all the ditto? I never got none of it.' . . . he got that nickname."

Monkey: "So small, oh, a wee, small man."

Two Ticks: "That was a sayin' of his: 'Mr. N., could you give me the time?' 'Just in two ticks.' "

Dates: "He used to bring a lot of dates into the mill. The cattle wanted the dates. And at night . . . he looked

after the cattle. And if we'd get into an argument, and they wanted to beat him . . . they woulda all done the cows and the calves and the sheep. 'Baa-aa' and roared. And then he'd stop talkin'."

Rum Hot: "His father drank rum, hot . . . whiskey and water."

Pinto or *Harkaway:* "The heart of the west. There's two nicknames for that one. . . . His father-in-law made bicycles, and there was a stamp on 'em . . . Harkaways. . . . I don't know whether Pinto come from because he went to Yankee land a while and come back."

Travers: Just a nickname. "Funny thing about him. He married a Roman Catholic, and the whole shop never spoke to him except E. . . . They were so intense that he cleared out. . . . In them days, you just had to go out. You were ruined. . . . This was in the roughin' shop [where things were different]."

Dido John: See the explanation for Dido Jack.

Shoit: No explanation.

Soup: "Very fond of soup."

Tut: "He talks all backwards. . . . couldn't get it out—'tut, tut, tut.' One of the roughers took him home to try to learn him how to talk."

Waxey: "That come from his father. I just couldn't tell you. If my father was livin', he could tell me all them. . . . One would tell the other, you see."

Source: Respondent #2.

Note: The figure is meant to suggest two rows of men in their berths, facing each other, and the separation of hackling shop and roughing shop by means of a plate of glass. It was drawn up in this way by respondent #2.

placed most of the boys in the Machine Room was, when first introduced, "Iron Man," because that piece of equipment "could do everything a man could do." The name was passed on. Machine hackling, in both earlier and later stages of development, involved the placing of pieces of flax in specially designed holders that were then set in a conveyor system. As the holders were moved forward and, simultaneously, subjected to a raising and lowering action, the flax within them was combed through hackles, gradually increased in fineness. On the Iron Man, levers which pulled the holders back and forth came to be known as "banjo levers" because, with their long necks, their shape evoked the image of that instrument. "Monkey levers," so called because of their forms, lifted the heads which raised and lowered the holders. Still another set of levers were called "fingers," both "pushin'-in fingers" and "pullin'-out fingers," because they resembled those appendages. A gear which opened and closed part of the apparatus was designated "shark's mouth."

That the use of specialized terminology was not confined to the Hackling Shop is illustrated by an example from the Spinning Room. There, the metal covering at each end of a spinning frame, which could be raised and lowered to expose the toothed gears behind, was affectionately referred to as the "horse's head."

The lexicon of the hacklers encompassed other facets of the hackling process. A flax dresser who had labored at his trade in a number of mills before and after the First World War confirmed the fact of the industry-wide use of some terms, which had been reported on in a printed article of nostalgic nature,[13] and explained them further:

> *Sidey:* "in roughin' and hacklin'. . . . The man who wrought beside you. Them's your sidey."

> *Crow:* "I'll tell you what a crow means. Well, now . . . the parcel you got, on Thursday night or Friday mornin'— well, whatever you had done of that parcel, you had to give that in for to make your week's wages up. You hadn't the full parcel done. . . . you crowed what you had done.
> "Say you had twenty or thirty pounds of flax done. Well . . . the foreman woulda . . . took that and then he took out what you done all week and added that—what they called a crow—till it to make your wages up. Then, whatever was

left of that parcel started your wages for next week. That's the way it was."

Bee's knees: "It's a sort of shou [small particle] in the flax—flax not properly cleaned. And the wee shous in it, you called it the bee's knees."

Goose: "You're goosed if he [foreman] finds fault. . . . or anything like that in it. . . . But . . . if a hackler [foreman] brought flax back to you, and it wasn't properly done, you daren't do it over again. . . . the union wouldn't allow you. . . . if they started to do that, they'd bring it all back to you." (#49)

He was not familiar with the expression reported on in the same article: ". . . a sorter preferred a 'crow' to a 'goose.'" But he enjoyed, and as an insider understood, the play on words. He was also amused by the fact that the idea—a sorter preferred having wages for an only partially completed parcel of hackled flax added to his pay packet over having a foreman fault him for his work—was expressed in that way.

Serving one's time, therefore, meant for the novice not only the acquisition of the technical skills of the trade but also the absorption of the preceding and other terms into his vocabulary. In the country mill, the apprentice, in addition, was exposed, or re-exposed, to a type of lore which did not originate in the mill, but for which the Hackling Shop served as a center for dissemination. Thus, Old Nell customarily waylaid all newcomers in order to pose to them a number of "conundrums"; from their responses, he formed his estimate of their basic intelligence. His attitude itself may well be a part of a broader Irish tradition.[14] At any rate, a typical example of a conundrum, prefaced by his usual introduction, follows:

Could you answer me this question?

Bible character without a name,
Who never to corruption came;
She died a death none died before,
And part of her shroud's in every household store.

Answer: Lot's wife. (#2)

The roughers also shared their stock of this verbal lore:

Some of the boys woulda told different ones—and different yarns. . . . I'll tell you a conundrum. I don't know whether you heard it or not:

There was two brothers,
They were born in March,
Their birthday was in June,
They both married,
And died single.

Answer: Two clergymen, twins, born in March, England, who performed the marriage ceremony for others. (#36)

Still another took the form of a "neck riddle": [15]

Another conundrum which I thought was a good one. . . . In those days, they woulda hung you for thievin' or stealin' or anything like that. Well, now, this fella, accordin' to the conundrum, he was sentenced to death, and there was a courthouse, and they were tryin' him. And outside there was a graveyard. So, the judge told him if he could give them a conundrum that the jury couldn't answer, he would let him go. And if they could answer him, he would be hanged. So they gave him five minutes to walk around a cemetery—a little cemetery outside—and he come back in. And the judge asked him had he got one. He said he had, so this is it. He said:

As I walked out,
As I walked in,
I saw death that life was in.
There was six sat,
And the seventh flee.
Riddle me that,
And hanged I'll be.

Answer: Skull, containing six baby robins and the mother, who flew away. (#36)

"An apprentice kept silent in them days. You listened in" (#2). And the good listener was able later to pass on some of the amus-

ing things he had heard. Verbal word play, as just illustrated by
the conundrums, and the witty, or perhaps humorous, remark,
have long been features of Irish speech,[16] and the individual
whose talk includes outstanding examples has been, and still is,
greatly admired. Whether or not, more than other groups of
workers, "all old hacklers were great wits" (#2), a number of
their remarks did circulate widely. A sample of these and some
additional humorous anecdotes help to reveal something of what
appealed to the sense of humor of those craftsmen.

> In those days . . . when the mill was stopping, the lights
> went down. . . . And there'd a been a fuss at night, rushin'
> past one another, gettin' their coats on. And one old fella put
> his hand down the sleeve of his coat, and it went into the
> hole of the linin', and he couldn't get it on. And he remarked
> to the next old hackler, "Boy, won't we have a terrible time
> on the last day, puttin' our coat on over our wings?" And this
> old wit says, "Not atall. You'll have no trouble in the wide
> world. Your job will be puttin' your hard hat on over your
> horns." (#2)

A picturesque comment could be evoked by almost anything.
Therefore, when the first light bulbs appeared in the mill:

> They were very red lights—dull, dead bulbs. And [Cuckle
> Eye] says, "It's the first time I've ever seen red hot hairpins
> in a bottle." (#2)

To mitigate complaints made about heat in the Hackling Shop:

> It was very warm one day. And [Old Nell] says, "Wait'll you
> go to hell. You'll have to go in backwards, or the sparks will
> cut the eye out of you if you don't." (#2)

An evaluation of a coworker's appearance:

> I mind an old fellow [Two Ticks]. . . . had a wee mustache,
> and they used to call it a football team, about five hairs on
> every side. (#2)

A characteristic misuse of words was considered very amusing:

> He [Ditto] put everything backwards. . . . for instance, there
> was a blackbird. . . . He says, "A blackbird flew over the

half-door this mornin'. I couldn't tell you if it was a thrush or a swallow." And then he says, "My britches were blowin' this mornin' when I was just puttin' on my horn." (#2)

Laughter could also be called forth by remarks and antics which bore scatalogical overtones. Sometimes the reaction was aimed for:

> When we'd run short of a parcel—there may have been one or two just comin' off the machines, and the foreman just wouldn't give it to you right off the reel. Maybe you'd have to sit for half an hour, until they got you one . . . suitable for that type of flax you wanted . . . to do. And maybe you had to sit there and just clean your hackle out and have a bit of a gabble. So that's when these capers came off. . . . Davey would have said:

> Mademoiselle, I love you so well,
> I fain would kiss your toe.

> And . . . [Dr. Watson] made a great bow and he would say:

> Monsieur, dear, and my arse so near,
> Why should you stoop so low? (#2)

On other occasions, an intended rebuke secured the opposite effect:

> Maybe I shouldn't tell you this, but he [Two Ticks] used to say this when he was in bad tune. [Wee Ape] . . . was on one side of him . . . and he was a small man. And I was on the other side. I was a big, tall man. I would say, "Can I have the time, please?" And he would look up at me, "This bastard here, he's lookin' up my arse all day, and you're lookin' down my bloody throat." (#2)

A number of anecdotes circulated about hacklers who had been to "Yankee Land" and back. Many of those men had probably had their passages to America paid for by the Flaxdressers' Trade and Benevolent Trade Union. One of the earliest founded within the linen industry (1872), it was "one of the most important unions in late Victorian Belfast."[17] Suffice it to say that, in an industry that was not organized in an overall way to any great extent until the 1940s, the flax dressers' union provided benefits for its members in the early years of this century that, for the time, were rather unusual. The union's balance sheet for the year 1906 (Figure 2) states the circumstances under which money was paid to the flax dressers.[18]

Pertinent here are the references to emigration in both the income and the expenditure columns. Members of the union who chose to leave the country, for various reasons but particularly during periods of economic depression in the industry, were assisted in their efforts to locate elsewhere. A substantial number, apparently, availed themselves of this aid between the years 1900 and 1912. Thirty are shown here to have been provided with financial aid during 1906; this was, seemingly, double the number usually helped annually.[19] While the report does not state the name of the mill from which each emigrant left, it is reasonable to assume that emigration from some areas over the years was heavy. In the country mill town, a street, Briggy's Brae, which had once housed a number of flax dressers, was known locally as "California Street," in recognition of the fact that so many hacklers had departed from it for America.

The sum of ten pounds granted to the emigrating hackler was often an outright donation. At the same time, it was understood that arrears in union dues would be paid if the man returned to Ireland and resumed his trade. The worker who defaulted was not permitted into the flax dressers' union again and was, therefore, deprived not only of work but of all benefits.

Many emigrants never undertook a return voyage, even for a visit or retirement:

> Some of them didn't like to come over on the boat again . . . in them days it was rough. . . . I suppose they didn't want to face the journey. Some used to say if there was a road we'll walk it . . . walk back. (#2)

A few ventured back, and the stories circulated about them contain references to an umbrella and skyscrapers, motifs frequently found in anecdotes about any kind of returned Yank. One hackler, who came to see his old friends in the Hackling Shop, carried a symbol of his financial success:

> This fellow went to America. . . . And he hackled there, and when he came back, he was a real American hackler. Well,

FIGURE 2.

Flax Dressers' Trade and Benevolent Trade Union:

Balance sheet for the twelve months ending 31
December, 1906

Income

To cash in bank and on hand, 30 Dec. 1905	£1,561	12 3½
Contributions	1,490	6 6½
Returned emigrants	29	18 6
Bank interest	27	0 7
Readmissions	1	0 0
Discount	0	17 9
Fares repaid	0	9 0
	£3,111	4 8

Expenditure

By cash in bank, 31 Dec. 1906		£1,229 16 5
Ailment—Out of Work	£362 4 11	
Sick	530 13 0	
Lock-out	7 11 0	
Trade grants	48 1 8	
		963 10 7
Funeral allowance—15 members and 13 members' wives		205 17 8
Emigration (30 members)		300 15 0
Secretary		104 0 0
Shop clerks' salaries		40 15 11
President and committee		42 0 0
Treasurer		12 0 0
Auditor		6 6 0
Trustees		4 16 0
Tylers		3 16 0
Printing		25 9 5
Hall rent (including 10/– to hallkeeper)		12 5 0
Members' fares		4 6 0
Bond on treasurer		1 5 0
Postage and transmission, inward and outward		16 12 0
Deputation and lost time		13 0 0
Trades council and municipal elections		5 10 0
1,500 rule books		9 6 6
Registration		0 10 0
Insurance on trade banner		0 2 0
Balance in hands of treasurer		104 5 2
		£3,111 4 8

I have examined the above Accounts with the Books and Vouchers,
and found them correct.

JAMES GLASGOW, Public Accountant

he come down to the mill yard here with his umbrella up,
you see. Everybody was cheerin' him because it was somethin' unusual. . . . And then when he come to the Hacklin'
Shop door, he woulda backed in and knocked the drops out
of it, hung it on the arm, and everybody cheered him when
he went up the Hacklin' Shop. (#2)

Another carried back Yankee tales, "a lot of lies." When asked
how things had been for him in "Uncle Sam's land," he is said to
have replied:

"Everything's so big out there," he says. "When I went to
Uncle's place, I'd come down to the bottom in the morning,
and get into the lift. It was about half nine," he says, "and
you didn't arrive in Uncle's," he says, "until about half past
twelve. It was that high up." (#2)

Again, he is reputed to have said:

When you were at supper at night, the whole house shook.
And so I says, "Uncle, my heavens, what sort of a place is
this?" "Now, William," he says, "control yourself. I forgot to
tell you. The moon sticks on—the new moon mostly sticks
on the house here on a black night, and you've got to push
her off." (#2)

With the installation of machines to do all the roughing and
hackling came the gradual demise of flax dressing as a trade.
Hacklers in one mill received severance pay in the amount of one
pound for each year of service, but not all the displaced men were
so fortunate. With the retirement of the craftsmen came an end
to their customs and to the creation and perpetuation of lore associated with them. The disappearance of the berths at which
they worked and the replacement of skilled artisans with young
men trained just enough to feed the machines with raw materials
changed the character of the trade and broke the chain of tradition. If the shop continues to serve as an arena for the dissemination of certain forms of folklore—forms which were not
investigated—their nature is surely quite different. What remains
of the old is to be found only in the heads of a few remaining individuals, and about them it is said: "You wouldn't get a day's
shooting at them—so few hacklers today." Even some years back,

"An old fella used to say, 'You wouldn't get a football team—five a side, five roughers and five hacklers. They're all gone'" (#2).

Perhaps they are not too far away. According to Sam Hanna Bell, the apprentice at the shipyard in Belfast learns "that he must not clod bolts at the seagulls for are they not old fellow-workmen, joiners, painters, loath to leave the scene of their earthly labours?"[20] It is maintained that many hacklers shared the same fate, and a statement, even if slightly skeptical in tone when it was made, makes reference to the alleged metamorphosis:

> I'd go out to the yard maybe in the evenin'—along by the carpenter shop there, and . . . [a carpenter] was a bit of a wit. And all the seagulls come up there and warm their feet. This was a warm pond in them days. I said, "All them seagulls. What's them?" "Them's old hacklers. One's William John Moore, and one's so and so, and so and so. . . ." And he said, "One day I'll join the band up above and come over on top of ye." (#2)

FIVE

"And Her Scissors in Her Hand": The Weavers

We were the "e-lite." We were the "swanks."
They were the "down."... We weren't really better
than they were, but you thought you were
above all that. (#35)

Some of the same levity, sport, and earthy behavior that were
found in the Spinning Room of the mill characterized the Weaving Shed of the factory. But the lore of the latter, while widely
disseminated throughout that part of the industry, not only was
somewhat different in kind, but also was, in general, less varied;
particularly did there seem to be a lack of songs originating there.
This picture of life in the factory, reflecting primarily the views of
one group of workers, will, I hope, make clear why this was so.

Although men have always been employed at various jobs in
the factory, it was mainly women who worked as warpers, winders, and weavers in Belfast in the early years of this century. Not
so in certain places outside that urban center. In a few areas,
where there was to be found almost no industrial work except
that available in weaving factories, a substantial number of jobs,
including that of power-loom weaver, were held by men; their attitudes must be considered here. But the experiences of female
factory workers in Belfast are the ones that are emphasized, in
order to make a comparison between the lore of the spinners, almost without exception women, and weavers most meaningful.

Well, that first day that I went to the weavin'... was desper-
ate.... It's what you call the fever you take. Well, it's the

awful blunderin' of the looms. . . . I couldn't right describe it. Well, comin' out . . . awfully knocked about . . . an awful feel over you. . . . You only have to be in a Weavin' Shed to under- stand. . . . It's sort of fear on you. . . . I was very sick. . . . That sickness was on me nearly a fortnight. Every night I went to bed . . . at 7:30. (#32)

A recording made in a Weaving Shed confirms the description of the deafening noise which assailed the ears of the novice. The "blundcring" was, of course, produced by the whirling power belts of the machines, plus the racing of the shuttles and the banging of the sleys—also, where damask was woven, the com- plicated Jacquard card machines (see Photo 17)—of hundreds of looms turning out various kinds of linen cloth.

As well as noise, the prospective weaver encountered heat and dampness, the former generated by, often, hundreds of gas jets, the latter a result of the need for induced humidification when weaving with linen yarns. The amount of moisture required dif- fered according to the type of cloth being woven, and for this rea- son a factory generally contained more than one Weaving Shed. Thus, in one firm, there were found two sheds devoted to the weaving of damask, in which the humidity was strictly con- trolled; there was one *plain* shed; and a fourth room contained looms operating with very fine yarn and was kept extremely moist.

The number of looms in a factory also varied, with perhaps 150 in a small firm and 1,000 in a large one. The sizes of the indi- vidual machines—three-quarter, four-quarter, twelve-quarter, etc., in reference to the width of cloth cach wovc, a *quarter* yield- ing textile nine inches wide after bleaching—and the way in which they were placed determined the quantity that could be accommodated in any one shed. A typical placement of machines was in rows arranged across the room, each row containing groups of, perhaps, three looms, with the groups separated by passes which ran the length of the shed. Machines in every two rows faced each other, allowing a weaver to stand between two looms and operate the one in front and that behind her. The space between the rows which contained the work areas, or stands, was sometimes in the early years of this century so narrow that, while the operator could turn in it, others, seeking to squeeze past her to gain access to another part of the room, could not do so. (See Photo 18.)

For purposes of illumination, the Weaving Shed was built with a characteristic saw-tooth "north light roof" (see Photo 19). This style of construction provided for one side of each "tooth" to be covered with slates and for the other to be made of glass and positioned so as to admit the least amount of direct sunlight. The transparent portions were whitewashed during the summer months to cut down on the heat and glare.

Under the roof was found the central power shaft from which emanated the belts which, attached to pulleys at the side, drove the individual looms. (See Photo 24.) While a machine was in operation, the belt was placed on the tight pulley; when the weaver stopped her loom, she pushed a handle which transferred it to the slack pulley. The expression "works on the slack pulley," applied to a lazy individual not working up to capacity, arises out of the distinction between the performance of the two wheels.

The half-time system, under which so many were employed in the mill, was not, at the time the men and women with whom I spoke began to work, associated with the factory. Jobs there were considered by most people to be more prestigious than jobs in mills and, therefore, were more difficult to secure. Families in dire financial straits and anxious to supplement household incomes with the earnings of their children could not wait until a job opening appeared in the factory, a waiting period which might have allowed their youngsters to complete their schooling before commencing work. The mill, always the more labor-intensive of the two—that is, employing a greater percentage of workers in relation to machines—was there to absorb the children at an earlier age as half-timers, a situation that was deemed fortunate by the more needy families.

It was usual for a girl to enter the factory at the age of thirteen or fourteen. It was also customary that she be brought in by someone already at work in the firm:

Photo 17. Damask weaving shed, containing power looms fitted with Jacquard machines, in Broadway Damask Company, Belfast, 1923. From the Welch Collection, by courtesy of the Ulster Museum, Belfast.

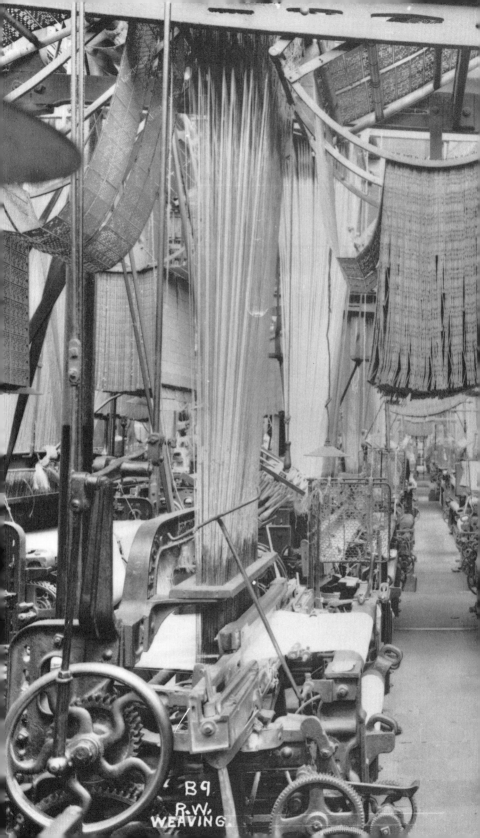
B9
R.W.
WEAVING.

You were a neighbor's child and your mother came and said, "I would like Mary in to learn the weaving." And then, the woman would say, "Well, my daughter will ask for her." So, they spoke to the foreman and Mary was taken in . . . right into the Weavin' Shed. (#10)

The best situation was one in which a close friend or interested relative, a person willing to supervise the learner closely, did the asking:

My aunt, my father's sister . . . a weaver [asked for me]. There's not many would want to learn ye, because you're a—keep them back, because you have to learn too much, where they have to be busy and quick. You're lossin' time when you're takin' in a learner. . . . but I was learned right for she was better than a stranger. (#32)

There was no set pay for the weaver as there was for the spinner. The wages paid the former were based on the amount of cloth she was able to weave during the week. Therefore, any time she spent as an instructor was time taken away from full production, and the effects were visible in her pay packet. Only a person devoted to the work itself or to the individual being taught would be motivated enough to demonstrate weaving techniques thoroughly and provide adequate explanations for what was to be done.

In some places, another person was immediately affected by the presence of beginners. The *tenter* in a Weaving Shed was an overlooker in charge of a number of looms, the quantity being dependent upon the type and width of the machines. It was the tenter's responsibility to keep looms in optimum working order, to provide assistance when the weaver experienced technical difficulties and so ensure maximum output, and to "light the weaver's way"—to light the jets of gas on dark wintry mornings before the working day had begun and, again, late in the afternoons. It was also his permission that was sought when one wished to bring in a beginner. Normally, where looms lay idle, the tenter had no objection, provided the applicant met with his approval. But it was the practice in some firms to supplement the man's basic wage with a bonus, calculated on the amount of cloth produced by the weavers whose looms he tended:

Photo 18. Damask weaver at Jacquard power looms in Brookfield Linen Company, Belfast, ca. 1930 (?). By courtesy of Dr. W. A. McCutcheon.

Photo 19. *A large flax spinning and linen weaving company (Bessbrook, County Armagh), ca. 1900. Note saw-tooth roof of weaving shed, at right. From the Welch Collection, by courtesy of the Ulster Museum, Belfast.*

It was piecework in my time, too, for the tenters. They had twenty-four shillin's a week and a shillin' to the pound for what the weavers threw off. I mind workin' . . . in [a factory in a small town] . . . and there was no set pay there. . . . If the weavers earned a pound, the firm allowed me half a crown. Or if they earned ten shillin's, they earned me one and thruppence. Well, I mind workin' a week . . . after the July holidays, and all I'd a lifted at the end of the week was half a crown—didn't pay me free and fairly. (#11)

A good tenter anywhere tried to minimize interference with the work of his weavers but, in addition, in those places where the bonus situation prevailed, it was to his financial advantage to do so. As a result, he often looked with disfavor upon requests of his weavers to bring in untrained workers, especially if there were a number already undergoing training.

Not all prospective weavers went directly to the looms. At one time, particularly in smaller concerns, newcomers were started as *givers-in*, passing threads coming off new weaving beams to highly skilled *drawers-in*, women who completed the process of putting ends through the *heddles* and *reed* (see Photo 23), in readiness for insertion into a weaving machine.

The learner who did go directly into the shed stood at the looms of her instructor and gradually picked up from her the rudiments of weaving. Before she could be put on a loom of her own, she had first to master three basic skills: how to change a shuttle, the way to draw-in broken ends of warp, and how to tie a *weaver's knot*. Learning the weaver's knot, shared with the handloom weaver and taken over by reelers and, later, some winders, occupied much of the time of the novice. The distinctive steps in tying it have been described elsewhere.[1] It was difficult to master, but the end result was a very flat knot—"more divided, as much on the bottom as on top"—which was almost undiscernible and which permitted smooth intermeshing of warp and weft yarns.

Broken warp threads forced a weaver behind her loom, where she had first to locate the loose ends. Then, with a weaver's knot, she attached each to a piece of yarn, drawn from her supply of *thrums*, or extra threads of the same quality kept on her loom for such purposes. An anecdote revolves around the use of thrums:

There's an interesting story I heard about a lad who was startin' to weave . . . on power looms. And he didn't like weavin'. . . . he tried it for about three or four weeks, and he was gettin' fed up. So, one mornin' he didn't go in to his work and his mother come up to call him—he was in bed—and she says, "Why? You're not goin' in to work today." He says, "I can't go today," he says. "I have no thrums." He couldn't go to his work because he had no ends to tie on to the broken threads. It's unbelievable. . . . He never became a weaver. (#74)

It was the next job of the trained operator, and a second skill for her charge to learn, to discern the proper eye in the heddle and the correct split in the comblike reed (see Photo 23) through which to draw-in this end in order to join it to the one from which it had broken off.

A considerable part of the weaver's time was also spent in *shuttling*, the art of which some women mastered so well that it was said of them that they could accomplish a change of shuttles without even stopping their looms. But, in the beginning, the ability to judge when a pirn bobbin in the shuttle was running out and, therefore, when it was necessary to substitute a new shuttle containing a full pirn of yarn had first to be acquired by a prospective loom operator. A step in the complete operation was the actual threading of the yarn on the bobbin through the eye of the shuttle. This was done by hand, or, to be more precise, by mouth, for it was customary to place the pirn into its holder, close a cover over it, place one's lips against an opening and, with a light intake of breath, suck out the end of the yarn. The action was known as "kissing the shuttle" (see Photo 20). It could, how-ever, be alluded to in a less delicate way at times, as was fre-quently done by spinners—seizing upon something which gave them an opportunity to make fun of those who generally looked down upon them—in their taunting shouts of "Holy Weavers, suck your shuttles!" (#58).

This means of threading a shuttle was deemed to be a possible contributory factor to the spread of tuberculosis, or consumption, as it was commonly and more acceptably termed then. In some homes, the custom was looked upon with disfavor: "My mother always scolded me for helping my friends by sucking their shut-

Photo 20. "Kissing the Shuttle." The shuttle shown here is a newer type than the ones used during the years covered in this study. Posed for the author in the Ulster Weaving Company, Belfast.

tles" (#32). The use of shuttles requiring mouth suction was officially terminated in 1958,[2] but the memory of the practice survives in still another expression, similar in origin but now widespread in the larger culture of the north of Ireland. "Weaver's kiss," dating from the days of the handloom weaver and perpetuated by power-loom operators, is used to refer to the strength of something: a coat of paint which chips off at the slightest touch is said to be as strong as a weaver's kiss, or the light flick of the wrist needed to brush off specks of dust from clothing is described as being like a weaver's kiss.

The learner's education was not confined to gaining proficiency in the techniques mentioned above. She also learned how to start and stop a loom, how to remove woven cloth, and to keep a sharp lookout for broken *shots* of weft and for *floats*—caused by broken warp threads—both of which necessitated her ripping out the improperly woven sections of textile. And, in the same way as the spinner had to overcome her fear of stopping whirling flyers with her hand, the young weaver was taught to regard the active sley with equanimity: "The sley went like Billy-o, and I was afraid to touch it. I thought it was great when I could put my hand on it" (#32).

Estimates of the duration of the initial learning period ranged from a fortnight to eight weeks. A statement made by one weaver reflects a fairly common length of time: "It was exactly six weeks before I was given a loom. . . . At that time you never got a farthing for learning" (#32). Later, a small payment was made to learners in some places, and the teachers began to be compensated for their loss in production and for the instruction they provided.

In one factory, what followed the initial learning period for the novice weaver was assignment to one of four looms in the "Black Hole." There, in a small recess, with the jet of gas above each machine and the light from a window opening onto the finishing room furnishing the only illumination, she practiced, for a set wage, her newly acquired skills under the guidance of a skilled operative. Utilized for many years, the room was condemned about 1905.

More typically, once her charge was deemed ready, an instructor recommended that the girl be given a loom of her own in the main shed, although she continued to assist and supervise her at the machine. At this time, the young weaver was paid according to the amount of cloth that the single loom turned off.

How long it was until she was given her share of two looms varied. If a girl "had it at her," if she "had the eye for weaving," she might advance in three months, although a year on a plain loom, or longer on a fine one, was a more likely period of time. Whatever type of loom she was provided with at the beginning, the tenter would eventually try to "marry" for her a coarse loom, which required much shuttling, with one weaving fine yarn. In this way, he was said to be giving the weaver "a good stroke." When he did not, outcries of "That bloody tenter wouldn't give me a good stroke" (#27) were directed against him by the annoyed woman, hard pressed in minding two coarse looms, both of which needed frequent replacements for pirns quickly emptied. The story is told of the fortunate weaver, on looms which turned

Photo 21. A weaver and her heddle hook, carried in the traditional way. Posed for the author in the Ulster Weaving Company, Belfast.

out a very fine grade of linen cloth, who could put shuttles into her machines in the morning, go off for a cup of tea, come back in time for dinner, and only then have to replace them.

The tools of the weaver were a *heddle hook*, used to draw-in broken ends of warp, and held in her mouth as she moved about (see Photo 21), a *ripper*—sometimes only a darning needle but at other times a more elaborate instrument with brass handle, made for the women by male employees in the factory—and scissors. The weaver's scissors were small and held in the hand, when not being used, in a characteristic fashion. (See Photo 22.) They were often carried home from work for fear that if "left behind they would be taken by somebody," and they became almost an extension of the weaver's body:

> I could work and sew with the scissors in my hand till this day. . . . I could take my tea and all, and the scissors didn't

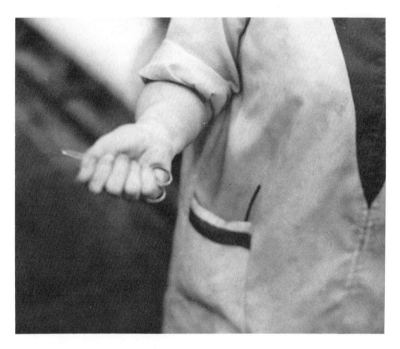

Photo 22. "With her scissors in her hand": a weaver. Posed for the author in the Ulster Weaving Company, Belfast.

matter. . . . I could—with the scissors—open my purse and take my money out. . . . If she's a weaver at all, you'll see her goin' along with her scissors. (#32)

So closely associated with the weaver were her scissors, it is to be expected that they would be mentioned in this variant of the "Doffer Song" (see p. 35), sung by a factory worker:

You'd easy know a weaver,
When she goes down to town,
With her long yellow hair,
And her apron hanging down.
With her scissors tied before her [like the winder's],
Or her scissors in her hand,
You'll easy know a weaver,
For she'll always get her man.

Chorus: Yes, she'll always get her man, *etc.* (#35)

A winder in a factory explained:

> ... the doffers were in the mill. Well, they were a more rougher type person, and they sung all those songs. Well, ... whenever we woulda sang, we woulda sang their songs, but changed the name. But never really had a song of our own. (#35)

To whom the song really "belonged" is a matter of conjecture. An unusual version concerns a quite different type of linen worker:

> Och it's aisy knowin' the flowerers/whun they go into town,
> Wi' their long masled skin and wi'/their perricoats hangin'
>   down,
> Wi' their boots half laced an' their/piercers be ther side;
> An' sez oul' Mr. Crutchley, 'Ye've made yer holes too wide.'

> "Ye see, that song wuz made be some naybur weemin that had somethin' again' the flowerers. The flowerers wuz ivery bit as good as them an mebbe betther, an' ivery bit as well put on, too, but somebody wanted to try to make little o' them ov'er jealousy about boys or somethin'." [3]

When spinners sang about the factory workers, they changed the words in order to "get their own back" on the weavers and winders who belittled them so much of the time, and they saw to it that they never got their men:

> You will easy know a weaver,
> When she comes into town,
> With her oul' tatty hair,
> And her stockin's hangin' down,
> And her apron tied before her,
> And her scissors in her hand,
> You will easy know a weaver,
> For she'll never get a man.

> *Chorus:* No, she'll never get a man, *etc.* (#30)

If any part of the weaver's dress could be considered traditional, it was her apron, mentioned in the song.

> ... snow white apron, every Monday morning. You bought the material yourself and made your own. ... you were so

proud of your white apron, you didn't put it around you . . .
comin' to the factory. You carried it over your arm . . . and
when you put your shawl on the nail or your coat on the nail,
you then undone the strings of your apron. . . .
    The stiffer the apron the better. Some of them used to put
a taste of sugar in it—woulda done without it in their tea, put
the sugar in their starch. . . . you wouldn't a wanted them
startin' your looms on Monday mornin' with a crushed apron. If it got crushed afterwards, that was all right. But it
was just a throwback from the past; you come in and you
had no creases in your over apron. (#10)

The apron (not always white, despite the preceding remarks) protected the weaver's skirt, worn with a blouse, from soil rubbed off
the breastboard of the loom. Underneath, in the early days, she,
too, wore a shift, made from the ever-useful flour bags.

    . . . we were slaves at the weaving in those days 11 pennys
    for 100 yds of linnen and we had to make 10 shillings thin
    days then you got 2/6 bonas but it was a lovely trade and all
    the linnen factorys are closed here and I am 84 on the 21st of
    August but it is a trade I could not forget. . . .[4]

Wages for the weaver were calculated on the *cuts* of cloth she
wove during a week. A cut varied in length, depending upon the
quality of linen—the more threads per inch, the finer the
weave[5]—being woven and the width of the loom. When the requisite number of yards had been turned out, a colored mark several inches long appeared on the warp threads, and the weaver
stopped the loom, cut the yarn at the marked point, and removed
the roll of linen in folds, or *laps*. She carried it on her shoulder,
sometimes to a table where it was collected by boys employed for
the purpose, but more often directly to the *cloth passer*, whose
office was located at one end of the shed. "In [one factory], we
had to work seven feet underground, and we had to go thirteen
steps up into the Cloth House—the Cloth Office" (#32).
    In the hands of the cloth passer, whose job it was to check for
faults in the cuts of woven cloth, rested the monetary fate of the
weaver.[6] For it was within his power to assess fines on the operatives when he deemed them responsible for cloth of substandard
quality. For many weavers, extremely conscientious, the embar-

rassment of being called to the Cloth Office and being informed
of the assessment was as worrisome as the actual loss in pay:

> If you didn't make perfect cloth, the boy came with a big
> sheet. . . . Here's the way they called you—"Whoo-oo."
> "Me? Murder. I knew." . . . It was the shame of it. You were
> ashamed to be caught goin' up the stairs . . . but then there
> were others that didn't give that [snap of fingers]. . . . Well,
> then, they woulda took maybe sixpence off you. . . . It was
> such a disgrace on you. (#32)

In part, this feeling was related to not wishing to be considered a
bad worker, for whether one did or did not turn out cloth which
merited a fine figured into an evaluation of one's skill as a weaver.
The statement made by a man employed in a factory where male
weavers predominated was echoed by the women in Belfast:

> This chap that learned me to weave. . . . he was a real good
> weaver. He was noted for his weavin'. In fact, I never mind
> . . . J. M. gettin' fined for bad weavin'. He was one of these
> —a very, very conscientious worker. (#18)

Such attitudes and evaluations reflected the Protestant Ethic, so
much a part of the character structure of many workers of all re-
ligions in the linen industry.[7]

The good weaver was required to pay constant attention to the
way in which the warp and weft were fed through her loom. The
machine contained a forked device that, the instant the weft supply failed, was supposed to lower and automatically "knock off"
the loom. Nevertheless, frequently the mechanism failed, and
the machine went on without weft. The worker, when she
noticed the error, had to rip out the flawed portions of cloth. As
regards the warp threads, the automatic drop device which today
stops a machine the instant there is a break along one of them
was not then present, and the weaver's eye alone could catch a
break. Immediately she had to knock off the loom and do what
was necessary to rejoin the ends.

> Every time you turned around, there was another—what you
> call the gear gone. It was weavin' away. You fixed that one—
> it made a hole . . . and you had to rip that all out and start

all over again. And by the time you had that, you turned
around and the same thing had happened on the other loom,
and then you started on that. (#28)

The curse of the weaver was bad yarn: "I have yet to meet a
weaver who says her yarn is good" (#10). *Slubs* on the threads,
caused by improper piecing of ends by a spinner or careless tying
by a reeler, and not caught by a winder, were potential breaking
points. Also, yarn that was not properly dressed could dry and
split as it moved off the weaving beam. It was maintained that
many weavers spent as much time behind their looms tying ends
as in front. Unfortunately, I have been able to recover only two
portions of a song lamenting this condition:

> From six to six,
> I'm in a fix,
> Tying [or weaving] rotten yarn. (#28)

> *and*

> With your heddle hook and shears,
> And your head up in the gears,
> Rotten yarn, rotten yarn. (#18)

A male power-loom weaver claimed to have heard the first part in
the factory, where "a chap I knew . . . put a bit on it. . . . it was
about [the firm]" (#28), and throughout the countryside, where
"the saying" was generally known. A handloom weaver, who had
worked in the past in his home and later at a handloom in a factory, said the verses were part of a long song, once widely circulated among craftsmen like himself. The words "from six to six"
suggest either that the song originated in a factory, where regular
hours were maintained, or that this verse was added after the
transition from home to factory. At any rate, one of the few active
handloom weavers at present heard "with my heddle hook and
shears," etc., sung by power-loom weavers as they marched
while on strike in 1948 in County Armagh, the area from which
the song is reported. It does seem to be an example of a tradition
passed down from handloom to power-loom weavers.

It did not seem to be known in Belfast. But this was true of
many songs: "The weavers didn't sing. They were only makin'

the money" (#40). The factory girls, too, mentioned the nature of
their work and the lack of opportunity for singing during working
hours:

> Because we had to work harder than the spinners. We never
> had time to sing. That probably was it, I think, because
> everybody had to try and earn their pay while the work was
> on. They didn't have to work as hard as we had, and their pay
> was goin' on all the time. We had to work very hard. If we
> had . . . relaxed any time, our pay was goin' down. (#35)

Even if the yarn was satisfactory, a loom not in proper working
order could cause imperfections in the cloth. The Truck Act of
1896 stated not only that the weaver should know in advance the
circumstances under which specific fines could be levied but also
that the penalties were to be fair and reasonable.[8] Individual
interpretations of the latter stipulation were the cause of continuous vexation to most operatives. It can probably be assumed that
many cloth passers attempted a fair assessment of work done.
They were all considered to be very strict, however, and about
those who were deemed to be excessively critical—and here one
allows for bias on the part of the teller—anecdotes circulated for
years. Representative of this genre are the following:

> When you were six years old, all you heard was people curs-
> in' A. S. . . . . I heard this from J. P., who I worked with, was a
> cloth passer himself. He said that a young boy went in. . . .
> As soon as [A. saw him], "Hi, my boy, I'll fix you. If you
> haven't that cloth right, I'll pound you."
> And sure as it went in, he fined him every time whether
> the work was right or not 'til the boy's heart was broken be-
> fore he started. So, we had the best recruitment man ever
> Britain had in A. S. And it's true. It seems they did die cursin'
> him on the battlefield, for he sent them there. Now, that was
> from J. P., a Christian. (#28)

> Now in another instance. . . . They were so afraid. He was so
> particular, and he took so much money off them that they
> kept it [the cloth] 'til the dark would come . . . and they
> thought he wouldn't see some small defects. And they left it
> down, for perhaps they were ready at two o'clock, but they

didn't bring it up until four o'clock or half four. He took six-pence off and said, "Damp and cold, lyin' on the floor, six-pence." They couldn't do anything about it. And that cut was perfect. (#28)

An old man told me . . . when I was about sixteen. . . . he was about seventy. He was standin', warpin' at the machine at the time, and he told me about a woman weaver. . . . And they went to fine her a shilling. . . . And all she could hope for was two cuts. . . . If they fined a shilling out of that, it meant an awful lot, for they were just existing and nothing more.

Well, she objected. There was no appeal against that. If the cloth passer fined you, you'd had it. She went up to this firm—there were no phones at that time—and they sent a message boy up to tell them not to start her. . . . They didn't start her, and she went to Belfast, and they followed her to Belfast, and she couldn't get a start. . . . That happened before my time. (#28)

I suspect that some of the misdeeds ascribed to particular cloth passers or firms are legendary, but I have been unable to locate analogues to support this surmise. On the other hand, it is a fact that similar grievances are of long standing.[9]

Although talked about, the harsh judgments of cloth passers did not, apparently, prompt anyone to ridicule them in song in the same way that personnel in spinning rooms made fun of figures of authority there:

They [spinners] made all that, but you couldn't a heard that in the factory. You see, now, you could stand in the Spinnin' Room and you could shout to the next person, and you could call over to this one. In the factory, you couldn't do that for the rattle of your shuttle. . . . That's what has me hard of hearin' now, is the rattle of the shuttles. (#56)

Nor were many barbs in verse and song directed against tent-ers. One reason for this may be that "tenters have never had the same power and authority over the labour force as that vested in Mill Overlookers who, historically, were practically demagogues. In weaving factories the 'man management' function was the prerogative of the Foreman Tenter." [10] Still, if one was unpopular, operatives were known on occasion to "sing him up," and in terms that it is often assumed only spinners used:

> Our oul' lad has a wooden one,
> Wooden one,
> Wooden one,
> Our oul' lad has a wooden one,
> And it wouldn't work. (#86)

The women also joked about the behavior of some of the men among themselves:

> In this factory here there was a tenter—I'm not going to name no names to you—and he used to come in and sit with his big bottle away at the back of my looms and drink it—any time. (#78)

The amount of money credited to the weaver was entered in a book kept for that purpose. Each woman came to know how much cloth she could produce weekly, given favorable circumstances. As the weekend approached, if it seemed that she could not reach the quota she had set for herself, she experienced added pressure and was likely to resent any intrusions upon her time. The expression "on the push" (see Photo 23), voiced as holidays approached or as the week's end grew near, was one understood by every weaver:

> It used to be that you coulda put your hand on what we call the sley . . . a rod across the top of your loom. And we used to get that and [motion of pushing faster]. "Ah, I'm on the push." . . . And you weren't pushin' anything, for you couldn't go any quicker than the engine. You didn't want anybody to come into your stand to keep you back, talkin'. . . . you'd been a hurry, maybe, to get it for your pay. (#56)

In factories, wages were computed for the cuts taken from the looms by a specified time, usually on Friday afternoons or Saturday mornings, although that money did not come into the hands of the workers until the end of the following week. A weekly sum of ten shillings in the years immediately preceding the First World War and of twelve shillings in the year 1915, mentioned as typical wages, must be viewed with caution. To arrive at a truly

heddle

heddle

sley

reed

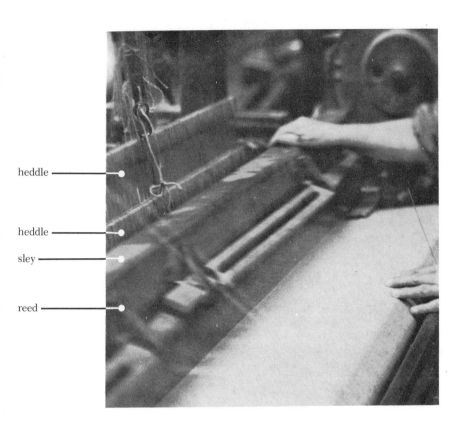

Photo 23. A weaver "on the push." Posed for the author in the Ulster Weaving Company, Belfast.

meaningful amount earned weekly in the years 1910–1930 or for a single year within that period is very difficult, because here, as with the spinners, wages varied in urban and small-town factories and from weaver to weaver; net wages also reflected various bonuses and deductions. It is possible to point out a few differentiating factors, however. For one thing, damask weavers tended to be better paid than plain, in part because they had to work much harder. For another, the weaver of fine cloth was paid more per cut than the weaver of coarse cloth, but each cut also took longer to produce. Furthermore, allowances were made to those who had to work with particularly coarse or bleached yarn. In general, it may be said that those setting wages tried to balance all relevant factors in order to provide similar pay for similar amounts of effort expended. But, if it had been possible to make all else equal, there would have been still the matter of the motivation, attitudes, and skill of the individual weaver with which to contend.

It cannot be stated with certainty that weavers were underpaid, all things considered. That some, particularly men, considered themselves to be can be sensed from the actions of a power-loom operator who, although working outside of Belfast, probably could not help viewing his pay in the light of, say, that received by shipyard workers in that city:

> One time he was standing, and there was a handbill which said THE WAGES OF SIN IS DEATH. And he had worked in J. and A., and he walked over and wrote below it BUT THE WAGES OF J. AND A. IS A DAMN SIGHT WORSE. (#28)

There is some indication that male weavers, in factories where both men and women wove, consistently earned more than most of their female counterparts.[11] But less discontent was voiced by women weavers, who were usually not the principal means of support for their families and, furthermore, could compare their pay favorably with that of female mill workers.

It was not illegal, or uncommon, for pregnant women in either the mill or the factory to continue working until almost the moment of delivery. The Factory Acts of 1891 and 1901 did state that a woman was not to be re-employed until four weeks after she had given birth to a child, but in Northern Ireland the regulation was frequently disregarded, for reasons of poverty.[12] An inci-

dent with both sad and humorous aspects, described in the unpublished memoirs of a tenter and reworded here, refers to the
then prevailing practice: The foreman in a weaving shed, concerned about a possible negative reaction from the factory inspec-
tor who was soon to visit the plant, asked one of his tenters to
inquire of a very pregnant woman when she would be taking her
leave of absence. Upon being questioned, the woman burst into
tears, saying she could not afford to do so until it was closer to her
time. She explained that she had little money and other children
(all illegitimate) to support. She went on to say that she neither
drank nor smoked and that this "was the only weakness she had
and could not overcome it." Later that week she did leave, but
resumed her duties after a few months. (She eventually married
a blind soldier with a pension, who was good to the children, one
of whom learned weaving when she came of age.)[13]

Despite their remaining at work until far along in their preg-
nancies, few women remember being involved in accidents
which precipitated an early birth, as was the weaver in this anecdote, related by another tenter:

> There was a woman wrought with me, and she was goin' to
> have her first baby. . . . And I was workin' . . . up on the ma-
> chines. And I happened to put my foot on a bracket, and the
> bracket broke, and I come down, and I just slid down her
> back, like that. Well, I was annoyed. And she said she was all
> right. But she wasn't in at her work the next mornin'. And I
> was worse annoyed. And I went to her father. Says I, "What
> about Maggie?" "She has a young son." (#11)

More to be expected were injuries from shuttles: "Used to be
they weren't as well guarded as what they are. . . . I've seen many
a one gettin' their teeth knocked out of them—eyes out" (#11). A
weaver who actually suffered an injury agrees and reveals a certain acceptance of the situation: "I got hit with a shuttle in the
eye. . . . They have shuttle guards up now that keeps 'em from

*Photo 24. Weavers at nonautomatic plain power looms in Brookfield Linen Com-
pany, Belfast: at left, in her stand; at right, tying broken ends at the back of her
looms; ca. 1930 (?). Note whitewashed walls to reflect light. By courtesy of
Dr. W. A. McCutcheon.*

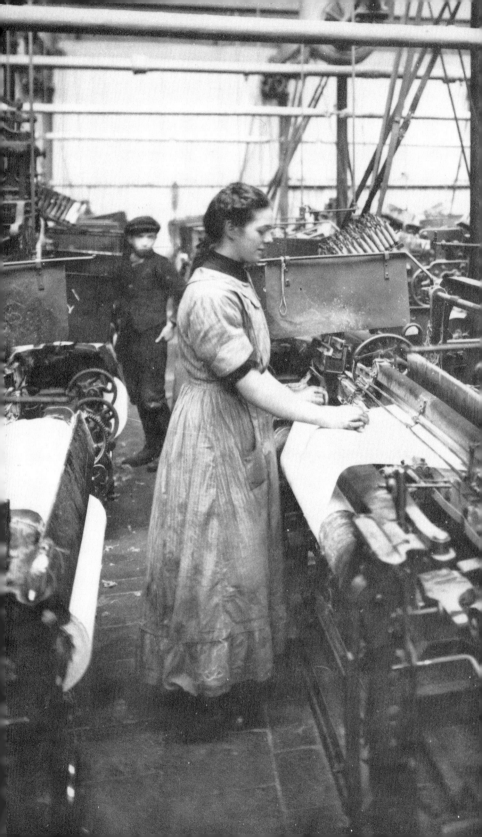

flyin'. Many's the time you got cracked on the side of the leg—you never bothered about it" (#56).

Most workers also seemed to adjust, if imperfectly, to the heat and steam in the shed. In order to keep the yarn moist enough to prevent it from breaking, an attempt was made to prevent air from entering, especially on those summer days when there was a "hard, dry wind" blowing. Most rooms, therefore, were without side windows, illumination being provided by light streaming in from glass skylights in the roof or by artificial means. In addition, it was customary in the early decades of this century to raise the humidity in some rooms by blowing saturated steam from nozzles located about eight feet high throughout the shed, causing the moisture to circulate around the weavers and their looms. The result:

> I saw . . . what we call the pass wringing wet. That was with the steam. It had to be that damp. And, in good warm weather. . . . you woulda saw, at dinnertime, "There's such a one. There's Maggie away today again." Fainted, and then they carried her out to the yard. (#32)

Noise was most often mentioned as the factor to be overcome before one could successfully adjust to work in the Weaving Shed, but one eventually acquired ability to withstand even ill effects from the rattle of the looms. After that, it was a matter of learning to communicate, despite the din, using traditional "signs." "We had a special call" and gestures:

> Now, if you asked me the time, and it was quarter-past four, I would do this: [right hand raised, fist clenched, index finger curved to form a C = "quarter"; swift motion, with hand postured as above, to the right across body = "past"; four fingers of right hand up straight = "four"]. . . . If you wanted to say something, I coulda shaped my lips so you woulda understood. . . . or if the foreman had been comin' through the shop—and we always wanted each other to know—there was a certain whistle you'd a given between your teeth. And then you touched your head—that was the hat. The foreman wore a hat, and everybody knew. . . . the foreman was comin' and you were on your best behavior. . . .

Photo 25. Pride in herself and in her work: a damask weaver in York Street Flax Spinning and Weaving Company, Belfast, ca. 1923. By courtesy of Mr. and Mrs. William Topping.

That was always used in the industry. . . . You see . . . no-
body really teaches you. You pick it up from the other girls
doing it. (#10)

The precise form of these signs and motions may have varied
slightly from factory to factory, but the three types of
communication—lip reading, a signal to warn of the approaching
foreman, and telling time with gestures—were requisite knowledge for a weaver. As for the arrival of the boss, a shrill "Whoo-
oo" often replaced the whistle and could be distinguished from a
similar one that was used only to attract someone's attention.
One could pass on other times of the day by raising and lowering
an appropriate number of fingers; for example, those on both
hands lifted and then dropped twice meant "twenty," and then
one indicated whether the minutes so shown meant before or
after the hour by a move with the right hand to the right, signaling "past," or toward the body, designating "toward." The past-
toward gesture seems to have been standardized. In much the
same way, one could indicate half past the hour in two steps: the
index finger of the right hand run down across the palm of the
left to show "half," and then the correct number of fingers to tell
the hour.

The ethos of the weaving subculture does not emerge as
clearly as do certain values, attitudes, and emotions of those employed at spinning. On the surface, however, the characteristic
spirit which dominated the Weaving Shed appears to have been
less colorful than that which ruled the Spinning Room. This may
well be because there was a deliberate attempt on the part of
weavers to project an image of themselves as a more serious and
dignified group of workers, a point to be enlarged upon shortly.
But, whatever the majority of workers were like, the Weaving
Shed did, apparently, harbor its share of "characters." Indeed,
more people with idiosyncratic behavior seem to have been at
work there than in the Spinning Room of the mill, or so one might
conclude from hearing the greater number of stories of those persons which emanated from there. At any rate, accounts about the
deviant behavior of four women, designated as "characters" by
those who described them, provide an added dimension to the
picture of the weaver and, also, serve to emphasize what was

considered to be more normal or appropriate behavior for the time and place:

> We had one woman, a bit better off than the rest of us because she had no family, and her husband was always in constant work. . . . she was a law unto herself, and was a person if you told her not to do a thing that was the very thing she would do. Management was not too happy about this. So, way back . . . the Prince of Wales, who is the present Duke of Windsor, was comin' to visit at home, in Northern Ireland, and of course he came to the firm where I was employed. . . .
>
> So the manager sent for me and said, "Now the Prince of Wales is comin' tomorrow and we don't want Jenny speakin' to him. And see that she doesn't." I said, "I wouldn't undertake to say that Jenny wouldn't speak to him, and to tell her, that's the thing she'll do." Well, the day arrived and the gentry were all here, and the Prince of Wales arrived.
>
> Now, in the weavin' factory, there's always a surplus of ends for a weaver, because if one end goes short, you have to fall back on the surplus. And these ends are rolled up in a ball. . . . when the Prince was a couple of yards away, Jenny let this ball down and it rolled onto his feet. He looked up to see where it was going, and Jenny winked at him . . . and he just walked into her stand, you see.
>
> Now, in the weaving factory, it's very noisy, and if you're going to speak to a person, you've got to speak into their ear. So, she had her arm around his shoulder. And she was talkin' to him, and he was talkin' to her. Now it didn't last any more than three to four minutes, but to us, it was an eternity. . . . when it was finished, Jenny curtsied, and, of course—you woulda thought he was in India—he put his hands up and he bowed. Well, away they went, and as soon as the Prince went away, I went up to speak to her, and she just put her fingers on her lips, waved me off—she was speaking to royalty, and she wasn't going to speak to me. So, she took her shawl and away she went, walked out. Now that was unknown in mill or factory, because you had to get permission by the foreman.

So, the next morning . . . I was sent for again. . . . I could
see it getting newspaper headlines: WEAVER SPEAKS TO
PRINCE, GETS THE SACK. So, we went up to the office and the
management says to me, "Yesterday was wonderful. I think
you behaved very well yesterday. When the Prince was sign-
ing the visitor's book, he turned around to the managing director, and he says, 'You know, I've traveled the world over
and never was asked such a homely question. Because that
lady down in the weaving shop said, "How's your mother?"' "
Well, in those days, it would have been, "How's Her Maj-
esty?" or "How's Queen Mary?" She said, "How's your
mother?" Now, when his father and mother, the late King
George V and Queen Mary, were married, the linen that Ulster give was woven in this factory, and her mother had had
a hand in the weaving of it. And she was telling him this, you
see. Well, I'm telling you, we haven't lived that story down.
(#10)

I remember one they called M. T. She . . . kept a bad house.
. . . That means that married men took women to her house.
Well, she was about the oldest worker there, and she
wrought the longest. . . . this day, she was just into the factory, and she come, lookin' a pass. Says she, "Will you let me
out now?" "Well," says I, "I'll get into trouble for lettin' you
out." Says she, "I'll be back again before breakfast time. I
want to go down to. . . . There was a gentleman there last
night, and whenever he went out this mornin', he left his
keys." And it was the director. But that happened regular.
Most of the workers knew about it but [the owner] didn't.

Well, she was a real good worker. So she wrought on 'til
she took bad. And, she woulda said, "I'm gonna leave all my
money to you and D. W." Well, we didn't think she had any
money at all, for we knowed she had big parties and things.

Anyway, whenever she died [the owner] give her ten shillings of a week of a pension—but six months after it, there
was a bit in the paper where Mary had left 500 pounds to the
cat and dog home. . . . [the owner] sent for D. W. and me,
and he says, "What do you think of it?" says he. "I give her
more of a pension than ever I gave any other weaver that was

here. And," says he, "there she left 500 pounds to the cat and dog home." "Well," says I, "she built the foreman and me up," says I. "We were gettin' it." (#11)

Well, Celina was one of the characters that is outstanding. Celina was a very good weaver, but she was completely mad. One of her peculiarities was a belief that she had got to insulate herself against electric shocks which the so-called electric man who was hiding on the roof had sent down—the electricity down. And, of course, these went through her.

And she had pieces of silver paper and the tops of mineral-water bottles, pieces of wire—her looms were festooned with these things. And Celina wouldn't weave—if you'd taken them off, she woulda—she wouldn't weave. She said she couldn't weave unless these things were there to protect her. But she was a very good weaver, made excellent cloth. (#13)

M. B. was a type weaver. And she, like Celina, was also batty and was always quarreling with people. Celina was very placid, but M. B. was always quarreling. And people gave her a wide berth. On an occasion . . . the managing director of the company was taking a visitor through the works. And they had stopped at a group of looms not very far from where M. B. was.

And [the managing director] was explaining and the man was feeling the yarn, touching it. . . . when suddenly M. B. came over from her looms and caught the man by the arm. And she said, "Never mind what he's telling you about that," she said. "You just come over here with me 'til I show you the hay they expect us to make cloth of." (#13)

Neither the social distinctions nor the verbal sparrings which existed among various groups of workers in the mill were found to any marked degree in the weaving end of the industry. Although the weaver, warper, and winder agreed in feeling themselves to be "above" the mill girls, there was no unanimity of opinion as to which one of the three occupied the highest position. One individual might feel that warping was a better job than winding, for there was more dust associated with the latter;

another might list weavers as being more important in that they actually produced the cloth; a third could cite the fact that damask weaving was better than plain in that it paid better. However, in general, all the women considered themselves to be on the same status level and described the jobs as being mutually interdependent.

Some of their male associates might tease them:

> The fellas used to carry on with the girls in the factory, and they used to say, "C'mon, you old "creeshie weavers." . . . they were working at the looms and all and sometimes they were dirty, you know, with oil and all. And they used to say, "You're a creeshie weaver. That's what you are." (#37)

But such teasing did not represent any real depth of sentiment.

Even when there were hard feelings between the weaver and the other two, whom she might blame for faulty weft bobbins or warp yarn full of slubs, her sentiments did not erupt into derogatory songs and rhymes.

> We never done that. We just give an argument. . . . hard talk. They'd tell the winder . . . to "make better weft, for there's nothin' to sell in them hard, bad-shaped bobbins. . . ." You'd have your arguments like. . . . The weaver's not supposed to come to the winder's machine for weft. . . . They used to come and curse me. I used to say, "See the foreman." You'd a had words like that. (#35)

As for the weavers themselves, except for the occasional flare-up and some personal dislikes, a spirit of comradeship existed among women who, for the most part, enjoyed their work, difficult as it might be. The closest bonds formed between those working in close proximity to one another, for the din in the shed made intimate communication at a distance impossible, and the necessity of watching one's looms intently kept one bound to a limited area. Good friends watched one another's looms when it was necessary for one of them to make a trip to the office for weft or to visit the lavatory, and they supported one another's efforts to make their pay: "Hurry back. You're on the push. You've got to make the mark" (#32).

Repeatedly, the women I interviewed spoke about their work in terms similar to the following, which appeared in a linen trade journal:

> My happiest hours were passed in the factory, so they were. I loved my work and my looms. I always got a thrill when I saw the pattern forming; often it would be flowers that took me back to my childhood's days. Some say it's slavery, but I always liked it; and cannot tell of my feelings of satisfaction as I carried my web to the Cloth Office, and knew I had little to fear from its inspection.[14]

Liking her work was no guarantee that a woman would remain satisfied with one place of employment, however, and there was a fair amount of mobility. Young weavers might move, within a limited area of Belfast, with their friends until they found a factory and looms to their liking; among the others, "some just couldn't settle down." It was not unusual for a tenter to find several weavers waiting on him when he arrived in the morning with the usual request, "Give us a pair of looms, Mister," and from among them he selected those he felt could work harmoniously with the other workers. These weavers, moving about restlessly, helped to pass along the lore of their coworkers from factory to factory.

Whether it was through the travels of such weavers or mainly by means of the printed word that poems came to be transmitted, we may never know for sure. But a verse known by many weavers and associated with them, though not exclusively, has for years been attached to the death notices in newspapers of many:

> Not 'til the loom is silent,
> And the shuttles cease to fly,
> Shall God unroll the canvas,
> And explain the reasons why.
> The dark threads are as neatful,
> In the weaver's skillful hand,
> As the threads of gold and silver,
> In the pattern he has planned. (#63)

Photo 26. Pirn winders and foreman in the New Northern Spinning and Weaving Company, Belfast, ca. 1910. By courtesy of Mr. Charles Morrison.

"That was the first thing my mother [a weaver] learned me when I came out to the weavin'" (#63).

Although the women who were weavers did not in their recollections repeatedly stress, as did the spinners, the good-times aspect of their days in the factory, they seem to have derived sufficient satisfaction from their work—whether from a sense of pride in what they produced, or from spending their time among congenial companions, or simply from having the opportunity to bring in money to their households—to speak in fairly positive terms of past times. The same cannot be said of the men. While individual personality factors undoubtedly accounted for some of the negative attitudes, equally important were the sense of confinement and frustration which seemed to overwhelm them at their looms and the realization that they, often the primary wage earners for a family, were undercompensated when compared with men laboring at other jobs in areas where there was alternative employment. Some male weavers in Belfast were recruited from the country. Being called in the city "old ladies" for undertaking what was there considered to be women's work did not improve their self-image.

In certain towns, the demand for power-loom weavers exceeded the supply. There, men without family responsibilities chose to be idle rather than confined to the looms:

> Before the First World War, the tenters used to . . . stand
> outside, watchin' to see could he coax anyone in—any
> weaver. Some of them naturally . . . young men that perhaps
> had some intelligence or more spirit, and they didn't go into
> their work. They stayed out and . . . loafed. They were up
> against it, and they just quit—didn't go back when the horn
> blew. . . . And the tenters were goin' out and watchin':
> "Would you like a start? I've got a good loom here, a good
> pair of looms. There's good cloth." (#28)

Efforts made to improve the financial lot of the weaver were supported mainly by men. In the areas outside of Belfast where male weavers were found in large numbers, union organization came about relatively early, and the men's tendency toward disputatious behavior, shared with their counterparts in the city and marked in contrast with the behavior of their female coworkers, earned them the label of "buck weavers" by management.

Photo 27. Workers posed by their looms in a plain weaving shed in Loop Bridge Weaving Company, Belfast, ca. 1912. By courtesy of Mrs. Margaret Smyth.

What may have been a typical male attitude toward weaving, and one which echoes sentiments of a hundred years past,[15] is summed up effectively by a man who had been for a time a weaver outside of Belfast:

> It was not man's work. . . . It was really women's work, a weaver's work. . . . In the first place, there was no money. On the other hand, it was a nimble job for the fingers; it didn't let a man express himself or use his energy. It was frustration all the time, and a woman has more patience than a man. . . . I've known them to go behind the loom in their frustration and . . . the man went behind it, and he just took his knife and he slashed it along, and he took it in his arms, and he threw it on the pass. And then he went out and joined the army. . . . It was just against man's nature to be stuck between two looms while he was gettin' no physical exercise. (#28)

The contrast between his disposition and the feelings of a woman in the city is striking. To her, as to many like her, the work was an interesting challenge:

> If I went to do the thing I went and done it. I couldn't be annoyed. And if I got a bad beam, it worried the heart out of me, even the very thought. But I wouldn't let anybody see that I couldn't master it. (#32)

However representative were the stances taken by that man and woman, at least one member of management viewed the merits of each sex from a slightly different perspective:

> Women were much more nimble with their fingers than men, but strangely enough, when you come to the very fine end of the trade, the very, very fine handkerchief . . . it was the men that did that. . . . a woman . . . has about ten things in her head at once. In ordinary weaving which is just a matter of attending a power loom, they can talk about their boy friends and what's going . . . but when it comes to real craftsmanship, a man is more used to putting his mind to one thing. (#27)

Some men did adjust and settle down to work quietly and patiently. Others left weaving to try for jobs in Scotland and other places; many of these, unable to adapt to new environments or types of occupations, returned to the factories after varying periods of time, but they remained disgruntled with their lot. If noise, heat, and the necessity for concentration were sufficient to deter women weavers from creating and singing their own songs, composing verses, and bantering back and forth, it is not surprising that those factories dominated by men harboring such negative attitudes nurtured a climate even less conducive to the creation and perpetuation of lore.

Still, a fragment of a rhyme which circulated in at least one small-town factory and which concerns a job utilizing men was recalled by a former weaver, later a warper and then a winder. A man, working as a dresser, would say to her "when he'd had a wee drop of drink":

> Never marry a dresser,
> He'll always give you pain,
> For his hands are always tallowed . . . (#37)

"He had a whole song made of it." A variant on the verse sung by the spinners (see p. 72), the words allude to the trying conditions under which those men worked and their resulting bad-naturedness. "Tallowed hands," is, of course, a reference to the pastelike sizing put upon the threads of the warp beam so they would pass through the loom more smoothly.

The fact that a detailed consideration of status has been left until last should not lead one to minimize the importance of the topic to this study, for no account of the female weaver is complete without providing an understanding of that motivating force behind her behavior. I cannot say for sure when the belief arose that the workers in the factory occupied a higher status position within the industry than those employed in the mill.[16] What can be stated with certainty is that, once the distinction had been made by the workers themselves, it was reinforced in several ways. Helping to perpetuate the notion was a recognition that it was more difficult to obtain a job as a weaver, winder, or warper than to be hired as a spinner:

> In the factory at that time, you were, like, awful, as they say, select like. . . . At one time in the factory, you nearly had to

have a line from your clergyman or your doctor, for to get in. But anyone could get into the mill. (#34)

I must point out that the high regard with which weaving was held was relative only to certain jobs:

> My mother wanted me to be a stitcher . . . and I went in for a wee while to Smith's. . . . I did go on to a machine, but I was pretty slow at it. Well, then, there was two sisters who wanted to go to the weavin', and I went with them. And my mother cried. Oh, she cried because I was goin' to the weavin'. And my father says, "I don't know what you're crying for. Wasn't your father a weaver? And wasn't Davy a weaver?" Well, I went to it, and I'm glad I did. (#63)[17]

When a woman did become a weaver—or winder or warper, which earned her the same prestige—she made sure it was known that her job was in the factory, not the mill. It was imperative that one use proper terminology when speaking of the place of employment:

> One thing be careful about. . . . Never, never, never say to a weaver, "You work in a mill." Look! You'll be down there with them. That conveys to a weaver that you don't know the industry. I don't mean to be offensive when I say that.
> But, remember, spinning is a mill, weaving is a factory, and stitching is a wareroom. You'll be "on a pig's back," as we say here, if you know those three technical terms. (#10)

Another distinction in terminology was made when referring to the lavatory. In the factory, women usually spoke of going to "parliament"; in the mill, the place was called the "wee house." I was unable to determine how long the names had been used, but suggestions were offered as to the reasons for those designations. As for "parliament":

> In parliament you can say what you like. And I could call you what I like, if you were in the opposition party. . . . you can say what you like, and it's not told. And we could say what we like in parliament about the foreman or the manager. And there was that loyalty, it wasn't carried into the workshop. It wasn't told. You could give your secrets there and

what you thought about the boss, and they weren't always pleasant things. (#10)

To be sure, the parliament in the factory was a place for conversational and other exchanges. Once within it, the women expressed not only their dissatisfactions but also current gossip. In addition, they could learn there the words to a current song and how to dance and crochet, as well as take a puff on a cigarette (a practice still highly disapproved of in those years). No matter that management attempted to limit such visits or restrict the number within the lavatory at any one time, even to the point of giving fines—or dismissing violators—when there was an infringement of rules.[18]

The wee house served the same social function in a mill, although the derivation of the name is quite different. The term apparently stems from the nature of the structure, in some mills a small unit at the end of each room and in others a cubicle located in a kind of tower alongside the main building and reached from the lobby off each floor.

Although one might know the terms used by workers in the other end of the industry, a person traditionally used the one in common usage by coworkers:

> The weavers called theirs parliament. And you know what
> we called ours? The wee house. . . . My mother was a
> weaver. She called it parliament. My sister [weaver] called it
> parliament. I used to say to my mother, "We call ours the
> wee house." "Well," Mother replied, "we call ours parlia-
> ment." (#40)

Some understanding of the underlying prestige distinctions contained in the terminology may be gained from noting the words of a graffito that was written on the walls of one "bog," the lavatory used in a mill by male employees:

> It was always the custom in Parliament House,
> When a member enters, he uncovers his head,
> In this little house, it is quite the reverse,
> When a person enters, he uncovers his arse. (#2)

It was only in later years that the factory-mill and parliament–wee house distinctions began to break down. A rover, now retired, always referred to the lavatory in the traditional way; her daughter, still at work in the mill, became accustomed to saying "parliament." A firm in the country had always been spoken of as a mill by the workers; in the last few years of its existence, younger people had begun to call it Drumaness Factory, "because that was a nicer name than mill" (#51). Similarly, in that place, "parliament" had begun to replace "wee house." It is important to note that the change in terminology was upward, toward those words associated with a higher status. In only one instance did I hear a factory called a mill, that by a weaver in a small town who also referred to the wee house.

Whether one is employed at a clean job or a dirty one has long been a criterion to measure relative social standing among the women in the linen industry: the cleaner the conditions under which one works, the higher one's status.[19] Even among the wet-spinners, at the bottom of the hierarchy, those spinning fine yarn felt themselves to be above the women producing coarse yarn, since the latter encountered more spray, mud, and "all the stuff of the day." Similarly, a dry-spinner was ranked higher than a wet one: "I worked in the dry-spinnin' end. . . . I held out I didn't want to be a wet-spinner. I wanted a wee bit more social upliftin'. It was still the mill, but . . . we worked with our shoes on" (#23). Those who worked in the preparing rooms, although their work was the unhealthiest, were considered to be somewhat better than the spinners, and the reelers, as has been pointed out, were at the top. Factory work was all comparatively clean, and so it could be said of the winder, warper, and weaver, "They were all aristocrats" (#56). Medical authorities, concerned with health hazards, would, I believe, have ranked the jobs somewhat differently.[20]

Going without shoes was a mark of poverty in the culture outside the mill and factory. One of the early objectives of many female wage earners was to provide themselves with proper footwear to be worn in public, and it was not long before this item served as one of the measures of social acceptability of a job in the industry,[21] tied in as it was with dry, clean working conditions. The weaver worked in shoes, although she might change at the factory into an old pair or into slippers. She also went to and from work properly shod, partly to maintain her image, one might assume. The mill girls, by which term was usually meant the wet-spinners, suffered by comparison on both counts. Not only were they forced to work in their bare feet, but, whether through habit, greater poverty, or simple preference, many continued to travel to their jobs barefooted.

The shawl also came to symbolize poverty and low status. Once, both weavers and spinners, along with other female members of the working class, had gone about wrapped in that useful article. But the factory girls, either to differentiate themselves from those they considered to be inferior or because they acquired sooner the means to imitate the dress of the "gentry," adopted the coat much earlier for everyday wear. The spinners, on the other hand, may have had a coat to wear to town but used the shawl for work. By the mid-thirties even they had put aside the shawl almost completely, to the dismay of Conor, who had painted them so often in the garb.[22] Until that time, however, the coat was one of the significant status symbols of the female linen workers:

> In the factory, they always went with their coat on them.
> Well, the other went with their shawl on them. And that's
> why one thought they were higher than the other. (#56)

To understand the feelings of social superiority which weavers and other factory girls felt and endeavored to maintain in various ways is to come still closer to an explanation of why there was so little singing among those workers. For, just as the wearing of the shawl and going barefoot were associated with the spinners and low status, so the singing of those girls and women acquired the same significance. A weaver might sing to herself, despite noise in the weaving shop; the individual winder or warper, working where there were fewer distractions, might also now and then break out in song. But the songs were the come-all-ye variety, songs of the day—war hits were popular—and, especially in country firms, hymns. Not for the factory girls the kind of rollicking, boisterous, simple worksongs which pervaded the typical mill during working hours and before, at meal breaks, and at party times. And, when leaving the factory and walking home, the majority did not emulate the daily arm-in-arm group singing which characterized the doffers and spinners. The "residential" weavers in one section of Belfast did not appreciate either having their hats knocked off almost daily by the passing doffers, the "roughs" who lived "at the other [bottom] end of the street," or the kinds of songs those young girls sang, in this case one about the "leader" of the boisterous group, newly married:

> Sara Murray
> Was a fool,
> She married a man,
> Without a tool. (#86)

The comments of a worker, quoted in part earlier but reported more fully here, sum up the attitudes of those like herself:

> There wasn't much singing or anything like that. All the singing was the doffers. . . . The mill girls were always coming out "bawling" a song. You'd be ashamed to be caught with mill girls. . . . We were the "e-lite." We were the "swanks." They were the "down." When you come out, you see, we work in the factory—we had hat and coat on—they wore shawls—we were above that. They, mill, they run about in their bare feet. . . . They were the low type. We weren't really better than they were, but you thought you were above all that. (#35)

Most of the weavers with whom I came in contact were no longer at work, many of them having received, much to their regret before they were ready to retire, letters similar to the following:

> TO WHOM IT MAY CONCERN
>
> This is to certify that [name] has been employed with us for the past number of years as a Damask Weaver. Owing to the closing down of the firm in the near future, we will have to dispose of her services. She has at all times carried out her work thoroughly, and has given good service to this firm, and we would recommend her to any future employer.

(The women in Photo 28 are pictured just prior to their forced retirement.) Nevertheless, I was able to speak with a group of women, employed in a factory still in operation, who compared a few of the conditions in the "old days" with present ones. They all applauded the elimination of the practice of "sucking the shuttle," liked being paid for the amount of cloth (measured on an in-

Photo 28. Weavers at York Street Flax Spinning Company, 1961. By courtesy of Mrs. Mary Johnston.

strument attached to each loom) woven each week rather than on the number of cuts produced, and approved of automatic stop devices which helped prevent serious faults in the cloth they turned out—although one woman, in her late seventies, preferred older types of plain looms to some of the newer models. Yet, despite these improvements, and, in recent years, the relaxation of rules governing their behavior while on the job, as well as the presence of foremen who are less strict, they agreed that they had had more fun at work in the past: "Right enough, it was good then" (#78).

SIX

Lore of Mill & Factory

Thus far, I have presented the life and associated lore of the Spinning Room, Hackling Shop, and Weaving Shed so as to emphasize what was unique to each. There were, however, certain practices which cut across both mill and factory, generally, if not in all specifics. I turn now to certain folkloristic facets of those which loom large in the minds of persons who labored in weaving and spinning concerns and which can supplement specialized research into the matters.

PRACTICAL JOKES AND HAZING

Few men and women escaped being the object of practical jokes during their working days. Most young people were subjected almost immediately to hazing, aimed at the newcomer making a transition from the ranks of the unemployed to the employed, and many also fell victim to pranks directed against certain categories of persons or engaged in at special times. The harassment of coworkers for the sheer sake of devilment was commonplace as well, but it is of less significance here, except as it reveals still other dimensions of mill and factory life.

One of the most common forms of hazing in the linen industry, as elsewhere, was that of sending the novice to procure a non-existent, and therefore ridiculous, piece of equipment.[1] Topping the list of items frequently sent for was a bucket of steam, sometimes blue steam so as to make the request seem more plausible. A variety of workers might send the child wandering to a logical place for it, but always the result was the same: embarrassment for the unsuspecting and laughter on the part of those already initiated. Standing at the head of their stands, all the women in one room watched a young doffer who, sent by her spinner ostensibly to clean the shoes of the spinning master, was told by him to procure a shiny new bucket from someone and then to have the oiler fill it with steam:

> Now there was cleeks on the steam pipes hangin', and that's
> where you hang this bucket on to get boiled water. . . . to boil
> the rollers. . . . It was all bubblin' up, really boilin'. And he
> took the bucket off me. And he hung it on one of these
> cleeks, and he let it hang for a couple of minutes. And he
> says, "There you are, Luv. That's enough."
> And I brought it to him [the spinning master], and I said,
> "There you are, Sir. That's enough." And he said, "Yes." And
> the laugh—everybody had the best laugh. The bucket was
> still at me, and I thought, "God bless me" . . . I didn't under-
> stand, see? I thought it was invisible or somethin'. So he took
> the bucket off me, and he says. . . . "I've cleaned me shoes
> myself, now that you got away, on account of getting me the
> bucket of steam." So I hadn't to clean his shoes. I got off well.
> (#47)

There were numerous requests for left-handed objects. The novice, usually a boy, who would ordinarily be working with tools, was sent for, perhaps, a left-handed screwdriver, a left-handed saw, or a left-handed monkey wrench.

Hammers—leather- or rubber-headed or -faced—were to be obtained from the Carpenter Shop, Blacksmith Shop, or Mechanic Shop. In the factory, youngsters were sometimes sent to their tenter for a cloth one. Often, several trips were made before the ruse was revealed to the new recruit:

> Well, there was a young fella come in to . . . serve his time.
> . . . I mind my husband, this mornin' he says, "Will you go
> to the Mechanic Shop, Charlie, and tell such a man to send
> me up the loan of the leather-faced hammer. . . ."
> Well, he come back. . . . and says, "The man says he's
> never seen a leather-faced hammer." "Ach! He's dopey," he

says. "He served his time in the Mechanic Shop and he
doesn't know what a leather-faced hammer is. Go ye back
and tell him."

Well, he had that wee fella back three times, you know.
And he got the best laugh out of it. And then . . . one of the
mechanics come, and he said, "Why are you takin' a hand
out of the wee lad for?" And then, whenever he knowed they
was only takin' a hand out of him, he says, "I'm not angry at
ye, Mr. M. It's a good laugh. I must mind that." (#37)

Requests for rubber screws and round squares were less frequent. A few people remembered seeking in vain a can of striped
paint, striped ink, or a striped pen or pencil. One mother, her
curiosity piqued when she observed her son wandering around
the factory, rescued him from further searching for the "half
round" for which he had been sent. Where diaper was woven, it
was customary to send the employee for a bird's-eye pattern book,
"bird's-eye" being a reference to a design consisting of a diamond
with an "eye" in the middle of it.

Another youngster was warned in advance that she might be
subjected to pranks: "I was put up till it, you see, before I went in.
Because I was inclined to be a wee bit nervous. And my father
says, 'Now, anything you're sent for, just say you haven't time'"
(#56). So, when she was sent for a "long wait," she knew what to
answer and warned her friends as well. Had she obeyed the order, she would have been sent from one person to another, until
one of them would have asked her to wait while he checked on
the matter. Upon his return, she would have been told, "Well, I
guess you've waited long enough." Interestingly, the term *long
wait* was usually employed in the factory, while *long stand*—
with sometimes the reply to the request being "Stand as long as
you like"—was the phrase used more often in the mill.

Mill workers report that newcomers were told to get various
kinds of keys. Spinners sent the doffers to procure a "key for the
flyers" or one for the troughs. Out of the hackling shop the unsuspecting emerged, looking for "keys to the hackles."

From the Carpenter Shop, it was said that one could obtain
baldy-headed nails or baldy-headed screw nails, but the dupe was
more likely to be told to get ones made of rubber. Sometimes, the
trip took the youngster right out of the mill:

> They woulda sent . . . the dopey ones . . . over to the Carpenter Shop for rubber nails. And B. M. said, "I have none. If you go over till the barber." And the barber woulda sent him over to A. B., the shoemaker. And then—all these old boys knew—A. B. woulda sent you over . . . as far as you could get, to J. D. And says, "J. D. . . . has them used." "What for?" "For puttin' on oilcloth." "Very thing." (#2)

Hazing of another sort served as a kind of initiation rite undergone by those entering the mill and factory. With women dominating the textile industry—at least in numbers— it is not surprising that the victims of many of these pranks were young boys:

> There was a custom—it's funny, it happened to me. Now, at the time, it's what . . . we call a tub. It was as long as this kitchen. And . . . what they call wet waste came off the frames. It was made into a ball about this size, and it was threw into this tub. Now, them was all wet. And the spinners, they woulda got the foreman in one part of the room. They got hold of you and put you in the box along—that was your baptism of fire. Your clothes were all wet . . . 'til you went home. That was done with nearly everyone [boys] that went into the spinnin' room. . . . "duckin' ye." (#43)

The custom was known as "dippin' 'em" in another mill, but there the "wee larners" were dipped into vats in which rollers were soaked overnight to keep them from cracking.

The newcomer may not have enjoyed such an experience, but the one he, in common with young men working in certain other industries in Northern Ireland, dreaded was that known as "oiling them." Each lad "knew their time had to come" (#47), and one small boy, warned in advance, went home and announced to his mother, "My trousers are comin' down tomorrow" (#32). When the moment was propitious, the spinners or weavers seized their victim, removed his breeches, and proceeded to grease his genitals with oil. A lad could not set the matter right until he reached home and could lather the afflicted areas. Sometimes, it was not until a party day when the young, and not so young, boys were seized, and occasionally paint was substituted for oil, but the principle was the same. Not even an apprentice manager could be sure he'd not be waylaid, although one who was would appear to have escaped relatively unscathed:

> When I was a young man, seventeen years of age . . . we had in those days what were called lighting-up parties. . . . it would be about . . . half past five in the evening, and the lights went up. And the—saving your presence—but the women used to put the young boys down and take out their private parts and paint them with red lead. It was probably an old fertility rite. . . .
> Anyway, they surrounded me in the Weaving Shed, among the looms. Fortunately, I'd been well briefed, you see. I never was more than ten-and-a-half stone, stripped. I— they put me down, you see, and started to fumble at my trousers.
> And—again, saving your presence—but in those days women wore drawers that were split. So, I just stuck up my hand and got her by the pubic hair. And I said, "For Jasus' sake! Let me up or out comes the bloody sod!" And . . . that was the end of that. It was a ritual kind of thing, you see. But I'd been warned, as I say, by my father, and he'd been warned, by his grandfather, what to do with them. They were virtuous women. It was a—sort of ritual thing—I don't know. (#27)

For a very long time, many persons outside the industry have held the belief that there was much immoral behavior on the part of female textile workers, that many engaged in illicit coitus, often through being subjected to assaults by managers upon whose good will their employment depended, or with men with whom they came in contact in the mill or factory. Neil J. Smelser discusses similar accusations that were directed against employees in the cotton industry in England in the mid-nineteenth century, and some of the causes for them. He concludes that the charges "stand unsubstantiated in the light of historical research," and he cites documents which suggest that those people differed little from others living under similar urban conditions.[2] Over a hundred years later, such insinuations are still circulating in Northern Ireland and seem to be unfounded in reality today as then. Men and women alike testified emphatically that, if there was such behavior in the industry, it would have been only an isolated case, definitely not a common occurrence, and probably participated in by a female known to be "loose" in her behavior outside work as well as in. There is complete agreement with the man who declared, "Ireland is the chastest country in Europe! No, never in my time, ever, ever" (#27). What did transpire was most likely the kind of earthy hazing just described, which was undertaken in the spirit of merriment. It may well be that stories which indicate otherwise reveal an element of wishful thinking on the part of, mainly, male tellers. The fact remains that women, not men, seem to have initiated most of what might pass in other contexts as predominantly sexual activity out of motives somewhat less sexual in nature.

Girls suffered anxious moments on different accounts. It was not uncommon, for example, to tell a newcomer in the mill, who was due to pass her physical examination, usually a minimal inspection of hair, teeth, etc., that she was required to take with her a urine specimen and to provide her with a bottle for that purpose. In one instance, a child was told that she must fill a bucket by the end of the day, and she wept continuously until the demand was shown to have been made for sport.

Farm laborers who entered the mills when there was no other available work found themselves the butt of many jokes. "You see, we were only in the village, but still we felt we were more superior, see, than the country fellows, and, of course, we used to keep them goin', you know" (#7). Probably not institutionalized was the "welcome" accorded them in one firm:

> We had one woman. . . . She used to—the country ones I was tellin' you about—well, she woulda called 'em down to her stand and she woulda been—the children were all breast fed then, you know—she woulda pulled her breast out and squirted it in their eyes . . . for devilment, more or less. (#7)

More usual was the practice of plastering various objects to the shirts of those young lads. Frequently used were wet laps, formed when broken ends wound themselves around the rollers of the spinning frames. In other places, where anyone might serve to provide the older hands with "a queer laugh," such items as bones and pig's feet were attached to their backs.

Men weavers, who "were always up to tricks of some sort" (#18), frequently tied greased cords from one shuttle gate to that of the loom across the pass. Any person who walked that way would be struck in the face by an almost invisible obstacle.

> You always kept water . . . at your loom. And . . . the winders used to go down what they call the main pass, down to the Windin' Shop. And maybe some fella woulda . . . been "blued" by a girl the night before. Maybe had a sat with her and she didn't turn up. And whenever he seen her comin' down—he used to have a tin, and he used to have it strung up on—don't you know—and as soon as she come he cut the thread at the top of the loom. . . . it dropped down on top of her, water and all. She knew why. (#18)

WEDDINGS

The marriage of a textile worker prompted hazing of another sort, and, although the bride- or groom-to-be often took great pains to keep news about the impending ceremony from reaching the ears of coworkers, few managed to escape the harassment customarily reserved for the occasion. The experience was one shared with employees in other industries, but the forms of the pranks played were largely dependent upon the materials at hand in the various departments within mills and factories. One was, of course, taking a chance in other ways: "There was a saying at Doagh Mill—'You're taking an awful risk getting married.' 'Well, it's better to be a poor woman than a poor girl!'" (#68). Still, numerous weddings took place, and, traditionally, many women worked after marriage.

Obviously, the makings for both good and bad wives were found among all workers, but it was the spinners who frequently boasted of the qualities they were known to bring to a marriage. The capacity for hard work was one of these, and one which stood them in good stead when comparisons were drawn between the girls who worked in the stitching end of the industry—considered to be of higher status—and themselves:

> The fellows always said, "Oh, she's a wareroom doll. She'll not make a good wife. For God's sake, don't marry a wareroom doll if you're wise. You'll never be able to get your supper. They can't cook and they can't clean. They would only

be good for doin' their faces and manicurin' their nails.
If you're lookin' for a wife, get somebody out of the mill.
They'll know what they're doin'." Every man wanted a mill
girl, who looked after you and kept a clean shirt on you.
(#47)

No matter how valid the distinction, the "wareroom doll" had
been rated low in this respect for some time.[3]

It was verified that at least one suitor was attracted by the
virtues of hard work:

She was a spinner. . . . And when I went to the mill, they
were giving the workers there at Christmas time . . . five shillings, ones that had not missed any time. She had been getting it for ten years, and I told her, "Ellen . . . if you do that
again, I'll give you ten shillings." . . . the eleventh year she
did it. And I told her if she did it another year I would give
her a pound. A pound was a lot of money in those days—this
over fifty years ago. So, she got the pound, but she only got
the pound once.

But she had done it for twelve years, and she walked to her
work, for four miles every morning, and walked back home.
And she had that record for not missing an hour in all those
years. . . . did it for very little money. All she was earning,
nine and sixpence a week. . . .

The peculiar thing was, some fellow in Dundee. . . . he got
the local paper, the *Down Recorder*. And . . . he wrote her a
letter and said he'd been looking for an industrious wife for a
long time. And he proposed marriage to her, without seein'
her. . . . At that time, she was a woman, well over sixty. (#1)

Males in the mill voiced their preferences in a musical way, but
it is doubtful if the negative statements they expressed toward
the rovers, covered with fluff and pouce from the flax they handled in the Preparing Room, bore much relationship to their actual choice of a mate:

Hairy rover,
Skin and bones,
I would rather lie m'alone,
As lie with a hairy rover-o. (#48)

> Greasy belly,
> Full of fat,
> I would rather lie with that,
> As lie with a hairy rover-o. (#s 55, 57, 58, 59)

About the rovers it was said:

> The rovers generally looked more dried up. . . . A child goin'
> in the Rovin' Room in no time lost any good color hardly. . . .
> Their skin shriveled more, dried up more than in the Spin-
> nin' Room. Because the Spinnin' Room was warm, but
> like—if they sweated there—they seemed more dried up.
> (#38)

The rovers' male counterparts were the "tow-pows," boys who
handled flax after it had come from the hackling machine and
deposited it in the tow stores. Coming out of work at night,
covered—shoes, hair, and all—with the short fibers, they were
objects of derisive taunts: "Here's the tow-pow boys; let's make a
beeline for it" (#33).

Even rovers married, however, and they, like spinners, reelers
(who most often remained single, it is claimed), warpers, winders, and weavers, were given a traditional sendoff, late in the
afternoon when the girl was due to take leave from her job. Typically, where coats were worn, they were filled with objects of all
kinds and the sleeves and bottoms sewn shut. When carts—
"trucks, we called 'em trucks" (#43)—were available, the hap-
less victim was dumped in "along with all the bobbins of the day"
(#21) and wheeled around the room, being bumped into pieces
of machinery along the way and, perhaps, taken outside into the
yard: "Sure, we were always pushin' trucks around" (#15).
Sometimes the bride-to-be was adorned with a veil; if she was in
a mill, it might have been made from strands of plaited flax. Or
she was given dolls and placed in a truck decorated to resemble a
pram, "and the wedding bells hadn't taken place atall" (#23).[4]
Another common practice was the presentation of a chamber pot,
filled with various objects, including salt; the decorated pot—to
one was tied a sign which read WASH MY FACE AND KEEP ME
CLEAN, AND I WON'T TELL WHAT I HAVE SEEN—had to be carried
home by the recipient.[5]

The customary "carry-on"—"They've been doin' that right

down the ages" (#47)—was described by a Spinning Room worker:

> When anybody was gettin' married, they carried on terrible.
> They tied your sleeves at the bottom and filled it full of rove
> bobbins. And the day you were stoppin' your work, they . . .
> wheeled you out in a handcart . . . on the Falls Road, singin'
> songs and makin' a fool of ye, in an old hat and all. But you
> had to enjoy the joke. You daren't refuse it; it was custom to
> the mills then to do that. . . .
>
> I mind one day there was a girl . . . gettin' married—God
> forgive me for laughin'—and they wheeled her down in the
> handcart. And they were singin'. Now he was a bus conduc-
> tor and his wife—he was married like, and this woulda been
> his second wife—and she wasn't that very long dead. And
> they sang comin' down:

> > Charlie, Charlie,
> > No matter what you do,
> > Don't let Mary shove it on to you.
> > If you do, you will rue,
> > Cheer up, Charlie,
> > No matter what you do.

> Dear! What do you think? Charlie died in a fortnight after
> that. Died very sudden. And we—God forgive us—we en-
> joyed singin' after him. (#47)

She went on to provide an explanation of the song's meaning: "Charlie mustn't be soft with Mary, or she would rub it into him. She would be havin' the trousers and Charlie would have the petticoat." And then she recalled:

> And they used to go out **on the** streets—say a weddin' in the
> street, and the mill workers all comin' out. They used to
> gather and shout, "Throw out the bun money." Throw a lot
> of coppers . . . for to buy. And the groom woulda come and
> tossed the coppers up in the air, and everybody was runnin'
> to get a ha'penny and a penny. "Throw out the bun money."
> (#47)

The weaver, also put in a truck, could expect still other goings-on:

A weaver has to go to the Weft Office to collect her weft. . . . Well, they'd a got her away. There used to be . . . a breast-board . . . across the looms . . . to keep the cloth clean . . . because you do get the front of you soiled. . . . they'd a taken this breastboard up, off the loom. It was as tall . . . as any of us. . . . And they woulda dressed it up in all kinds of funny things. . . .

Maybe somebody woulda hurried up and printed THE BRIDE TO BE or somethin' not too complimentary to the groom-to-be. Oh, yes—oh, dear, yes. It was always great fun at weddings. . . . When she come back again, she couldn't get into her stand. . . . And then everybody woulda gathered around and there was chuckles and a laugh until somebody, "Whisshht!" That meant the hat was comin', you see, the foreman. (#10)

FOOTING

Although the sleeves of men's coats were sometimes stuffed and sewn up, the customary "standing your footing" was, in a way, the male counterpart of the ritual undergone by female workers at the time of marriage. The practice, less frequently referred to as "payin' the footin'," was engaged in, generally, on two occasions: "when an apprentice finishes his apprenticeship, when he got his first pay as a journeyman" and "when 'he got a start,' as we call it—that was a job as a journeyman and in a year or two decided to get married" (#38). There is some indication that the first of the two instances was the more traditional and that the second came only later to be designated in the same way.[6] At any rate, the focus here is upon "footing" as it related to the attainment of journeyman status. A hackler explained it this way:

. . . payin' the footin'. When a fella come out of his time and had his first full pay, and all his mates would say, "You have to stand your footin' tonight." He had only to stand them all pints apiece. Of course, pints was only a tanner in them days. It didn't amount to a lot, you know. . . . I came in . . . to serve my time in 1927, and I never got it finished. . . . [you bought for] your mates, one on each side of you. . . . Anybody you knew well, you—gave a hand to pack tow or tie bunches up. You give this fella a hand at takin' out his parcels, and you give him a hand—work to one another. We call 'em mates. (#2)

What was true of the hacklers, as well as the roughers and the journeymen in the Mechanic Shop of the mill, may be similarly said of the men who served their time in the factory. There, it was the tenters, dressers, slashers, joiners, electricians, and other mechanics who stood their footing when they became journeymen, fully qualified.

The custom differed slightly from one footing to another, but the basic pattern remained the same. The number of mates actually taking part could vary. Sometimes all of one's associates in a shop were invited; where large numbers prohibited this, only a few would be asked to join a group, but among these would be the man directly under whom the apprentice had worked. Teetotalers could go along; in fact, the new journeyman himself might well be a nonimbiber. It was usual in some places for a man to give a sum of money to the oldest person in the shop, who invited other workers there to go to a public house, selected because it was convenient to a mill or factory and not because it was traditional for the purpose. However the money was handled and invitations extended, once there the members of the group drank to the health of their new equal, who might, for one reason or another, not even have accompanied them. At the conclusion of such an occasion, the publican, if so disposed, might offer a drink on the house.

Although the origins of the custom are unknown to the men, a few suggested that the name derived from the fact that "you foot the bill" or that "you're now on the same footing" as your fellow workers. If there is a connection, it is more likely that the phrases reflect back upon the practice, however.

CLUBS

The amount of money in the pay packets of female textile workers was small during this period, and what was earned was usually handed over for disposal to the person in charge of running the household. Most of it went to help meet maintenance costs and to make purchases of a strictly utilitarian nature. The portion returned to each young girl to dispose of as she wished was not sufficient in any one week to allow her to obtain what might be deemed luxury items, and she found herself, in common with others in her position, unable to accumulate easily over a period of time the funds necessary to buy such items; this did not serve to diminish her desires, however.

A partial solution to the problem lay in the formation of clubs which, in essence, forced those who joined to save a certain amount of money weekly. It is uncertain when they began, but they were found in all mills and factories by the time of the First World War, as well as in other places of work. The clubs were continued out of tradition or in the spirit of fellowship long after the workers had access to savings institutions or received enough money in a single pay envelope to allow them to make the desired purchases.

Early in the century, the most prevalent were the "draw clubs," so called because each member drew for a number which determined the order in which she would receive merchandise equal in value to the total of the monetary contributions she made weekly for the duration of the club. In the mill, where it was often the doffing mistress who organized the group, the draw was also arranged by her:

> You see, she wrote out numbers—numbers one, two, three, four, five—she generally now got the first draw. She wrote them down on wee bits of paper, and she called youse all together, and she threw them down, and whichever one you lifted, then that was your draw—maybe number two or number three. And you used to say, "I got an early one," or maybe you got a late one, the last one. (#40)

Each club was formed for the purpose of enabling those who joined to acquire a specific item, designated in advance. Typically, the person who formed the association made arrangements with a local merchant who sold the object whereby she would hand over to him the money collected weekly and receive in return what might be considered a merchandise certificate: "She went down and paid that and brought you a wee receipt, and you

took that back and went down and got your [merchandise]"
(#39).

In return for running the group, the sponsor was rewarded
with number one in the draw or received her item from the merchant free. After the club had run its course, often ten or twelve
weeks depending upon the number in it, since only one person a
week became beneficiary of the contributions, it was disbanded
and a new one formed.

Clubs were customarily referred to by the name of the object
that they allowed the member to purchase. Thus, one spoke of
belonging to a "shoe club" or "sweetie club" or "delft club." Also:

> Some of us ran a wee club in the mill for sticky-backs—a
> penny a week for twelve weeks. . . . You run away out of the
> mill . . . to Turnbulls on High Street [or Mercers on Ann
> Street]. And you had to ask your mother would she allow you
> to take a penny out of your pay. You daren't open your pay
> docket. And then, the next week, you got them, and . . . you
> were cuttin' a wee one here and a wee one there, and you
> were givin' it to this fella—one of your sticky-back photos.
> (#40)

To obtain a place to keep a sticky-back received in turn from a
boy, the young girl joined a "locket club." When she earned more
money, she might have a larger picture taken. (One such photo
appears as Photo 29.)

It was common practice to purchase articles of clothing
through participation in these joint enterprises, and the most
ubiquitous of the groups were "jumper clubs." One shop made
mill blouses (jumpers) for many of the girls, whose goal it was to
have a different one, easily laundered, for each day of the week—
not the ordinary blouses in solid colors, sewn by one's mother,
but fancy ones with small checks and frills around the sleeves
and elasticized necks. Selling for three shillings sixpence, each
could be obtained by making a weekly payment of three, six and
a half, or nine pence, depending upon the makeup of the group,
toward its purchase. When a girl's turn came, she selected the
material to be sewn by the shop dressmaker and looked forward
to owning the blouse a week later. When older, they joined "hair-
dressing" (later, "perm") clubs, run in the same way.

Photo 29. Studio photograph of teenage weavers: "We were the 'swanks,'" ca. 1906. By courtesy of Mrs. Margaret Smyth.

A somewhat different kind of venture, and apparently later to appear in most places, was the "money club," known also as "holiday club" and "tiddley club." Formed to make it possible for participants to accumulate funds to spend at Christmas or on other holidays, all of them unpaid at that time, it operated much as savings associations do in many places; one paid in a certain amount of money weekly and received back at a designated time the full sum in cash.

> I ran one. You started out with a penny and how many weeks was in it, every week you put an extra penny on it—a penny, twopence, and threepence . . . 'til it went up to five shillin's, till whatever holiday was comin' in. Well, then, you were all paid your money on the holiday week. (#47)

The persons who made the collections, the places where the money was kept, the length of time the clubs were in existence, and the amount saved by any individual varied, but in all firms the holiday clubs flourished, participated in by men and women alike. Today they are still found, as are, to a lesser degree, those of the "draw" variety.

JOINS

> There used to be joins at parties. This was in houses out to the country where there'd be a bit of a night on. They'd have a join, and they'd give whatever they could—maybe a couple of bob or half a crown—to the man, and they'd send into town, and they'd get whiskey, and they'd come out and have a bit of a night. They call that a join. (#29)

The preceding statement presents the essential nature of a join—the pooling of funds to provide the makings for a party. In a community where the provision of liquid refreshments at informal social gatherings was usually beyond the means of the individual who provided the house, the practice served a useful function. The term, most likely carried into the mill and factory from the culture outside, was similarly applied to the sharing of monetary resources for purely social purposes.

Join and *party* were frequently used interchangeably, but the words were not synonymous. A party need not necessarily be a join, in the sense of all participants' contributing funds toward the food and drink consumed at it, and there could be joins without there being actual parties. The former were less structured:

> . . . that's the sweeties—join—we called it joins. . . . there was a wee woman called Ellen Spots at the corner. And we used to get joins in there. We used to get the big bag of sweeties for tuppence, and we only got a shillin' out of our . . . pay packets. . . . But it was great, anybody givin' you a sweet at work. Then we used to sing all day. . . .
>
> Somebody that was trustworthy . . . they were responsible to get your money in, you see. Well, then, they come around to us on Friday night and got our join money and paid it in on a Monday morning. Then we got our join fresh again [bag of sweets picked up], Monday at dinner time. For we always used to say that Monday was a long day in the mill. So, when we had our join, it sort of broke the day up. You give me a share and I give you a share. . . . This was during working hours. . . . if you missed your week not payin' your join, well, that was you finished. But if you were a good constant payer, you were sure of your join. (#69)

HALLOWEEN

Typical of joins associated with parties were those festivities which took place at the time of calendar holidays. One day celebrated in almost all mills and factories was Halloween:

> Hallow Eve was good in the mill. We'd a had a join. We'd a hurried up and got squared up. And then, you come around, and so and so come around, and had a bit of a do. And then, we'd a sung away. . . . It didn't matter whether you were drunk or sober, you just sung away. . . . It was always in the afternoon, from about three and maybe went up to five o'clock. (#52)

Where little time could be taken away from work or where management tended to discourage such frivolities, the partying was done during the meal hour. Regardless of the time allocated, a part of the carry-on might continue throughout the day, behind the back of the foreman.

Generally, workers in a particular room broke up into smaller groups, each having its own join. It was customary to "lift" money, perhaps sixpence, from all participants and to send one member of the group out to purchase food and drink. Sometimes bags of goodies were made up at a nearby shop and left at the mill or factory gate, where at mealtime the workers would pick up their own refreshments. At other times the purchased items were brought in and divided up at party time. When the function was less organized, the join might consist of little more than the sharing of foods brought in by individuals or a mixture of these and, perhaps, one foodstuff bought cooperatively. Whatever the procedure, some combination of nuts, sweets, pastries, "minerals" (bottled lemonade, soda water, etc.), buns, and, of course, apples—fresh, candied, or baked in tarts—was always found on the menu. Drink, usually wine and smuggled in, and tea formed a portion of the fare for older workers. Often the food was consumed as one stood at loom or frames, but, in a few places, the occasion was considered festive enough to warrant a sit-down party. Where that was the practice—more likely in the mill than the factory—the women often began weeks in advance to scrub their stands and polish their machines.

As well as singing, there was set dancing, although the time element for the weavers and the often oil-spotted floors in spinning rooms ruled out much of that. In general, parties in mills, especially among the spinners, seem to have been more exuberant and to have lasted longer than those in the factory, where so much depended upon making one's pay. However, if a few spinners wore some decorative object, perhaps on the head, many weavers came to work wearing some sort of costume beneath their ordinary clothes or carrying a garment that might be donned when the time was appropriate. The cleaner conditions under which a weaver worked enabled her to continue to weave while dressed up in "a great velvet cape her great-granny wore, with bugle beads" (#10) or in, for example, a bathing costume, trousers, or even a football uniform.

What were called "freits" were performed among all the workers to some degree, especially at Halloween, but, the spirit of the

spinners and their parties being what it was, the best accounts of
these come from the mill. The purpose of the freits was to foretell
the future, in particular that aspect of it dealing with one's
husband-to-be. Women who were young at the time speak for
themselves:

> They used to get a bowl of water or somethin', and they put
> [boys'] names in it. . . . And they rolled the paper up in a
> piece of white bread and put it in. And . . . it would sink, and
> then it would come to the top. And she went around and
> everybody took a name, all drew out. And you opened it, and
> that was your boy. . . . during the time the work was goin' on,
> slipped around with it. . . . Stood and worked away and ate
> away. (#14)

> Clean water, dirty water, no water—you had three tins. And
> you blindfolded yourself and walked up. Whatever bowl you
> put your hand in: no water was no man; dirty water was a
> widow man; and clean water was a young man. . . . in the
> meal hour. You daren't play 'em when the mill was on.(#47)[7]

> They would "brush the pass" and leave the brush . . . some-
> where, to see whatever boy went by . . . that was your boy.
> . . . only at Halloween. That's only a freit. . . . there was
> a girl worked with us, and she had a boyfriend round the
> polishin'. . . . we used to go around and tell him, "Maggie's
> brushin' the floor. Come on around." And he would come
> with a bobbin and walk past, quite the way he didn't know
> . . . and we'd all cheered and yelled, whenever he come. And
> Maggie didn't know him. (#14)

> There was a girl worked beside me. She pretended—I'm sure
> she wasn't a bit anxious about a man, but she pretended she
> was near dead to know. And her and this other girl brought
> in a big, long, black snail and some flour—you know, you
> bake bread with. And they spread it all in a corner. And they
> put the snail on. . . . they put a lid over the top of this, to keep
> the snail from gettin' away. And whoever come in in the
> mornin' was the first one to lift the bin lid—the initials of
> their boy friend—the snail had made the initials. And we
> used to get queer fun out of that. . . . That was really an old,
> old Irish thing. (#15)[8]

Salt was sometimes substituted for flour.

Another well-known prognosticating custom,[9] one combining Christian belief with older traditions, was widely performed in mill and factory:

> We done what you call "turn the key in the Bible." . . . they got what you call a widow's key—at that time they had a big long key. It was more like for openin' a bank than it was for a door. . . . you had to steal it. And somebody brought in a Bible, and it [the key] was tied in till the chapter of Ruth. And this was tied up—with anything. You see, it was so supersti—the Irish are superstitious anyway.
>
> And whoever was doin' the turnin' . . . I always done it, you see. One tip of the key was on this middle finger here, and the girl that was gettin' it done—the other was on her middle finger. And you said:
>
>> "Ruth says, 'Entreat me not to leave thee, or to return from followin' after thee, for whither thou goest, I will go, and where thou lodgest, I will lodge. Thy people will be my people, and thy god, my god.'"
>
> Well, then, you said, "If 'A' be the first of my true lover's name, turn, key, in the Holy Bible, turn." You went up the whole alphabet, sayin' that, until it came that you knew that was her initial, and she was so engrossed that she didn't see you movin' your finger, and that woulda turned right around, and her mouth woulda been right open. "Oh, that's his name." (#35)

The quotation from Ruth 1:16 was repeated by the girl who was learning of her fate, but the utterances pertaining to the letters of the alphabet were spoken by the teller alone. Using a widow's key was said to be tied in with the fact that Ruth was a widow; for tying up the Bible with an orphan's garter, a requirement in at least one place, there was no explanation.

Tea-leaf reading, telling fortunes with cards, and palm reading were done throughout the year, but there was a special emphasis upon those activities at the time of the October holiday:

> And then on Halloween. . . . an old woman . . . used to tell us our fortune and read our cups. . . . She was an old woman, and she worked outside, and they had a great tub. And she

used to wash the waste. . . . Well, we used to make an excuse to carry around the dirty waste for Mary to wash. And
Mary woulda read our hand or told us our fortune. (#23)

One freit included the use of hazel nuts:

We carried on—got nuts and all in your bag, and cracked the
nuts, and tried to burn two nuts on the trough lids with a
piece of paper. And if the two nuts woulda burned together,
that was your boy, and you was gettin' married. . . . and then
somebody woulda been watchin' to see the spinnin' master
comin' in. And then you woulda blew them out, and you
were standin' as innocent as a lamb; you were doin' nothin'.
(#47)

At home, at the fireplace or on a shovel along with a hot coal,
there were other portents to be learned from observing the nuts:
if the nut designated as a boy burned and jumped away from the
one selected to represent the girl, it meant "he" didn't want
"her"; or the person represented by the nut which burned out the
soonest was said to be going to die first. It can be assumed that,
where the foretelling was carried on at work, the same signs were
evident.[10]

The raising of the age at which one began to work, the dying
away of the traditional Halloween practices at home, and, at an
early date in one place, the coming from England of a new boss
"who didn't know about these customs" (#22) and did not permit
them were a few of the factors leading to their gradual disappearance from mill and factory. But well into the 1920s, "We played
queer tricks, right enough" (#47) at Halloween.

ST. PATRICK'S DAY

Saint Pat's was best because you got your shamrock down.
That was the day you were sure of a mouthful. Like, bad and
all as he was, like, he allowed us to drink. Oh, Paddy was all
right. (#53)

St. Patrick's Day does not seem to have been observed in all
firms, but, where it was celebrated, it evoked a great amount of
boisterous behavior on the part of the celebrants. In many mills

on the Falls Road, a predominantly Catholic area, it was customary for girls to go to work that day with blouses and hair ribbons of green. Where a firm (especially in Belfast) was located in a "mixed" (religious) area, the wearing of the green by the workers was tolerated if they also donned a bit of red, white, and blue. As for the join, the mechanics of the typical one remained the same: money was collected, sometimes one amount from younger workers and a larger sum from older employees who consumed alcoholic beverages; the party took place formally in the late afternoon or during the dinner hour; workers in each room formed "a clutch here, a clutch there, drinking, talking"; and foremen, although they might be given their share, absented themselves from the scene. But this join, in particular, was notable for the consumption of alcoholic beverages and for Irish dancing and the singing of "Danny Boy," "Come Back to Erin, Mavourneen," "Dear Little Shamrock," and other songs considered to be "Irish."

A doffing mistress describes a typical celebration in the mill where she worked:

> On St. Patrick's Day, the doffers. . . . all brought in a wee drop of the good stuff. And . . . I used to say, "Margaret, go down and slip that into Sammy's press" and I'd a slipped . . . two black bottles [Guinness] and a wee taste of the other stuff—the hard tack, as they called it. And they used to go in there and say, "Sammy, take it away at the back end . . . of the room." . . .
>
> And he used to sit there, and we used to watch for the head spinnin' master . . . over him. . . . we'd never maybe seen Sammy until quarter to six that evenin', and we were stoppin' off work. And there we were singin' away like a good 'un. And we used to sing "Tears of an Old Irish Mother." . . . That would be about a quarter to five, whenever I'd be gettin' rightly settled with it, gettin' half of my work done. And then, we'd a looked up to see if Sammy was comin', get myself lovely and tidy, for fear the boss seein' 'em. Oh, dear, many's a good laugh we had. . . .
>
> Each one of us put up so much. . . . And we got it. And then, we woulda turned around, and they'd say, "Have you any more frames to doff, Margaret?" "No, I have only two." "Well, hurry up and get them and come down to my stand."

And we had apple tarts and all. . . .

My doffers woulda done that, and the spinners, they
woulda had one among themselves. They'd a come out
of one frame into that frame, and maybe they'd a looked
through the creel . . . and said, "C'mon over. I have this for
you," and all, you know. . . . We always had a wee shandy,
they used to say. We called that a shandy. (#33)

Although the festive observance of this "set time" was more a
feature of the mill than the factory, there were some mills in the
country where the day passed by almost unnoticed.

At the same time, in at least one firm in Belfast, almost no work
was done at all because of what came to be a day-long observance
of the calendar holiday:

When I was down in [name of mill]. . . . that was one day the
workers took things in their own hands. . . . It was there they
started at half six in the mornings, and the public houses
opened at seven. Well, somebody went out, and they started.
And the procedure seemed always to be everywhere in all the
mills. Each room had their own, and . . . they sent for the
fitters, of course. There was generally a half pint of whiskey
put in the overlooker's desk. . . .

Well, early in the mornin' it was all done—sorted away in
the mill. . . . when it came dinner time, everybody was sort of
elately. And . . . they used to throw their frames off. And
then, it was a hooley, party. The manager kept out the road.
He knew he could do nothing about it. And what he didn't
see, he didn't know. And the overlookers, they took their-
selves away out of the road somewhere. Oh, it was good. . . .
That would be 1913, and St. Patrick's Day 1914, 1919, and
1920. . . . It was all Guinness and whiskey. In [that mill] it
went on all day long, but in most other places it woulda generally started, maybe about three or four o'clock in the afternoon, though they'd a been maybe nibblin' up previous to
that. . . . They danced and sang, sang all the Irish songs, and
one thing and another. (#38)

As to how some of the parties ended:

When they got the first drop of wine, it wasn't the second
drop. For they had only lifted, like, what bought so many bot-

tles. They took their petticoats off them, and . . . they'd put
their aprons all around them, the front of their apron around
to the back and put their . . . glazer in the front . . . and over
they went to White's pawn and got a shillin' or sixpence on
their petticoat. That got them another taste of wine. . . . That
was the finish of the parties. (#47)

LIGHTING-UP

Seemingly unique to the linen industry were what were known
as "lighting-up parties."[11] A feature of both mill and factory, they
were mainly a Belfast phenomenon.

There was no fixed date for the party, and the time varied from
firm to firm. But the workers anticipated the event as the days
began to grow short. According to a man who had enjoyed the
occasion in many mills:

> You had to know when it was comin' off. . . . Now, in the old
> Bath Mill, it wasn't electric light. It was gas and compressed
> air. Well, now, when the clear weather come in, we took all
> them fittin's off the gas tubes, and the belt was taken off the
> compressed-air thing. When it begin to come in for winter
> time, late August, we went up, and we fitted 'em in the room.
> . . . we made sure everything was clean. Then we went
> around, and we lit them. When we put the mantles on, they
> were due for lightin'-up.
>
> Now [later] in Ewart's—in where's electric . . . the bulbs
> used to be taken off the electric every summer. And when
> the "sparks" come around and started puttin' the bulbs up,
> you knew you were gonna have lightin'-up time. (#38)

Sometimes celebrations took place on the day the lights were actually turned on. In other places, where artificial illumination always started on a Monday, the festivities were held the previous
Friday, a more suitable time for them. Occasionally, a lighting-up
party was combined with the Halloween carry-on, and, when this
occurred, costumes were worn. A weaver, now in her eighties,
recalled her own actions on such an occasion, a sort of behavior
generally assumed to be indulged in only by those in the mill: on

that day, she paraded into the winding area wearing "my brother's knickerbockers with a half pound of sausages dangling from the front opening" (#86).

Although late afternoon was the more usual time to celebrate, some used the meal hour to acknowledge the event. Typically, there was a join:

> A tenter's share was forty-eight looms. Whenever we were havin' the party, there was two girls collected the money off each weaver. And there coulda been two or three shares in that. Well, whenever it come time for the lighting-up party, the girls bought the material, put it in bags and . . . we all sit down at the top of our share, and we had a party.
>
> And we gave the tenter a bag. And so many shares would fit up a bag and give it to the foreman. But he had his in his office. Well, we'd a had about an hour of that. And then a good sing-song of Irish songs. And maybe some of 'em woulda got up and had a bit of a dance and a carry-on. Well, that finished and the lightin'-up—the lights went up. (#56)

"Fruit bags," consisting, perhaps, of an apple, dates, a bit of dulce (dried seaweed), and a currant square were common fare. Sometimes a bag of sweets, with brown and pink "old fellows" or "licorice all-sorts," was added. Whiskey and Guinness might have been provided for tenters and spinning masters, but, in earlier days, most of the women seemed to have had minerals, or even tea. A few preferred stronger drink, and it became the practice to bring in Red Biddy, an inexpensive red wine—some said Australian—which was especially potent when mixed with methylated spirits: "You couldn't a whacked it [Red Biddy] for the flu" (#38).

In the closing decade of the last century, it was the custom, in some mills on the outskirts of Belfast, for the mill owners, at lighting-up time, to provide treats for their employees to consume at home. This would attest to the fact that there was even then some special significance attached to the event; whether it also indicates that parties at work, as they have been described here, were instituted industry-wide only at a later period cannot be as easily inferred.

It is interesting to note also that, in one mill located well out-side Belfast, Halloween but not lighting-up parties took place. However, what were known as lighting-up parties were recalled by a spinner, now well into her eighties, to have been held at night in a hall maintained by the mill for recreational purposes; she had no idea why such a name was given to the event. Inas-much as that particular mill had provided employment for many years to spinners from Belfast who, for various reasons, were un-able to secure work there or chose not to work in that city, it could be maintained that those women carried the tradition with them, even though perpetuating it in a different way in the country.

Lighting-up is no longer observed among linen workers. A fac-tory manager, who felt that the initial inspiration for the parties at work had come from local shop owners who commissioned work-ers to buy the ingredients for the festivities from them, expressed his belief that they were eventually prohibited when, because of the bringing in of spirits, especially Red Biddy, the proceedings got out of hand and became too boisterous. He suggested also that other kinds of entertainment outside replaced the earlier so-cial forms in the lives of the workers. It is equally probable that when year-long artificial lighting came into effect there was no longer anything to celebrate. It is possible, as was maintained by one man, that the widespread use of ring spinning frames to re-place the old flyer ones helped to hasten the necessity for the new lighting in the mill. For, whereas the flyer frames were placed across the room in such a way that each received light from a window along its adjacent wall, the ring frames were placed lengthwise in four rows, two on each side of the pass, and po-sitioned so that the inner row of frames next to the pass received little or no outside light.

QUEEN OF THE MAY CELEBRATIONS

Activities involving the Queen of the May were not carried over directly by the linen workers into the firms where they were em-ployed, but because certain aspects of the celebration help to ex-plain practices which occurred upon other occasions in the mill—discussed in the next section—they merit comment.

Of particular significance here are the daily processions, taken part in by numerous groups of children, which extended throughout most of the month of May.[12] Each small band, with its own queen and her retinue, among whom was typically a boy known as the Darkie, moved about a limited rural or urban area. Stopping at various places, they sang, danced, and performed stunts in hopes of receiving money from onlookers. Meetings of rival entourages, competing for limited funds, resulted in sham, and sometimes real, battles in which the Darkie acted to protect his queen.

Songs associated specifically with Queen of the May activities reflect the competitive aspect of the proceedings. There were, first of all, those stressing the merits of one's own queen, which were sung, with matching actions, to impress rival groups or older spectators:

> Our queen can burl [move in a circle] her leg,
> Burl her leg,
> Burl her leg,
> Our queen can burl her leg,
> Burl her leg.

> Our queen can tumble on her head, *etc.* (#52)

> Our queen is six feet high, *etc.* (#64)

Sung in the spirit of praise and insult but associated more with encounters leading to "battle" were these verses:

> Our queen's up the river
>   with your ya, ya, ya,
> Our queen's up the river
>   with your ya, ya, ya,
> Our queen's up the river,
> And we'll keep her there forever,
> With your ya, ya, ya ya ya.

> The other queen down the river
>   with your boo, boo, boo,
> The other queen down the river
>   with your boo, boo, boo,
> The other queen down the river,

And we'll keep her down forever,
With your boo, boo, boo boo boo. (#52)

With victory came further taunts:

Our queen won,
The other had to run,
Hee, ho, hi, ho,
Our queen won. (#14)

One other song bears mention here:

The Darkie says he'll marry her,
Marry her, marry her,
The Darkie says he'll marry her,
Because she is the queen.

Chorus: Hip, hip, hooray,
The Queen's birthday,[13]
You're welcome Aggie Savage,
To be the Queen of the May. (#4)

On Saturday afternoons and in the early evenings after work, the mill doffers joined younger children as they paraded about, or they formed their own retinues with one of their workmates as queen. Because the singing was not restricted to songs about the queen and the Darkie, it was commonplace to hear mill songs interspersed with the others. Thus, "A for Barney," "Doffer Song," and others became familiar to many who might never have encountered them otherwise. Furthermore, some children altered the song about the Darkie in such a way as to bring together mill and outside culture in still another way:

The Darkie says he'll marry her,
He'll marry her, he'll marry her,
The Darkie says he'll marry her,
And take her out of the mill.

Chorus: And take her out of the mill,
And take her out of the mill,
The Darkie says he'll marry her,
And take her out of the mill. (#47)

It is said that the Darkie was sometimes even referred to as the band-tier during the parades.

TWELFTH OF JULY

The principal exchange in the other direction—from the larger culture into the mill—took place more than two months later when the Twelfth of July (commemorating the victory of the Protestant King William III over the Catholic King James II at the Battle of the Boyne in 1690) came around. Joins at work were not necessarily held the previous day, but a few persons, anticipating the festivities surrounding the traditional parades held throughout the province on the twelfth and thirteenth of the month, began early to celebrate with drink that was consumed on the sly. The majority of women in the spinning rooms found an outlet for their high spirits in the act of "doffing-off," always done before the mill shut down for this or any other holiday.

Half-filled bobbins of wet, spun yarn could not be left to rot on the frames over the holiday period. In order to get the yarn to the reelers and to do certain tasks afterward, the women had to gauge carefully the size, and thus time, of every doff on their frames that day so that their last one, respectably large, was completed early enough. Each spinner in turn, as her frame was doffed, joined the doffing mistress and doffers in her half of the room in taking off filled bobbins from machines subsequently filled. The cooperative effort among those in any one half developed into a competition between halves to see which could complete its doffing-off first. The victory was hailed triumphantly:

> God be good to Lily Devlin and Paddy's sister, Rosie. . . .
> They done it down in the factory [*sic!*] whenever they were
> doffin' the frames. . . . Whenever her doffers were first, Lily
> went down then, and she took them out, like, "Ah ha, our
> half won! Our half won!" And that woulda started it. (#53)

They sang:

> Our half won,
> Our half won,

Hee, ho, pa diddy-o,
Our half won.

The other half lost,
The other half lost,
He, ho, pa diddy-o,
The other half lost. (#53)

"We'd doff-off, and one would be tryin' to get in front of the other, and this half here, maybe you woulda won, and the other half they would lie behind, and then we started to sing at 'em" (#s 55, 57, 58, 59).

Referring to the defeated doffing mistress, they also chanted:

Annie thought she had it
   with her ya, ya, ya,
Annie thought she had it
   with her ya, ya, ya,
Annie thought she had it,
But you see, she didn't get it,
With your ya, ya, ya ya ya. (#53)

Just as the Queen of the May was carried about the streets by her followers, the victorious doffing mistress was paraded up and down the pass on the shoulders of those who worked with her, and feelings sometimes ran high: "It nearly went into blows. Many's the time it woulda went to the riots" (#53).

They claimed that "We sung *ya, ya, ya* to everything" (#14). Sometimes the chant was used positively, in the sense of expressing the idea of being best, "the head of the pole." Thus, in a plant which produced linen thread, groups of workers were lauded with "The coppers up the river/with your ya, ya, ya" or "The bleachers up the river/with your ya, ya, ya," etc. (#14). Similar words could be employed in cheering for one's football favorites: "The Riggies up the river . . ." (#14), but I will not attempt to ascertain the direction of influence here.

In the mill, a negative connotation was attached to this version:

She is up in builders
   with her ya, ya, ya,
She is up in builders
   with her ya, ya, ya,

She is up in builders,
And we'll keep her there forever,
With your ya, ya, ya ya ya. (#52)

Sung by doffers, most likely to tease or to register disapproval of a spinner, the essence of the verse was: "The frame was full, and the doffers wasn't till it, and the laps was on, and the builders was all gettin' choked up with waste, you know" (#52).

The song, again in the competitive sense, was employed, at least once, at the conclusion of a quite different kind of battle:

Tillie thought she had him
  with your ya, ya, ya,
Tillie thought she had him
  with your ya, ya, ya,
Tillie thought she had him,
But you see she didn't get him,
  with your ya, ya, ya ya ya.

This is really true. There was two old girls over there. One of them was doffin' mistress, and she was about sixty-two at the time, and a lovely woman. . . . And the other one was an old widow, and she snuffed. They used to go till this pub, and there was some old lad. And this widow thought she was gonna hook him. But, unfortunately, it didn't come off. He married Mary Jane.

Well, Mary Jane had never been married before 'til she was sixty-two. . . . When she come in the followin' week, well, that place was in an uproar, that Number Three Spinning Room—"Mary Jane up the river"—Mary Jane up again. And Tillie, they called the other one Tillie somethin'. It got that bad she went and left that week . . . Tillie the widow woman. Mary Jane blued her. (#38)

The reasons for the dictum that "party songs," expressing political or religious (not erotic) sentiment, were not to be sung openly by the linen workers at their jobs were known to all. But on the afternoon preceding the Twelfth celebrations, the barriers were lowered to a degree, and a number of Orange (Protestant) songs, and others, were sung as closing time drew near and the excitement of the event pervaded mill and factory. Differences might be put aside for a brief time, and almost everyone joined in. A Protestant:

> Especially on the eleventh night. That's a hectic time. That was warmin' up time. They'd a come out and sung these—all these Orange things, you know, like Billy and all, like that. (#33)

A Catholic:

> When comin' out at July, everything was sung. "The Sash" [an Orange song] was sung. "The Shamrock" was sung, and "The Lily" [an Orange song]. It didn't matter what you were. You joined in. I sung "The Sash" oftener than I sung anything else. In fact, I learned a whole lot of them "The Sash." (#53)

Whether anything further occurred around the Twelfth was probably related to two factors: the ratio of Protestants to Catholics working in a mill or factory or at a particular job and the vigilance of foremen and management in preventing outbursts of sectarianism. For a recurring, if not traditional, feature of the month was the possibility of the manifestation of hostility between groups of workers who could work in reasonable harmony—even consider themselves friends—most of the year. In some rooms where those with Unionist (Protestant) sympathies predominated, "celebrating" might begin as early as the first of July and extend until the twentieth of the month. Machines were festooned with red, white, and blue flags or streamers, which action in itself caused no trouble. But celebrants, carried away by the spirit and significance of the impending event and by party songs sung too early and freely, might turn to more physical means to express their sentiments.

An incident which occurred in 1916 in the Reeling Loft of a mill located in a mixed area in Belfast serves as an illustration of what could happen. There, fourteen Catholics, out of a total of sixty reelers, walked off their jobs and out of the mill after being tormented by the waving of small Union Jacks in their faces and being chased with brushes used to clean the reels. In this instance, management stepped in to settle the dispute, but it took months before relationships between the two groups were no longer strained. That some of the participants never spoke to each other again was a less obvious result. During the same period, women in the spinning rooms and, presumably, elsewhere in the mill worked on as usual.

Sectarian outbursts were, of course, far more frequent at any time in Belfast than elsewhere; almost all to whom I spoke emphasized that fact. The reply given to a question I asked about the singing of party songs in a factory some distance from Belfast was:

> Oh, they weren't allowed to sing them. They didn't do it now. Not where I worked—in the "mill" down there, there weren't too many Protestants. And any that worked there were very nice people—and were all very great. . . . You wouldn't want to sing a song till insult them—to hurt them. . . . In Belfast there'd be maybe the same amount of people on both sides, you know. (#29)

Contrasting earlier with later times, and speaking of his experiences in one country mill, a man told me:

> Them was quare days, girl. There was no money, and there was peace. Oh, there was peace. Nobody knowed where—he didn't—nobody cared what religion—no religion in them days. (#25)

The two-day July closing and the shutting down of mills and factories on Easter Monday and Tuesday and Christmas Day and Boxing Day, which followed, are significant because of the relationship between those "holidays" and the transmission of linen lore. In trying to explain the presence of similar items in a number of places, a man who had worked in numerous mills remarked:

> They're sort of universal, because, like, long ago they shifted from one mill to another, all over the city. . . . it used to be a great game comin' on, let's say July—that there was no holiday for pay then. You see, it was a lock-out; it wasn't a holiday; you were out.
>
> Comin' on July, or even Christmas, to get extra money, they'd a give their notice in—for to get two weeks' pay. Well, once they got the two weeks' pay they were out of a job. Well, some of them woulda come up immediately after the holiday,

a lookin' to start again. Other uns hadn't the knack and went somewhere else. Of course, it was done all over for to get the extra two or three shillin's. That was an old game. . . . It was an accepted thing. (#38)

FIFTEENTH OF AUGUST

The Fifteenth of August, the Feast of the Assumption and a traditional day of Catholic celebrations, was not an official work holiday. Nor does the occasion seem to have been marked at work by joins or parties of any kind. What was done unofficially had its effects on the workings of at least one mill, however:

> I remember the time. . . . My sister Rose—we had nothin', as usual. Well, every Fifteenth of August, they all stopped early —all stopped out of work. And. . . . there used to be big brakes [long, horse-drawn carts]—you know, the old-fashioned brakes and horses? Well, all the women woulda had a round straw hat . . . one of them and a blouse and skirt. And they all went to Crossgar [a town five miles away]. . . . they thought that was great, gettin' away for that bit of a day. There was that many woulda stopped out that the mill had to be stopped. There was too much work and no workers to do it, and they all had to come out.
>
> That's years and years ago. . . . they all woulda cheered, woulda seen the others—the people comin' out. . . . And I remember one time, we stopped out with the rest of them. And my father was after us, and we had to take to the fields. He hunted us, and he was shakin' his fist at us—for the loss of the money. But we were afeared of goin' in cuz of the rest of 'em stayin' out. But they all took brakes and went away to Crossgar—every Fifteenth—and had a great day. (#42)

EASTER AND CHRISTMAS

Parties might be held before the Easter break, and there were minor festivities at Christmas—food and the decoration of machines—in a few places. But the celebrations at those times do not loom large in the minds of the men and women with whom I spoke. What is recalled is that the three sets of unpaid holidays placed a heavy financial burden on the workers: "The other holidays were very near upon us before the people got pulled up from the ones that they'd already lost" (#3).

CHOOSING A JOB

There is some indication that, overall, larger numbers of Catholics than Protestants worked in mills, while the opposite was the case in factories. Among floor-level operatives, however, the proportions varied from one firm to another and from job to job within each mill and factory. It may be a fact, as a Catholic maintained, that Protestants were not anxious to secure employment in a former mill, Catholic-owned, where the Rosary was said every morning and the Angelus recited each noon, and that Catholics were not "permitted" to work in another firm, although the man had himself worked there. But the assertion sometimes made that the general prevailing situation stemmed solely or even primarily from deliberate hiring practices oversimplifies a complex situation. One has to consider not only decisions made by those at the top but also the motivations of the people seeking employment to understand more fully why a particular individual labored at a particular job in a particular place.

Religious stereotyping was certainly engaged in by some members of management, but it also influenced the behavior of each group of workers toward the other. One result of this was the unwillingness of many persons to invade territory which might prove dangerous to them:

> We had one or two spinners at [name of firm] from the Falls, but, like, they were rare, very rare. In fact, you'd a got them comin' from the Falls up the Ligoniel quicker than you'd a got them up from the Crumlin Road, though it was only half the distance. . . . Well, sectarianism comes into it a bit. Now I remember a time there wasn't a Roman Catholic in [name of mill]. And when I was in the old [name of mill] in the

> spinnin' rooms there, there was only one Protestant girl in
> the two spinnin' rooms. There was no Protestant girl woulda
> went in there. . . .
>   [Why were the roving rooms mixed?] The rovers consid-
> ered themselves a cut above the spinners, and probably the
> spinners was more rough and more liable to break out. . . . I
> would say there was over half and half in the rovin' rooms—
> like, mixed Protestant and Catholic in the Rovin' Room—and
> in the Reelin' Room. (#38)

The implications of the fact that spinning was the more labor-
intensive end of the industry and attracted to it those in direst
need has already been discussed (see p. 123). The advantages of
piecework, with the possibilities of earning more money, probably played a part in the decision of some to work as weavers or, in
the mill, to become reelers, and can be considered along with
other purely economic reasons. In a quite different category was
a consideration of status, one of the primary factors in inducing
one to seek employment in a factory. It was often pressure from
the family which pushed a person in that direction, but not infrequently the preferences of the family were disregarded in
order to follow personal predilections. Such predispositions toward a certain job could have arisen out of situations encountered at play:

> We played in the streets after work to let all the pople know
> what we were in the Spinnin' Room. We used to get the wee
> ones that wasn't workin' at all and get them to doff their
> shares at the window. . . . We lived . . . right next to the mill
> then, and the mill windees was on that side—it was the din-
> in' room—and we used to say, "You doff there, and you doff
> there." And I had a wee whistle and all. So, you were doffin'
> mistress then, and you were only twelve or thirteen. (#40)

One mill girl, in that area and influenced by the play, was struck
by other things as well:

> We had no mother, and my father didn't want me to go into
> the mill. . . . He said the factory was best. But I couldn't get
> into the mill quick enough. . . . I was wantin' in the Spinnin'
> Room. Because the girls used to wear lovely wee silk hankies
> around their neck, and that's what took my eye. . . . that girl

lived over across the street . . . and she worked in the mill.
So, every night she come home from work . . . we weren't,
like, the age for work—she had us doff the frames. We were
runnin' up and down all the time. . . . I got interested. (#55)

Work experiences of family members who had preceded a person often determined what a youngster wanted to do, or was able
to do, but there were also instances where an individual rejected
the choices of those who had gone before and selected a job for
purely idiosyncratic reasons. One woman, with five sisters all
employed in the factory, chose to begin work in the Spinning
Room, and, even though she was later taken by an aunt to work
in a wareroom at stitching, she returned after a brief interval to
complete her working years in a mill:

I went back to the mill. You got a better laugh. You got a better laugh. I tell you, in the mill you got a good laugh. And you
were harashed—you were really harashed—but you got a
good laugh, and your pay was goin' on. (#47)

Another woman preferred weaving, although her family would
have had her work elsewhere:

My mother was a weaver, but she didn't want me to go. They
wanted me to be of some importance. They wanted me to go
to the dressmakin'. Well, that wasn't my style. I could never
sit that long, at peace, sewin'. So that ended that. (#32)

In the final analysis, where a floor-level operative worked, at
least initially, was probably determined mainly by whether a mill
or a factory was situated in the vicinity. To say, in addition, that
one's choice was often made on the basis of where close friends
worked does not make that assertion any less true, since one's
friends were likely to live close by and to work near their homes.
It would follow that one might well work where one's parents,
also raised in that locality, had worked. What must have been the
experience for many was stated by a former doffing mistress in
several long comments. If parents had been in a mill, their children usually went in

[because] that was all that was right around where we were
reared. It was always spinnin' at Jennymount and Milewater

Mill, and it was always spinners and doffers, and their husbands was band-tiers, oilers, spinnin' masters, and all. All
right round that whole district. Because the two mills just sat
there, and the houses—all right round. And you'd very rarely
hear of a man workin' in the shipyard. I had a brother, and
he was a rovin' master in Milewater. And then there was five
sisters, all worked in the mill. (#33)

A firm combining spinning and weaving (see Photo 1) attracted
some into the latter, however:

York Street Mill, there was a part of that for the weavin'. A
good lot went into the weavin' because there was more
money made at the weavin' than there was at the spinnin'. . . . And some didn't want to go into the spinnin' mill,
because there's an awful heavy smell of it . . . but it all de-
pends on the rooms. (#33)

Her explanation for why some chose spinning over weaving, regardless of opportunity, was as follows:

You see, maybe they wanted in along with their chums. . . .
It seemed to me like a wee gatherin'. I'd speak for my chum,
you'd speak for your chum. . . . Wherever they wanted to go,
their mothers just let them go there. . . . I could have been in
York Street Mill [as a weaver]. Well, that was further away
for us. That woulda took us ten minutes to run. Well, now,
I'd say about five minutes to Jennymount. . . . it's just
wherever you started like, and who you got friendly with.
(#33)

Outside of Belfast, too, one worked in a mill or factory according to which was located in the immediate area. As for the divi-
sion of jobs among those of either religious persuasion, much obviously depended upon the composition of the community. Beyond that, it is not known how typical the situation reported from
one mill in the country was:

At A., we had sixty-nine spinning frames. I would say there
were only five of those were Protestant spinners, and the rest
were Catholics. Now up in the Reeling Room, the reverse of
that was so. They picked their own jobs, you know. (#1)

TRADE UNIONS

As late as 1940, only a small number of textile workers belonged to unions in Northern Ireland. In an article of broader scope, Fred Dohr cites four factors which worked against unions' achieving a strong position: (1) wide distribution of the industry, making it difficult for organizers to operate effectively; (2) difficulties arising from the fact that not only were workers involved in a variety of jobs, but also groups engaged in similar work in different mills and factories had few contacts with each other; (3) large number of female employees who regarded their jobs as more or less temporary; and (4) religious sectarianism, which worked both to overshadow common grievances among segments of the working population and to make it difficult for Protestant workers to overcome religious convictions and join with Catholics in action against mainly Protestant management.[14] The lore of the linen workers contains nothing to contradict these assertions but does document a few incidents which might be overlooked in more comprehensive studies of trade-union activity.

Around 1893, the first union for female textile workers was founded; but, with the exception of remarks from women who became involved in an official way, attempts made to organize spinners and weavers in Belfast seldom were voiced in women's recollections of their work experiences, and what accounts were proffered were vague in content.

Conversations with those who did recall something about early efforts to unionize attest to the very scattered and localized activity which took place. Typical of what occurred is the following:

> I only remember tryin' for to start the trade union [in 1915].
> . . . There was a man. . . . used to work in York Street where some of my cousins worked. They were all reelers. And . . .
> they were all in the trade union. My cousins were sayin',
> "You should be in the trade union. There's no activity startin' the union . . . in [your mill]."
> J. M. that come into the house, and it was him that got the books . . . and I remember givin' him the money. . . . got a

free doctor and any complaints, and there was a sick benefit
if they had been out. . . . [small amount] for to get them
in—it was all softened down . . . for there was no union over
there. . . . About half them come into it. . . . [in] the Reelin'
Room.
    Only half the Reelin' Room, for there was nobody else . . .
for to try for to organize. . . . I contacted a girl . . . in the
Spinnin' Room. She was a spinner, and I contacted her to
see if I could get her to start it. She was too frightened—said
she was too frightened. She wouldn't take it on. I hadn't
enough sense to be frightened. (#64)

A name that stands out in the memory of some operatives is
that of Mary Galway, secretary of the Textile Operatives' Society,
who in 1899 was elected to the Belfast Trades' Council. Several
weaving factories along the Falls Road were relatively well organized in the first decades of this century, and Mary Galway is
said to have had much to do with achieving this, standing on a
box outside factories at 5:45 in the morning and urging workers
to join up. Some mills may have come within her sphere of
influence, but it was only female weavers who spoke to me about
belonging to her "society."
    Trade unions, as we think of them today, were, in these years
in Northern Ireland, often registered under Friendly Society Acts
and were frequently referred to as friendly societies, in part because they provided some of the services offered by those earlier
groups. Comparing the workings of one type of friendly society
with those of two unions makes the relationship clearer. The record books of Donaghcloney Weaving Factory Sick Society reveal
that in 1910 employees paid a one-shilling entrance fee and, typically, two shillings a week thereafter. Services of a doctor were
provided and, if approved by him and the other members of the
organization, five shillings a week, on the average, for up to thirteen weeks were paid out to members who fell ill and were unable to work; one pound for burial expenses was also forthcoming.[15]
    Unions often undertook these functions but also did more. For
example, new employees were allowed some time to pay into
"Mary Galway's" union. Then twopence, contributed weekly,

only maintained membership. For death, accident, and unemployment benefits, they paid in extra; according to one woman, an additional small amount helped toward a fortnight's vacation in a holiday home. The union also assisted with settling grievances; "being blamed for a fault which you were fined unfairly for" was a common cause of discontent. It is said that every time Mary Galway got an increase in pay for her women, the amount of their contributions was increased. Whatever the actual organization and its effectiveness in helping to settle claims, and however it was viewed by those administering it, "Mary Galway's Society" was generally related to in a personal way by female employees. It was not considered a remote force operating on their behalf but, rather, was looked upon as a friend to turn to in times of trouble: "You took your complaint to Mary Galway" (#32).

The Flaxdressers' Trade and Benevolent Trade Union was an older organization, as has been mentioned, and its workings were more formal and regarded in a more detached way by its members. In the late twenties, "the new hackler was given three months before being asked to join; then, sixpence kept you a member" (#2). For additional benefits, one paid accordingly. Of all the advantages which went along with membership in any type of union, the one which appeared to be of major interest to the majority of members, and a major concern since the inception of friendly societies, was the death benefit. Upon retirement, many continued to make payments toward this. Such was the practice among flax dressers, even when the trade which their union represented went out of existence and the organization was subsumed under another:

> All the old hacklers used to come to me when I was a young man. . . . when the hacklin' finished, they kept their old card goin' because they thought they would get a death duty on it. My father paid it, J. D. paid it, A. W. paid it, and two or three more. And they says to me, "You're sendin' your father's away." "Give it to me and I'll send it all together." They all gave me their thruppence, and I woulda got a postal order and sent them all away to S. P. for years and years.
> When J. D. died, I sent away the death certificate . . . the daughter . . . got the check for ten pounds. . . . A. W. was the

same, and somebody else. . . . And I says to my father,
"You're the only one left. There'll be nothin' left for you."
"Oh, pay it. It's only thruppence."
So I paid the thruppence, just to keep it up 'til my father
died. And I sent it away. S. P. sent me a great letter: "All the
old hacklin's faded away." And all that was in it was three
pounds. It wasn't worth it, keepin' it on for twenty years. My
father kept it on for twenty years. "Keep it goin'." You see,
them old boys had that idea—keep it goin' and you'll get the
death duty. (#2)

The negative effects of religious sectarianism upon efforts to
unionize those in the linen industry have been recognized by
many students of the topic, and a majority of the workers themselves were well aware of the problem. "The trouble in Ireland is
water. There's Holy water and there's Boyne water. The two don't
mix" (#10). Many also agreed that Catholics were more inclined
than Protestants to consider unions as allies in their attempts to
better their lot.

Lending support to such an assertion is one explanation offered for this song (air: "John Brown's Body"):

Old Rosie Lappin ate twelve currant baps,
Old Rosie Lappin ate twelve currant baps,
Old Rosie Lappin ate twelve currant baps,
And a twenty-five pound pot of jam. (#48)

Rosie was said to have been a Protestant doffing mistress who re-
fused to cooperate in the walkout of her fellow workers in the
Spinning Room and to whom lunches of jam and baps (a type of
bun) were brought in by the manager. An astute observation was
made by another man about the use of such a song as a social-
control device:

When you think on it, they were far more wiser than they are
today. . . . That story—anybody can take a bat on the job, but
very few people can take ridicule. You see? So, making up a
song about her—makin' her look ridiculous like—in their
innocence—instead of beating her, they made her look ridiculous, which is far harder to stand. If they'd a beat her up,
she'd a got sympathy. But makin' her look ridiculous, she
was laughed at. (#38)

The reasoning would be no less valid if she had been only a harsh doffing mistress about whom fun was being made, as she was also identified.

Organizers met resistance from both segments of the linen population at one time or another. A widespread anecdote, told here by a woman who, although she became seriously involved in trade-union work only in the 1940s, did participate in some of the earlier action, makes the point:

> We tried for many, many times to organize the textile workers in . . . Belfast. But it was absolutely impossible, because in our country there's a question of religion, and we're divided on it. . . . in 1929. . . . there was mass unemployment. . . . Now we tried to do something about organizing the workers then, because we were offered another machine to operate for less money. . . .
>
> Now we got them fairly well organized and then Joe Devlin died. There was a man called Bob Getgood, a famous man. . . . And Bob was looking after our interests . . . through the trade-union work. And he done many trades, and the textile industry was thrown into his lap, too. Well, now, Joe Devlin died—I think it was 1932 or 1933—and Bob Getgood, as a Christian, went to Joe Devlin's funeral. Joe was a Roman Catholic, and Bob Getgood was a Protestant. . . . Bob marched behind the hearse, as happens in Ireland, and the newspapers reported . . . that Bob was one of the mourners.
>
> Now, I went to collect the union contributions the followin' Saturday. And the Protestants . . . refused to pay me their contributions because Bob Getgood went to a Roman Catholic's funeral. So, our Roman Catholic people—girls—still continued to pay. Then we had another attempt to organize the textile workers, and I arranged a big concert in Ulster Hall. . . . textile workers are very talented. They can sing; they can dance; and they know all the folksongs. And it was the textile workers themselves that produced the program.
>
> Now, at the end of the concert—we had two thousand people packed in that hall—and at the end of that concert, the pianist, naturally, played the National Anthem. Now, our Roman Catholic friends . . . walked out of the concert. And

> when I went to collect the union contributions the following
> Saturday, they refused to pay their union contributions, be-
> cause the National Anthem was played at this concert. . . .
> So the whole thing was wiped out. (#10)

As elsewhere, one ran risks in being a union organizer in the
early days; sometimes subterfuge seems to have been used in
meting out punishment to an individual who was forward in this
respect:

> I got the union started all right at [name of mill]. . . . and
> then, the girls wanted somethin'—I can't remember what.
> . . . And I didn't get them all in, but somebody had told in
> the office that I had started a trade union. And I slept in one
> mornin'—and I was a good time keeper [usually prompt].
> I got my cards, for sleepin' in [once]. . . . That was the end
> of the union. (#64)

People gave other accounts of attempts to organize workers in
their mill or factory. Frequently, as in the preceding case, what
was established failed after a brief interval, and new efforts were
made. A few persons cited instances of work stoppages as a result
of various grievances. The specifics of those can be recovered
from other sources. But one strike, likely to go unreported when
larger histories of trade-union activity in the linen industry are
compiled, took place around 1913 in a mill located well outside of
Belfast. The spinner who recounts the incident was at the time
earning seventeen shillings sixpence a fortnight. Interesting because of what it reveals about the light-hearted attitude with
which the young women regarded strike activity, the account
also shows the risks they ran:

> I wasn't out in the morning, because I was lent into another
> room. And when we were after dinner time, this wee girl . . .
> said, "Well, you missed it. We were all out on strike." And
> she says, "We'll strike in the evenin' again." And her and me
> struck in the evenin' again and brought them all with us. . . .
> And we were havin' a good big ring around the clock [tower].
> And we were all dancin' and singin'. . . . First thing I saw
> was a fella in the office, and he comes up and he says, "Could

you tell me where Mrs. C. and Mrs. M. lives?" That was my mother and the other girl's mother.

We were all tellin' him, scared to death. And the next thing was they [mothers] come with their big white aprons, down into the office. And the manager said, "If you don't go in immediately, youse can all clear out." We went in right away. . . . We didn't want them all to leave. My mother, it would have killed her. Whenever the other girl was goin' in, the boss had her a big kick. He didn't kick me hard. All the doffers and all them reelers were out—just that one day, an hour or two. . . . fourpence [daily increase]. That wasn't so bad. (#4)

There were more serious strikes, but the numerous and prolonged encounters which marked disputes between labor and management elsewhere—in the textile industries in the United States during these same years, for example—did not take place on a wide scale among similar groups of workers in Northern Ireland. Nor does one find the same type or quantity of economic protest songs as have been recorded in other places.[16]

One walkout in Belfast had a direct bearing on the study at hand, if some of the reported incidents connected with it are true. In a biography of her father, James Connolly, Nora Connolly O'Brien relates that many mill girls had, about 1912, gone out on strike, for a number of reasons but in part as a reaction against newly posted regulations forbidding them to sing, laugh, and talk while at work. They had appealed for assistance, as regards their larger grievances, to Connolly, remembered today chiefly as an Irish patriot but acting at the time as an organizer in the north of Ireland for the Irish Transport and General Workers' Union. Apparently he was unable to procure concrete benefits for the women at the time, but he provided them with a piece of advice which would enable them to evade the rules when they returned to their work:

I've advised them not to go back in ones and twos, but to gather outside the mills and all to go in in a body; to go in singing. If when at work one girl laughs and is reproved, they are all to begin laughing; if one girl sings and is checked, they are all to sing. And if a girl is dismissed for breaking the rules they are all to walk out with her. They have accepted the idea enthusiastically, and before they left me tonight they were busy making up a song to sing as they go back. What wonderful, wonderful fighting spirit.[17]

The point has been made repeatedly that musical, and other, traditions, long a part of the way of life of many girls in the mills, persisted for many years after this incident. It is interesting to conjecture what part, if any, the counseling of Connolly played in the process. At any rate, his message is still recalled:

For instance, we used to be in the mills and factories—now I'm speaking between 1912 and 1913—they wouldn't allow the workers to sing. . . . This is where James Connolly—and he just said, "Well, sing on." And I can remember my father telling us, "Well, you can all sing, for they can't sack you all." . . . You see, you were there to work, not to sing. (#10)

Connolly was not frequently mentioned, however. In fact, there were many who claimed never to have heard of him or of James Larkin, well known generally for his efforts on behalf of workers in Belfast. And despite mill girls' proclivities for composing songs and rhymes about events and personalities that touched their lives, no spinner could recall having heard any song about either of the men.

But there is at least one, that recorded in O'Brien's portrait of her father:

Cheer up, Connolly, your name is everywhere;
You left old Baldy sitting in his chair
Crying for mercy; mercy wasn't there;
Cheer up, Connolly; your name is everywhere.

Praising the mill girls in return, Connolly remarked: "They've wonderful spirit. And they make up songs about everything on the spur of the moment. That's not the only song they've got. You should hear some of the others."[18]

One explanation was offered for the seeming dearth of verses about him: "They [spinners] never made up songs [about him] because Connolly never was an M.P. He was just an ordinary man" (#48). The implication is that creativity flourished more when politics was the issue.

POLITICAL ACTIVITY

This may well be. At any rate, there was one political figure whom almost everybody recalled readily and whose name appeared in songs of the workers. "Joe Devlin was one good man" sums up the sentiments expressed by the laborers in mill and factory alike. Reared among those whom he championed in Belfast, the man was almost idolized for his endeavors on behalf of the "laboring man," although it was probably female mill workers who benefited most from his efforts. One can doubt whether he alone accomplished all that he is given credit for, but one should be aware of what he is believed to have done. Thus, from various persons, one hears the claims that he "got the windows open, top and bottom, and got fans in" (#4); "was the man partly responsible for abolishing the half-time system" (#70); "got this rule passed in Parliament . . . you had to be in at six o'clock. He got that took off 'til eight o'clock, and he got Saturday's work took off" (#52); was "the very man who got the glazers for the spinners" (#41); and "got the spinners raises in pay and everything" (#55).

I need not set forth details of Devlin's political career.[19] The following comments pertain to the parliamentary elections held in the United Kingdom of Great Britain and Ireland for the years 1906 through 1914, in which Devlin, a Nationalist candidate representing West Belfast, was returned as a member. In the 1906 campaign, he won by sixteen votes. The story behind one of the ballots cast then is probably not known widely:

> Well, I never was interested about James Connolly. I was more interested in Joe Devlin. When I was eight year old, and that wasn't much, I voted for him. . . . up at St. Pat's School. I put big high heels and a long skirt on and an oul' hat, and I was Mary Ann O'Neill from Oranmore Street. Now I mind that from eight year old.
>
> And [a challenger of voters] was viewing me up and down, for he knowed me. For he used to run with our Paddy, come in till our house. . . . So . . . Mary Ann got her vote, and put it in the ballot box, and off she went. So there he come out after me and he says, "Listen here. Don't you come back to play

any more of your wee tricks, for," he says, "I'll give you
away." I says, "Jest you do, and I'll tell Joe Devlin." (#47)

The truth of the narrative can be questioned. For one thing, the
woman who told it was actually older in 1906 than she claims to
have been. For another, when she repeated the incident to me
some days later, she maintained that she was ten at the time of
the election (an age more likely to have been her real one) and
had assumed the identity of Ann Duffy of Kennedy Square when
she voted. Whatever its veracity, her story nevertheless reflects
the enthusiasm supporters of Joe Devlin felt for him at the time
he conducted his campaigns.

Although the singing of songs with political implications was
discouraged officially by management, "at election times it was
wild in the mill" (#4). Much of what transpired outside continued during working hours, and some activities begun at work
were extended into the night:

> The only consolation we had when we were stoppin' our
> work—"Hurry out tonight. Joe Devlin is comin' out with the
> bands," and we were all after him, singin':

> Joe Devlin won the West,
> Joe Devlin won the West,
> It's true, it's true,
> The West so blue,
> Joe Devlin won the West.

> And then:

> Don't be too hard on Joe Devlin, boys,
> Give honor where honor is due,
> Don't you think that he's no good,
> He is far too good for you.
> And when there's a meetin' in Clonard Street,
> I hope all the boys will be there,
> And they'll give three cheers for the hard-workin' man,
> And let any rebel interfere.

> We were makin' these all up in the mill. . . . we made them
> —you put a line, and somebody else put a line, and some-
> body else thought of a line. (#47)

Protestant and Catholic linen workers alike expressed admiration and affection for Joe Devlin. Protestants could say:

> Joe Devlin of Belfast—he was a Roman Catholic. And he done more for the Protestants than he did for the Catholics. . . . Oh, he was a household word. (#2)

> Like, he was a Roman Catholic, but he was a good man. He was for the workin' class people. It didn't matter what religion you were. (#41)

> He was a great man, you know. . . . He wasn't what now you'd call political minded. . . . I used to hear my mother talkin' about him. They said, "There would never be another Joe Devlin." (#23)

His Catholic friends remarked, typically:

> Joe Devlin was a real good man. I don't think he ever lifted his salary. And he got the poor children of Belfast—didn't matter who they were—and gave them holidays to the sea. (#45)

> He was a great Nationalist. . . . He did help the poor. . . . They all idolized him, and he didn't loss his head over being idolized. (#49)

> Joe Devlin loved the mill workers, and they loved him. (#47)

To admire Joe Devlin privately did not mean that a Protestant would, therefore, endorse an open expression of admiration for the man in a formal public situation; social pressures to insure conformity to group mores helped to prevent this being done. Nor did the nonsectarian popularity that he enjoyed among the workers carry over to the ballot box, where traditional political loyalties persisted. Yet the singing at work seems to have continued with Protestant support: "We sung all them songs in the mill about Joe Devlin. . . . Everyone had to sing them, Protestants and all" (#47). One of these was heard when Boyd Carpenter opposed Joe Devlin:

> Good-bye, Josie, when you're away,
> Every night, Josie, for you I'll pray,

When you meet Boyd Carpenter,
Don't be afraid,
For every voter in West Belfast,
Will vote for you again. (#4)

"You woulda met the doffers—a whole squad of them. You woulda met them all comin', singin' that up the pass, and all that stuff" (#4). That was true outside of Belfast as well.

In 1910, an American doctor, "Peter" Crippen, murdered his wife in England but failed in his attempt to escape on a ship with his mistress, Ethel LeNeve. The fact that wireless was used for the first time in a murder hunt helped to give the case an added amount of publicity.[20] Four years later, the incident was recalled in songs associated with a political contest between Devlin and Sir John Smiley, Protestant and Unionist. This time, the singing of the mill girls was more partisan in nature, reflecting more accurately political realities on the outside. Those with Nationalist sympathies sang (a parody on "Dinah"):

Smiley's in the hall with Miss LeNeve,
Smiley's in the hall, I know,
Smiley's in the hall with Miss LeNeve,
Playing on her old banjo. (#30)

"The doffers went down the pass, when they were doffin' frames, singin' things like that" (#52). In one sense, the retort of Smiley's supporters contained an additional sting, being a verbal attack on the man who was almost a "folk hero" to so many:

Devlin's in the hall with baldy nuns,
Devlin's in the hall, I know,
Devlin's in the hall with baldy nuns,
Playin' on their old banjo. (#30)

I should not leave the impression that those employed in weaving factories never participated in demonstrations for their candidates. The fact that songs and rhymes, of which these are only a sample, were carried primarily into the mills, and may even have had their origins there, is merely consistent with all that has been said previously about the activities of the various groups of workers.

PATERNALISM

A development of the last decades of the nineteenth century, "The family firm in the form of the private company has remained the typical business organization in Northern Ireland,"[21] at least into the early 1960s. At the time this study was made, in the 1970s, only one linen firm remained in private hands, but the men and women whose lives are depicted here worked in mills and factories organized in such a way. Evidence of the paternalistic attitude displayed by owners toward their employees—a sentiment which originated much earlier but continued under the newer economic arrangements—is revealed in the reminiscences of the workers. Men and women might speak very critically about a mill or factory manager at a lower level, but they expressed feelings of respect and admiration toward owners of firms. Attitudes reflected individual experiences, and men, more than women, were inclined to blame certain undesirable practices on general company policies, but, in general, those who criticized directed most of their complaints against foremen with whom they had daily encounters.

In a firm where three or four hundred people worked, an owner could come in contact with most of his employees: "My grandfather knew every worker by name" (#88). The workers, rather than resenting the owner's superior position and attempts on his part to direct the course of their lives in ways consonant with his own standards, usually reacted with pleasure when he evinced interest in them: "If a manager or owner spoke to you, it made your day" (#42). Comments such as "Are your teeth original? Now you look after them" (#23) might be treated humorously in the retelling, but they were repeated proudly. The mother who told her daughter how the owner cuffed the ears of an individual who at work behaved in ways he did not countenance did so, not resentfully, but rather as a warning to the girl to conduct herself properly on the job. One man, contrasting several mill owners under whom he had worked with other more typical "linen lord" types, spoke of them as being "the very kindest I ever had, decent men" (#48) and proudly showed me a letter received from one of them, praising him for his willingness to serve the firm.

Photo 30. Decision-makers in the private office of the Barn Mills of John Taylor and Sons, Carrickfergus, County Antrim, ca. 1916. By courtesy of Mr. John Weatherup.

Several individuals told stories of visits made by owners to their employees who fell ill. And the owner of one mill, located some distance from Belfast, was said to have maintained a ward in a hospital nearby to which those who worked for him were sent, one penny being deducted from each pay packet to help cover the cost of the doctor and nurse in attendance. The same man paid visits to the homes of those he suspected of stirring up sectarian emotions, threatening to put troublemakers out of mill houses if they persisted.

Where restrictions against certain types of carry-on at work were in effect, they were usually accepted as reflecting the fact that a particular individual "was a Christian gentleman and didn't go in for them" (#23). Such men and their sons—"Master George," "Master Henry," or whatever the case might be—were known to permit frivolity when they ran yearly excursions to seaside resorts or gave "great parties" in social halls for their employees.

Furthermore, although people recognized that they might be turned out of company houses if they left their jobs with one firm to work elsewhere, they cited that as merely a minus factor to be considered when evaluating relative merits of places to work and did not assign blame for the practice to owners of particular firms. They also felt that in a family business they were less apt to be turned out of their jobs when the industry was economically depressed. Many people were eventually torn between longstanding loyalties to companies for which they worked and action demanded by leaders of trade unions.

I do not know how representative of mill and factory owners the following reminiscence about one member of a family firm is. It does, however, reveal aspects of the involvement with their workers which was characteristic of some:

> Master Sam, we called him. . . . he was very good to the workers, and if you were ill and things were very hard . . . they'd a said, "Well, I want you up for a fortnight. And I'm takin' you down" . . . till some kind of a home. . . . and fed them cod-liver oil and everything. . . . he used to make them wear the wee glazers and all for fear of the wet and all, fear of gettin' cold or anything. Then they abused it like. . . . took the stuff away and pawned it. He give them the docket for to go and buy out of a place in Orr Street, and they got them, and they abused him. You know what I mean?
>
> And then another thing that he done. The dinin' room was there, for the workers, and he used to give out wee tokens. Now, they were brass . . . and there was a penny marked on that. Well, you woulda went in at breakfast time, and you woulda got a cup of tea and a Paris bun . . . and what we called cold squares. . . . And at dinner time, you got a bowl of soup and two potatoes and a cup of tea and a bun after that. Never cost you anything.
>
> That was for anybody that was poor . . . the unemployment was that tight in Northern Ireland. . . . Whenever they had

no money to pay for their food, through the week, he give it
to them . . . in tokens, but they couldn't a took that outside.
. . . and then that was taken out of their pay on Friday. . . .
if he'd seen them in a very bad strait, he'd a . . . had a talk
with them. Maybe the spinnin' master woulda said, "They're
not able to pay their rent and all." . . . You woulda had to be
a worker before you got a mill house. For all, that mill house
was four and six.

    That was kept out of your pay every week, but on the con-
dition that whenever you left that place you were out of that
house . . . spinnin' masters, rovin' masters, reelin' masters,
and all had to do that. . . . That was . . . '14 to '18, some time
during the war. (#33)

The humane activities of Quakers who were involved in the
trade were often mentioned. But sometimes their well-inten-
tioned gestures earned unexpected responses. In an earlier day,
when, typically, employees of certain firms were not allowed to
remain in work areas during meal hours and there was no dining
room in which they might eat, it was customary for the workers
to bring bread from home and buy tea for a penny from households in the vicinity. A widely circulated story tells how the owners of one mill on the Falls Road instituted the practice of providing free breakfasts for linen workers who could not return home
during the morning break. What followed is that those who were
able to eat the meal at home directed taunts at the workers who
remained, suggesting they were too poor to provide their own
food. Somewhat later, the free meal came under another attack
when a healthier porridge was substituted for the more usual fare
of tea and bread, and the employees struck to make known their
displeasure.

POPULAR NAMES OF MILLS

That it has long been natural for many workers to associate a mill
or factory with a particular family or individual is evidenced by
names traditionally assigned to certain of those industrial concerns. After the official designation of a business was altered to
reflect a merger or other change in ownership, those connected

with the industry often continued to refer to the firm by its earlier name. A good example is the Falls Flax Spinning Company, traditionally called "Kennedy's," although it was taken over from James Kennedy and Sons in 1865. Another is the firm built by John Emerson in 1850, which later became the Ballysillan Mill of the Doagh Flax Spinning Company but continued to be called "Emerson's." In the late 1880s, the New Northern Spinning and Weaving Company was formed to acquire a number of mills, one of the original owners of which was A. W. Craig; the New Northern is still known as "Craig's Mill" or "Craig's Factory." [22]

Customary appellations based on the location of business concerns were employed as well: Hilden Mill, Bessbrook, and Shrigley fall in this category, as does Bath Mill, [23] so-called because it adjoined what were at one time public baths. More remote in origin are two traditional names still used by old-timers. "Tea Lane," applied to the Ulster Weaving Company, derives from the days when, on the "loanin," or lane, leading to the linen firm, it was customary to keep the half-doors on each house open and tea on the hearth, ready for those who might drop in at any time of day. As for the second of the two, if you had asked where an employee of Durham Street Weaving Company worked, he or she would most likely have replied, "The Pound," because of the company's location along a stream which once ran through a part of Belfast known as The Pound.

Such designations were very frequently though not consistently applied, and the few examples given here do not exhaust all the terms of reference. Yet they should be sufficient to document still another category of items which belong properly with other lore of the linen industry.

SEVEN

A Last Word on Folklore & Industry

Assuming that the reader subscribes to the broad notions about the nature of folk and folklore that are implied in the preceding pages, the material just presented provides evidence that a substantial body of lore could be and was transmitted in many flax spinning mills and linen weaving factories in Northern Ireland in the early decades of this century. Tied firmly to a specific context and viewed in their entirety, the traditional materials can be said to be unique to the linen industry, although some of the traditions in slightly modified form—clubs and wedding customs, for example—are found in Northern Ireland and England among workers in firms where different products are manufactured, and others, such as "fool's errands," sexual hazing, and songs of protest have been discovered among diverse industrial groups in several parts of the world. The preceding chapters also make clear that there was great variation in the lore, both in amount and kind, from one job to another and from one industrial plant to another, from which fact it is possible to conclude that it is the presence or absence of certain factors, alone or in combination, rather than industrialization per se that determines whether folklore will exist in an industrial setting.

In delineating age, gender, personality and religious differences, status distinctions, variant pay schemes, placement and type of equipment, degree of concentration required, atmospheric conditions and noise levels, availability of labor, and contrasting attitudes of individual foremen and members of management, I have indicated, either directly or by implication, the types of variables that seem to have operated to produce differences in the traditions of several groups of workers in the linen industry. Some of them were probably significant only in a Northern Irish context. For example, there is some indication that more Catholics than Protestants were employed as spinners, while the reverse was true for weavers. Because traditional singing, dancing, and storytelling seem to have been more vital in the lives of the Catholic segment of the population than the Protestant—or, as it was put to me, "The Catholics had more Culture than we did" (#28)—it is conceivable that the differing religious (and concomitant cultural) backgrounds of the majority of workers engaged in spinning and weaving was an important factor making for contrasts in mill and factory folklore. Other factors most likely assumed importance in many places, although this cannot be known with certainty until such time as the necessary comparative data are made available.

A number of generalizations, formulated after a consideration of the specifics of the variables mentioned above, can be made about the relationship between the linen industry and its folklore, as follows: females of all ages sang more than males; children, particularly girls, contributed heavily to the creation and transmission of a corpus of lore; traditions of high-status workers were less varied than those of low-status workers; dust, more than heat or moisture, was a deterrent to the development of lore; those whose services were in greatest demand had the richest bodies of lore; there was less lore associated with those on piecework than with those who received a set pay; noisy machinery precluded the transmission on the job of lore of a conversational nature; a relatively small amount of folklore circulated among workers whose jobs required constant concentration; and the amount and character of the lore associated with each job reflected the basic personalities of those who furnished the models and set the general tone in the rooms where they worked. These factors may suggest lines of investigation to those who undertake similarly oriented research.

Although I have tried to reveal facets of the linen industry about which outsiders had little or no knowledge, I have not meant, by the way I have organized my materials, to lead anyone to believe that life in mills and factories centered around the traditions I have just described. At the same time, I do not feel that the nature of my inquiry dictated that the workers overemphasize the lighter side of their work experiences. For one thing, there was no guarantee when I began my search that any lore I might discover would reflect other than sordid aspects of the daily routine. For another, I had no preconceived notions about the industry that might lead me to steer conversation in any one direction. By allowing those with whom I spoke to talk freely and spontaneously about a variety of topics rather than by limiting them to answering questions designed to elicit just one type of information, I was told about multiple facets of their daily routines rather than about only one segment of them; I have included as many of these as possible. If the total image that has emerged is less somber than previous portrayals, it is, I believe, mainly because the men and women who turned flax into linen cloth saw things that way. I reject the notion, frequently voiced, that they probably remembered most of the "good" experiences and forgot most of the "bad" ones. To those who still feel that the picture is somehow misleading, I can only say that at least it serves to temper impressions left by specialized investigations of another order, such as those directed toward revealing unhealthy conditions or toward improving relations between management and workers.

By 1929, radical transformations in the linen industry, brought about by new technology and changes in the wider culture, were leading to the disappearance of most of the traditions found earlier in the mills and factories. In previous chapters, I have mentioned some of the effects of the application of new methods and the introduction of improved machinery, but the outside influences which probably contributed to the demise of the traditions—such things as changing attitudes, social legislation, and the impact of radio, cinema, and television—are too numerous and the relationships among them too complex to plumb to any depth in this book.

The older lore which survives is usually modified—as are the hazing activities which take place before a girl is married—or transmitted in new ways (a few songs and reminiscences on tapes and records) and in new settings (music at social gatherings of retired employees, organized by firms presently in operation, and at church- and community-sponsored events for older people). To what extent and in what form new traditions have replaced the old in mill and factory is not known. A substantial reduction in the linen work force, a consequence of redundancies, retirements, and the availability of alternative employment, has certainly eliminated a number of possible bearers of traditional materials in any form.

It is maintained in some quarters that current renewed and increasing demands for the textile could be met more easily if there were enough men and women willing to operate the machines which produce the yarn and cloth. The lack of response to the call for more workers is related in part to the negative image of the linen industry which lingers in the minds of most people in Northern Ireland. This, despite considerable improvements in hours worked, employee benefits, and equipment, and despite efforts made by management to acquaint the public with the changes that have taken place.

As has been pointed out, people who have never been directly associated with the industry have usually dwelt on its dark side when speaking and writing about it. And those who, because of their personal knowledge of what it was like to work in flax spinning mills and linen weaving factories, could add other dimensions to the picture have until now refrained from doing so in clear voices, largely because they have adopted the stereotyped attitudes held in the wider culture and have tended to reject the favorable along with the unfavorable aspects of their past: "I loved it, but the people here don't really know what it was like, you see" (#47).

I have tried here to include some of the brighter facets of the work experience and, in so doing, to supplement the image. The end product is, I believe, more consonant with the perceptions and reactions of the linen workers themselves. For the majority of them in the early decades of this century not only found things in their daily routines that were acceptable to them but compensated for deficiencies they could not avoid in numerous ways, not the least of which was the development of the oral, material, and behavioral traditions just described. It is not likely that my words will persuade anyone to become a linen worker—nor are they intended to. But it may be that those who spent much of their lives producing linen yarn and cloth in Northern Ireland—and, perhaps, other types of textile workers elsewhere—will find something in what I have written to cause them to take pride in the work they did and in the lore that is so distinctively their own.

Appendix A

Respondents

1. Male; manager; born 1880; began work 1899; worked in Belfast and two country mills; Protestant.
2. Male; hackler; born 1910; began work 1927; worked in country mill; Protestant.
3. Male; electrician; born 1902; began work 1914; worked in country mill; Protestant.
4. Female; spinner; born 1895; began work 1904; worked in two country mills; Catholic.
5. Male; hackler; born 1893; began work 1905; worked in country mill; Protestant.
6. Female; spinner; born 1907; began work 1919; worked in country mill; Protestant.
7. Female; doffing mistress; born 1909; began work 1921; worked in country mill; Protestant.
8. Male; rougher; born 1899; began work 1910; worked in country mill; Catholic.
9. Female; spinner; born 1898; began work 1910; worked in country mill; Catholic.
10. Female; weaver, then trade-union organizer; born 1906; began work 1919; worked in factory in Belfast; Protestant.
11. Male; tenter; born 1893; began work 1907; worked in factories outside of Belfast and in the city; Protestant.
12. Female; reeler; born 1895; began work 1909; worked in mills outside of Belfast and in the city; Protestant.
13. Male; factory manager; born ca. 1914; Protestant.
14. Female; copper; born 1900; began work 1913; worked in thread mill outside of Belfast; Protestant.
15. Female; reeler; born 1900; began work 1913; worked in thread mill outside of Belfast; Protestant.
16. Female; various jobs; born 1898; began work 1911; worked in thread mill outside of Belfast; Protestant.
17. Female; various jobs; born 1897; began work 1910; worked in thread mill outside of Belfast; Protestant.

18. Male; weaver; born 1898; began work 1912; worked in factory outside of Belfast; Protestant.
19. Male; soft finishing; born 1893; began work 1905; worked in thread mill outside of Belfast; Protestant.
20. Female; ring twisting, then bobbin winding; born 1894; began work 1906; worked in thread mill outside of Belfast; Protestant.
21. Female; twisting mistress; born 1910; began work 1924; worked in thread mill outside of Belfast; Protestant.
22. Female; spinner; born 1910; began work 1922; worked in two country mills; Protestant.
23. Female; spinner; born 1905; began work 1917; worked in mill outside of Belfast; Protestant.
24. Female; spinner; born 1900; began work 1911; worked in country mill; Protestant.
25. Male; various jobs in mill as a young person; born 1902; began work 1914; worked in country mill; Catholic.
26. Female; spinner; born 1900; began work 1912; worked in mill in Belfast and two country mills; Catholic.
27. Male; management level; born ca. 1907; Protestant.
28. Male; cloth passing, weaving, dressing; born 1900; began work 1914; worked in factories outside of Belfast and in the city; Protestant.
29. Female; weaver; born 1900; began work 1914; worked in factory outside of Belfast; Catholic.
30. Male; folk singer with many family members in mills in Belfast; born ca. 1920; Catholic.
31. Female; spinner, later in machine room as sorter of flax and piecer-out; born 1908; began work 1920; worked in mills in Belfast; Catholic.
32. Female; weaver; born 1891; began work 1904; worked in factories in Belfast; Protestant.
33. Female; doffing mistress; born 1898; began work 1910; worked in mills in Belfast; Protestant.
34. Female; winder; born 1906; began work 1919; worked in mill and factory in Belfast; Protestant.
35. Female; winder; born 1919; began work 1933; worked in mill and factory in Belfast; Catholic.
36. Male; rougher; born 1901; began work 1913; worked in two country mills; Protestant.
37. Female; winder; born 1893; began work 1908 (after shop work); worked in factory outside of Belfast; Protestant.
38. Male; mechanic shop; born 1899; began work 1912; worked in numerous mills in Belfast; Protestant.
39. Female; spinner; born 1899; began work 1911; worked in mill in Belfast; Protestant.
40. Female; spinner; born 1902; began work 1914; worked in mill in Belfast; Protestant.

41. Female; spinner; born 1887; began work 1898; worked in mill in Belfast with brief interlude as winder in factory in Belfast; Protestant.
42. Female; spinner; born 1898; began work 1910; worked in country mill and mill in Belfast; Catholic.
43. Male; various jobs in mill; born 1900; began work 1912; worked in thread mill outside of Belfast; Protestant.
44. Female; twisting department; born 1904; began work 1917; worked in thread mill outside of Belfast; Protestant.
45. Male; spinning master; born 1904; began work 1916; worked in country mill; Catholic.
46. Female; warper; born 1903; began work 1916; worked in factory outside of Belfast; Protestant.
47. Female; doffing mistress; born 1896; began work 1908; worked in mill in Belfast; Catholic.
48. Male; mechanic-shop foreman; born 1901; began work 1913; worked in various mills in Belfast; Catholic.
49. Male; hackler; born 1887; began work 1899; worked in country mills and mills in Belfast; Protestant.
50. Female; reeler; born 1899; began work 1912; worked in country mill; Protestant.
51. Male; spinning master; born 1903; began work 1915; worked in country mill; Protestant.
52. Female; spinner; born 1898; began work 1910; worked in country mill; Catholic.
53. Female; reeler, after starting as spinner; born 1895; began work 1906; worked in mills in Belfast, with a ten-year interval as a winder in factory in Belfast; Catholic.
54. Female; rover; born 1900; began work 1912; worked in mills in Belfast; Protestant.
55. Female; spinner; born 1907; began work 1919; worked in mills in Belfast; Protestant.
56. Female; weaver; born 1903; began work 1916; worked in factory in Belfast; Protestant.
57. Female; spinner; born 1902; began work 1914; worked in mill in Belfast; Protestant.
58. Female; doffing mistress; born 1901; began work 1913; worked in mill in Belfast; Protestant.
59. Female; drawer; born 1902; began work 1914; worked in mill in Belfast; Protestant.
60. Female; spinner; born 1904; began work 1916; worked in country mill; Catholic.
61. Female; reeler; born 1912; began work 1926; worked in country mill; Protestant.
62. Male; management level; born ca. 1901; Protestant.
63. Female; weaver; born 1908; began work 1921; worked in factory in Belfast; Protestant.

64. Female; reeler; born 1897; began work 1909; worked in mill in Belfast; Catholic.
65. Male; various jobs in mill; born 1887; began work 1899; worked in Belfast; Catholic.
66. Male; various jobs in mill; born 1901; began work 1913; worked in country mill; Protestant.
67. Female; spinner; born 1893; began work 1905; worked in country mill; Catholic.
68. Female; reeler, then trade-union organizer; born 1912; began work 1925; worked in mills in Belfast; Protestant.
69. Female; winder; born 1907; began work 1919; worked in mill outside of Belfast; Protestant.
70. Male; physician; born ca. 1909; Catholic.
71. Male; trade-union official; born ca. 1908; Protestant.
72. Male; management level; born ca. 1907; Protestant.
73. Male; handloom weaver; born 1938; Catholic.
74. Male; university professor; born 1890; Catholic.
75. Female; personnel director; born ca. 1921; Protestant.
76. Female; reeler; born ca. 1926; Protestant.
77. Female; trade-union organizer; born ca. 1936; Catholic.
78. Female; weaver; born 1896; began work 1909; worked in factory in Belfast; Catholic.
79. Male; bundler; born 1907; began work 1920; worked in country mill; Protestant.
80. Male; general manager; born 1895; began work in 1911; worked in mill outside Belfast; Protestant.
81. Female; spinner; born 1908; began work 1920; worked in country mill; Protestant.
82. Female; reeler; born 1875; began work 1888; worked in country mill; Catholic.
83. Female; reeler; born 1888; began work 1901; worked in country mill; Protestant.
84. Female; spinner; born 1908; began work 1920; worked in country mill; Protestant.
85. Male; tenter; born 1890; began work 1903; worked in factory in Belfast; Protestant.
86. Female; weaver; born 1892; began work 1905; worked in factory in Belfast; Protestant.
87. Female; reeler; born 1906; began work 1919; worked in country mill; Catholic.
88. Male; mill owner; born ca. 1907; Protestant.

I have not included in the foregoing list facts about individuals who contributed welcomed but minimal amounts of information or from whom I obtained inadequate background information.

A number of respondents came from families many members of which had had work experience in mills and factories. Data provided by one male respondent, #38, make the point:

grandparents—four in the mill; one grandfather a hackler
mother—spreader
uncles—two hacklers
brother—preparing master
sisters—one reeler and weaver, one weaver
wife—rover
daughters—two, who worked at reeling, spinning, carding, and
  combing

Appendix B

Terms & Conditions
of Employment

(D.1882/2/1, Public Record Office of Northern Ireland)

NOTICE

The Truck Act, 1896, requires that a copy of the following terms and conditions should be handed to every worker.

WM. LIDDELL & CO., LTD., DONACLONEY.

TERMS and CONDITIONS under and subject to which all Workers are employed in this WEAVING FACTORY.

1. No person has power to engage or dismiss a worker except the Employer, Manager, or Overlooker.
2. No worker shall leave the employment without first giving a fortnight's notice, such notice to be given to the Manager or to some person authorised by him, before 8 o'clock in the morning of the notice day, and the notice must be worked up in 12 full consecutive working days. Any worker leaving without giving such notice shall pay a fine equal in amount to one week's wages, which, in the case of piece workers, shall be based on an average of the wages earned during the preceding three weeks.
3. No worker shall be discharged without receiving a fortnight's notice, except for breach of these terms and conditions or other sufficient misconduct.
4. Every worker shall be liable to instant dismissal who, in the opinion of the Employer, Manager, or Overlooker, is
    (a) Incompetent, or has been guilty of
    (b) Absence at any time from his or her place of work, without leave.
    (c) Disobedience.

(d) Loitering, smoking, idling, or assisting others to idle.

(e) Carelessness in discharge of duty.

(f) Annoying or quarrelling with other workers.

(g) Using obscene or blasphemous language.

(h) Acting in a way calculated to lead to a breach of the peace.

(i) Being under the influence of drink, or bringing intoxicants into the works.

(j) Doing anything likely to endanger the safety of the place or its contents, or the health of the workers.

(k) Interfering in any way with any machinery or plant, whether in motion or stopped, except when required or necessary in the discharge of some duty.

(l) Beginning to work before or continuing to work after the appointed time.

(m) Obtaining employment in the Factory by false representations.

(n) Introducing strangers into the works.

(o) Bringing into the works knitting, needlework, books, newspapers, or other articles likely to cause waste of time.

(p) A breach of any of these terms and conditions.

5. Each worker shall be at his or her place of work at starting time in the morning and after each meal hour, unless leave of absence has been granted by the Manager or some person authorized by him, or evidence satisfactory to the Manager of inability to work be produced. Any worker absent at the morning start shall pay a fine of 2d., and any worker absent after any meal hour start shall pay a fine of 3d. No worker absent at any starting period shall be entitled as of right to enter the works until the succeeding starting period, but permission may, at the discretion of the Employer or Manager, or any person authorized by either of them, be given to enter the works within 10 minutes after any starting period, and, if given, then the aforesaid fines shall be reduced to 1d. Instead of enforcing the foregoing fines, the worker may, at the discretion of the Employer or Manager, or any person authorised as aforesaid, be summarily dismissed for absence.

6. No worker shall take out of the premises any property of the Employer without permission of the Employer or Manager, and any worker suspected of having any property of the Employer concealed about his or her person may be searched by a person duly authorised for that purpose by the Employer or Manager.

7. If at any time any of the workers in any department shall strike or decline to work, it shall be competent for the Employer or Manager to discharge, without Notice, all or so many of the workers in all or any of the departments in the Factory as he shall think fit, and the persons so discharged shall not be entitled to any compensation in lieu of Notice.

8. In case the Employer shall stop all or any part of the works for holidays, whether local or general, or on account of injury to any part of

the works due to fire or other cause, or to enable alterations, additions to, or repairs of buildings or plant to be effected, or on account of religious or political excitement, or any other cause, which in the Employer's opinion, may effect the discipline of the works or their harmonious working, or on account of trade disputes in the works or in the trade generally, or in any trade or occupation upon which the works may be dependent in any way, or on account of shortage of coal, material, or work, or any other cause, workers shall not be entitled to wages or compensation during the time they shall be out of work for loss of time or otherwise.

9. Every weaver leaving must leave his or her yarn straight, in good order, and his or her looms clean, or pay a fine of 1/-.

10. Any weaver, unnecessarily stopping a loom, or refusing to commence work when called upon to do so by either Manager or Foreman, shall be liable to a fine of 1/-.

11. Each worker in charge of any machine or machinery shall, every Saturday and during the time appointed for such work, clean same to the satisfaction of the Manager or Overlooker, and for each breach of this condition shall pay a fine of 6d.

12. Any worker taking a guard or covering from any machinery, gearing, shafting, or wheels on any account, except when the belt is off the driving pulley or when the engine is stopped, shall be liable to a fine of 1/- for every offence.

13. The fines in these terms and conditions mentioned may be deducted from the worker's wages then due or that become due in the two pays next succeeding the imposition of the fine.

14. A deduction may also be made from the wages due or that may accrue due to any worker in respect of bad or negligent work by such worker, or injury caused by him or her to the materials or other property of the Employer. Such deduction will be fair and reasonable having regard to all the circumstances of the case, and in no case will it exceed the actual or estimated damage or loss occasioned to the Employer by the act or omission of the worker or of any person over whom he or she has control. The following are amongst the cases where such deductions will be enforced:—

WINDERS for bad knots, soft pirns or spools, mixing of yarns, excessive waste and dirt.

WARPERS AND DRESSERS for slack or improperly dried beams, sunk selvages, latched yarn, bad knots, missed marks, dirty threads, oil or other stains.

DRAWERS-IN for crammed or empty splits or wrong drafts, and in addition, the work shall be made right without further payment.

TENTERS for clouding, slack cloth, webs not containing the specified shots, or any other defect reasonably preventable.

WEAVERS where a beam of yarn is not evenly and well woven into good cloth and taken out only at cut marks, and is not free from

The Belfast Education Authority and Its Work (1923–73), pp. 14–15.

7. A medical interpretation of "mill fever" is provided by C. D. Purdon, *The Mortality of Flax Mill and Factory Workers and the Diseases They Labour Under*, p. 7, and *The Sanitary State of the Belfast Factory District during Ten Years (1864–1873)*, pp. 14–15.

8. David Hammond of the British Broadcasting Corporation in Belfast suggests that the tune is most likely of music-hall derivation.

9. With four shillings one penny or four shillings twopence to the dollar at the time, the pound sterling was approximately equal to five dollars.

10. Thomas Wright, *The Great Unwashed*, p. 143.

11. See section 3 of the "Terms and Conditions" in Appendix B. The document sets forth conditions under which those employed in a factory worked, but similar regulations governed the behavior of mill workers.

12. The material from which the petticoat was made seems to have been manufactured in Newtownards, County Down, since the late 1860s. See E. R. R. Green, *The Industrial Archaeology of County Down*, p. 14. However, I cannot say when the spinners adopted it as part of their traditional dress.

13. David Hammond suggests that the use of the name Barney Ross in this particular variant may have been a satirical reference to the owner of a mill, popularly known as Ross's. (Its formal name was William Ross and Company Ltd., Clonard Mill.)

14. Her variant begins: "Hold her slow/For we're all here." The BBC tape recording was not otherwise identified.

15. There are verses about other towns which contain references to the local mill, so often a dominant feature of the place. One, recited by a friend, tells how:

Tandragee is a nice little town,
It's built on a rising hill,
At the top of the town, situated a church,
At the bottom a spinning mill.

16. According to David Hammond, who heard it in Scotland, the tune to which the words of "Doffing Mistress" are sung are there associated with texts of derision directed against several types of individuals. The melody appears to have been used to express a variety of sentiments in Northern Ireland. See, for example, p. 56.

17. Hugh Quinn, "Notes to Children's Street Tunes and Games of Old Belfast." I thank David Hammond of the British Broadcasting Corporation in Belfast for letting me read this typescript.

18. Quinn, "Notes to Children's Street Tunes," posits that it was composed by an unknown mill girl, one of a crowd of young persons gathered in a sympathetic protest reaction at the home of a well-

liked doffing mistress who had been dismissed from her job. He states, furthermore, that mill authorities, frightened at the prospect of a strike of great magnitude, reinstated the woman. The explanation is, perhaps, a bit romantic.

19. So as not to offend either segment of the population, I have included variants, obtained from friends, which present the sentiments of both certain Catholics and certain Protestants.

20. Among other regulations, the Truck Act of 1896 made it mandatory for employers to inform those working for them of the conditions under which deductions from their wages could be made. The "Terms and Conditions" in Appendix B reflect conformity to that act.

21. Elsewhere, in the past, a policeman on his beat or a work mate supplemented the professional callers (Wright, *The Great Unwashed*, pp. 75–76). The tolling of a church bell was a less personal way to rouse late sleepers (William Dodd, *The Factory System Illustrated*, pp. 218–219).

22. In England, according to Thompson, *The Making of the English Working Class*, p. 338, a witness before Sadler's Committee of 1832 commented: "I have seen some children running down to the mill crying, with a bit of bread in their hands, and that is all they may have till twelve o'clock at noon: crying for fear of being late." See, also, Dodd, *The Factory System Illustrated*, pp. 218–219.

23. See, for example, Diana Hamilton, coll., "So Early in the Morning," as recorded on Tradition Records TLP 1034.

24. C. D. Purdon, *The Mortality of Flax Mill and Factory Workers* and *The Sanitary State of the Belfast Factory District*.

25. The air is said to be the same as that of the chorus of the well-known Irish song, "Biddy Mulligan, the Pride of the Coombe."

26. The verse was probably put together, using lines from variants of the "Snuff Box Song." See pp. 67–68.

27. Respondent #52, personal correspondence.

28. The following is one variant of the football song:

It's a grand old team to play for,
It's a grand old team to play,
And when you read the history,
It's enough to make your heart go sad.
Oh, I don't care where the money's coming from,
Dang the hair I care,
For all I know, there's going to be a match
And Hilden United will be there. (#44)

29. William Conor, 1881–1968. The titles of some of his paintings— "Weavers," "Laughing Mill Girls," "Hemstitching Factory," "York Street Spinning Mill," "Young Mill Worker," "Belfast Mill Girls," "A Spinning Mill," "Going to the Mills," "Mill Workers," "The Mill Girls Parading," "Mill Girl at a Window," "The Stitching Factory," "Bel-

fast Shawlies," and "Mill Girls Off to Work"—attest to his being a chronicler of the linen industry. (The titles are taken from several exhibition catalogues found among uncatalogued materials in the Linen Hall Library, Belfast.) One of his paintings appears in Photo 10.
30. In the early nineteenth century, according to Thompson, *The Making of the English Working Class*, p. 413, witnesses before investigative committees in England spoke of being shocked by "the coarse language and independent manners of Lancashire mill girls," the assumption being that the factory system was responsible for their behavior. Dodd, *The Factory System Illustrated*, p. 156, mentions "those filthy and obscene songs, so much in use in our factories at present." The latter reference is particularly interesting, not because of the characterization of the songs—which may or may not have been accurate—but because it points to the fact that the girls were even then singing in the mills, despite conditions there that appear to have been many times worse than those reported on in the present study.

4. "BUT THE HACKLERS . . . ARE OF THE BEST CLASS"

1. See Appendix C, Table 2.
2. Their elitist status may have been a carry-over from the early 1800s, when, as E. P. Thompson, *The Making of the English Working Class*, p. 237, points out, "in some industries, the [in general] craftsman's privileged position survived into workshop or factory production."
3. Shown by D. L. Armstrong, "Social and Economic Conditions in the Belfast Linen Industry, 1850–1900," *Irish Historical Studies* 7 (1951): 264. Documents of now defunct linen firms, located in the Public Record Office of Northern Ireland, Belfast, help to verify his findings. One limitation of tables such as that compiled by Armstrong is that the broad categories give no indication of the varieties of jobs, with differing pay rates, that are included in each. The charts in Appendix C show such a breakdown.
4. See Thompson, *The Making of the English Working Class*, pp. 717–719.
5. The explanation was one the men provided, but the disability may have had other roots. Writing about byssinosis, a respiratory disease, James A. Smiley speaks of the effects of exposure to the dust of flax and quotes from a report, probably produced in the 1860s: "the eyes often become sore, the margins of the eyelid being swollen and inflamed and the sight is said occasionally to become impaired" ("Background to Byssinosis in Ulster," *British Journal of Industrial Medicine* 18 [1961]: 5).
6. The verse meant is probably Isaiah 19:9—"Moreover they that work in

fine flax, and they that weave networks, shall be confounded" (King James Version).
7. Thomas Wright, *The Great Unwashed*, pp. 281–282.
8. Ibid., p. 282.
9. Ibid., p. 159.
10. My guess is that, if a song rather than a rhyme, it was sung to the tune of "John Peel."
11. The passing off of dung as a pill with special powers (Motif 114.3.1 in Stith Thompson, *Motif-Index of Folk Literature*) is well exemplified in this anecdote.
12. In this form, the song is a variant of "The Butcher Boy," P24, as categorized by George Malcolm Laws, *American Balladry from British Broadsides*, p. 260.
13. "Linen Workers of Long Ago Are Still Earning Praise," *Linen Trade Circular*, 29 June 1957, p. 14.
14. Vivian Mercier, *The Irish Comic Tradition*, p. 86, sums up his discussion of an illustrative riddle by saying: "The significance of this text for the history of Irish learning and wit can hardly be exaggerated. It expresses three archaic attitudes which have remained imbedded in the popular beliefs of the Irish: first, that wisdom can be demonstrated by the propounding or answering of seemingly insoluble riddles . . ."
15. The riddle seems to be a variant of that presented in Tristram Potter Coffin and Hennig Cohen, eds., *Folklore in America*, p. 160.
16. Mercier, *The Irish Comic Tradition*, pp. 78–104.
17. David Bleakley, "Trade Union Beginnings in Belfast and District with Special Reference to the Period 1881–1900, and to the Work of the Belfast and District United Trades' Council during That Period," p. 249.
18. *Flaxdressers' Trade and Benevolent Trade Union, Thirty-Fourth Annual Report, for Year Ending 31st December 1906.*
19. Ibid., p. 5.
20. Sam Hanna Bell, *Erin's Orange Lily*, p. 48.

5. "AND HER SCISSORS IN HER HAND"

1. Leslie C. Marshall, *The Practical Flax Spinner*, p. 221.
2. "'Shuttle Kissing' Doomed," *Linen Trade Circular*, 23 August 1952, p. 17. The article states that six years after regulations restricting the use of mouth shuttles come into effect, on 1 November 1952, they can no longer be used at any time.
3. W. J. Fitzpatrick, *An Old-Timer Talking*, 2d ed. rev., p. 61. The *flowerers* mentioned in the song were women who did hand embroidery at home; the *piercers* were sharp instruments used to poke holes in the cloth, around which holes the flowerers did fancy stitching.

4. Respondent #86, personal correspondence. Representative "Terms
   and Conditions" under which factory workers labored are contained in Appendix B.
5. The usual designations describing that quality were based, theoreti-
   cally, on the number of warp threads in forty inches of cloth. Actually, they reflected more closely the number of splits in forty inches
   of the reed, for usually two warp threads passed through each of the
   openings in it. In theory, one could count the threads per inch, mul-
   tiply the figure by forty, and then divide by two. A cloth described as
   20^{00} was, thus, one which contained 100 threads per inch; one designated as 10^{00} contained 50 threads per inch. The higher the
   figure, the finer the weave. In practice, however, specially constructed glasses were used to make the calculations for cloth, both
   on the loom and after bleaching.
6. See section 14 of the "Terms and Conditions" in Appendix B.
7. How the work discipline of industrialism came to be inculcated in the
   working classes in England in the nineteenth century, and especially the role of Methodism in the process, is a topic that has been
   effectively covered by E. P. Thompson, *The Making of the English
   Working Class*, pp. 355–400.
8. For examples of circumstances under which fines were levied, see
   section 14 of the "Terms and Conditions" in Appendix B.
9. See Thompson, *The Making of the English Working Class*, p. 200.
10. Respondent #75, personal correspondence.
11. See, for example, Documents 1133/A/WF/22 and 1191/62 in the
    Public Record Office of Northern Ireland, Belfast.
12. A. M. Anderson, *Women in the Factory*, pp. 150, 162.
13. Respondent #85.
14. William Haggan, "Weaver's Rubric—3," *Linen Trade Circular*, 24
    October 1959, p. 16.
15. See Ivy Pinchbeck, *Women Workers and the Industrial Revolution,
    1750–1850*, p. 158.
16. My own feeling is that the belief stems in part from the fact that ma-
    chine spinning preceded power-loom weaving; antagonisms even-
    tually extended to the new system of production as a whole were
    directed initially, and with lasting effects, toward the mill. It is
    possible, furthermore, that the practice in mills of employing large
    numbers of women and children (reinforcing fears of the break-
    down of the family) and, perhaps, as in England, the hiring at the
    beginning of many persons, frequently of low status, who were anx-
    ious and willing to leave other occupations for higher wages (see
    Pinchbeck, *Women Workers and the Industrial Revolution*, pp.
    184–185) soon gave rise to the belief that the mills were seedbeds of
    immorality and the haven, primarily, of the poverty-stricken. A
    greater degree of acceptance most likely accompanied the prolifera-
    tion of factories, people by then having grown more used to the in-
    dustrial milieu.

17. Nora Connolly O'Brien, *Portrait of a Rebel Father*, pp. 124–125, refers to this further status distinction between women factory workers and those who labored in the wareroom in the making-up end of the trade.
18. See section 4d of the "Terms and Conditions" in Appendix B.
19. Thompson, *The Making of the English Working Class*, p. 434, says: "The same character structure which made for application and skill erected also barriers of self respect which were not amenable to dirty or degrading tasks." The status distinction between dirty and clean work, made by linen workers, may somehow be tied in with this.
20. For instance, see Henry S. Purdon, "Flax and Linen," in *Dangerous Trades*, ed. Thomas Oliver, pp. 696–701.
21. In an earlier era in England, a female agitator, urging the working classes to assert their rights, described the contest between rich and poor as one, in part, "between shoes and wooden clogs" (Thompson, *The Making of the English Working Class*, p. 454).
22. Conor once remarked in a public address that the "mill lassies" wore the shawl, not out of necessity, but by choice, recognizing that it enhanced their beauty. He went on to advocate that women should abandon hats and once again adopt shawls, but he was, apparently, upbraided by women for his suggestion. (Uncatalogued material in the Linen Hall Library, Belfast.)

6. LORE OF MILL AND FACTORY

1. Examples of "fool's errands" (Motif J2346 in Stith Thompson, *Motif-Index of Folk Literature*) in other industries are to be found in Alan Smith, *Discovering Folklore in Industry*, p. 15; A. M. Honeyman, "Fool's Errands for Dundee Apprentices," *Folklore* 69–70 (1958–1959): 334–336; and M. G. Dickson, "Factory Workers' Philosophy," *Sociological Review* 28 (July 1936): 300–301.
2. Neil J. Smelser, *Social Change in the Industrial Revolution*, pp. 279–284.
3. As viewed by at least one male in the 1860s, "the young ladies of the needle-driving and cognate businesses. . . . are a class by themselves, are dressy, uneducated, frivolous, and affected, and are noticeable for trying to ape their betters. . . . and even when married, regard household work as degrading, and are ashamed to be seen in its performance" (Thomas Wright, *The Great Unwashed*, p. 37).
4. Similar hazing practices at the time of marriage are still common in England. For instance, see Smith, *Discovering Folklore in Industry*, p. 16; Margaret Baker, *The Folklore and Customs of Love and Marriage*, p. 19.

5. The custom is known in some places in Scotland as "creeling" the bride (Baker, *Folklore and Customs*, p. 19).

6. See Smelser, *Social Change in the Industrial Revolution*, p. 193.

7. Cf. John Brand, *Observations on the Popular Antiquities of Great Britain*, rev. Henry Ellis, I, 384 n. 2.

8. See Brand, *Observations*, I, 388, for an earlier example.

9. Brand, *Observations*, III, 353–354, discusses "Key and the Bible" as it was performed in an earlier period to determine the identity of a thief. Variant examples are provided by Baker, *Folklore and Customs*, pp. 9–10.

10. The burning of nuts for purposes of divination is an old custom in England. See Brand, *Observations*, I, 281 n. 3, 378–379.

11. The practice has certain features in common with a trade custom once characteristic of shoemakers in England: "on the First Monday in March they ceased to work by candlelight. The ceremony was known as 'wetting the block.' The oldest hand in the workshop solemnly doused the candles in ale and the rest of the evening was spent in drinking" (Smith, *Discovering Folklore in Industry*, pp. 32–33).

12. My description of Queen of the May activities is based on data I collected. The Ulster Folk and Transport Museum has distributed a questionnaire on the topic, the replies to which furnish additional information.

13. This is a reference to the birthday of Queen Victoria. In one area of Belfast, the party given by participants in Queen of the May activities was held on that day, 24 May.

14. Fred Dohr, "The Linen Industry of Northern Ireland," *The Textile Quarterly* 2, no. 2 (1952): 146.

15. Documents 1882/3/1 and 1882/3/3, Public Record Office of Northern Ireland, Belfast.

16. I was told by a trade-union organizer that songs were sung during strikes and that there were choice bits put in about overlookers, but "Old Rosie Lappin" was the only one brought to my attention.

17. Nora Connolly O'Brien, *Portrait of a Rebel Father*, p. 136.

18. Ibid., p. 133.

19. See F. J. Whitford, "Joseph Devlin," *Threshold* 1, no. 2 (1957): 33, for a brief sketch of his life.

20. Colin Wilson and Patricia Pitman, *Encyclopedia of Murder*, pp. 168–169.

21. E. R. R. Green, "Business Organization and the Business Class," in *Ulster since 1800: A Social Survey*, ed. T. W. Moody and J. C. Beckett, p. 117.

22. The traditional names, among many provided by my respondents, were verified by Walter T. Barbour, "Some Irish Flax Spinning Mills of Yesteryear," *Linen Trade Circular*, 25 July 1959, pp. 13, 15.

23. Bath Mill, erected in the late eighteenth or early nineteenth century

as a cotton mill, is said to have been the first mill in Belfast. Its official name was frequently changed, but to some old timers, it is still remembered as Campbell's Mill, called that after one of the early (1817) owners. (See "Sale of What is Probably Belfast's Oldest Mill," *Linen Trade Circular*, 11 January 1947, p. 3.)

Works Cited

Anderson, A. M. *Women in the Factory*. London: John Murray, 1922.

Armstrong, D. L. "Social and Economic Conditions in the Belfast Linen Industry, 1850–1900." *Irish Historical Studies* 7 (1951): 235–269.

Baker, Margaret. *The Folklore and Customs of Love and Marriage*. Aylesbury, Bucks., U.K.: Shire Publications, 1974.

Barbour, Walter T. "Some Irish Flax Spinning Mills of Yesteryear." *Linen Trade Circular*, 25 July 1959, pp. 13, 15.

Bell, Sam Hanna. *Erin's Orange Lily*. London: Dennis Dobson, 1956.

Black, R. D. C. "The Progress of Industrialization, 1850–1920." In *Ulster since 1800: A Political and Economic Survey*, edited by T. W. Moody and J. C. Beckett, pp. 50–59. London: British Broadcasting Corporation, 1954.

Bleakley, David. "Trade Union Beginnings in Belfast and District with Special Reference to the Period 1881–1900, and to the Work of the Belfast and District United Trades' Council during That Period." M.A. thesis, The Queen's University, Belfast, 1955.

Boatright, Mody. *Folklore of the Oil Industry*. Dallas: Southern Methodist Press, 1963.

Boatright, Mody, and William A. Owens. *Tales from the Derrick Floor*. Garden City, N.Y.: Doubleday, 1970.

Boyle, Elizabeth. *The Irish Flowerers*. Belfast: Ulster Folk Museum and Institute of Irish Studies, 1971.

Brand, John. *Observations on the Popular Antiquities of Great Britain*, revised by Henry Ellis. 3 vols. 1849. Detroit: Singing Tree Press, 1969.

Carter, H. R. *Flax, Hemp and Jute Spinners' Catechism*. London: John Ball, Sons & Danielsson, 1910.

Charley, William. *Flax and Its Products in Ireland*. London: Bell and Daldy, 1882.

Coffin, Tristram Potter, and Hennig Cohen, eds. *Folklore in America*. Garden City, N.Y.: Anchor Books, 1970.

Copeland, M. T. *The Cotton Manufacturing Industry in the United States*. 1917. Reprint, New York: Augustus M. Kelley, 1966.

Copp, Terry. *The Anatomy of Poverty: The Condition of the Working*

Class in Montreal, 1897–1929. Toronto: McClelland and Stewart, 1974.

Crawford, W. H. *Domestic Industry in Ireland: The Experience of the Linen Industry.* Dublin: Gill and McMillan, 1972.

Devine, Francis. "Early Slaves of the Linen Trade." *Liberty*, February 1976.

Dickson, M. G. "Factory Workers' Philosophy." *Sociological Review* 28 (July 1936): 295–312.

Dodd, William. *The Factory System Illustrated.* New ed., 1842. Reprint, New York: Augustus M. Kelley, 1968.

Dohr, Fred. "The Linen Industry in Northern Ireland." *The Textile Quarterly* 2, no. 2 (1952): 142–157.

Factory and Workshop Act, 1901. In *The Public General Acts*, 1 Edw. 7, ch. 22. London: H. M. Stationery Office, 1901.

Fitzpatrick, W. J. *An Old-Timer Talking.* 2d ed. rev. Newcastle, Co. Down: Mourne Observer Press, 1963.

Flaxdressers' Trade and Benevolent Trade Union, Thirty-Fourth Annual Report, for Year Ending 31st December 1906. Belfast: W. & G. Baird, 1907.

Gailey, Alan, ed. "The Flax Harvest." *Ulster Folklife* 19 (1973): 24–29.

Gill, Conrad. *The Rise of the Irish Linen Industry.* Oxford: Clarendon Press, 1925.

Green, Archie. *Only a Miner.* Urbana: University of Illinois Press, 1972.

Green, E. R. R. "The Beginnings of Industrial Revolution." In *Ulster since 1800: A Political and Economic Survey,* edited by T. W. Moody and J. C. Beckett, pp. 28–38. London: British Broadcasting Corporation, 1954.

———. "Business Organization and the Business Class." In *Ulster since 1800: A Social Survey,* edited by T. W. Moody and J. C. Beckett, 2d ser., pp. 110–118. London: British Broadcasting Corporation, 1957, 1958.

———. *The Industrial Archaeology of County Down.* Belfast: H. M. Stationery Office, 1963.

———. *The Lagan Valley, 1800–1850.* London: Faber & Faber, 1949.

Greenway, John. *American Folksongs of Protest.* New York: Octagon Books, 1970.

———. "Folk Songs as Socio-Historical Documents." *Western Folklore* 19 (1960): 1–9.

Haggan, William. "Weaver's Rubric—3." *Linen Trade Circular,* 24 October 1959, p. 16.

Hamilton, Diana, coll. "So Early in the Morning." *So Early in the Morning.* Tradition Records TLP 1034.

Hill, Christopher. "Political Animal." Review of *Cromwell,* by Roger Howell, Jr. *New York Review of Books,* 9 June 1977, pp. 39–40.

Honeyman, A. M. "Fool's Errands for Dundee Apprentices." *Folklore* 69–70 (1958–1959): 334–336.

Hughes, Everett Cherrington. "Work and the Self." In *Psychology at the*

Crossroads, edited by John H. Rohrer and Muzafer Sherif, pp. 313–323. New York: Harper & Brothers, 1951.

Jones, Emrys. *A Social Geography of Belfast*. London: Oxford University Press, 1950.

Joyce, P. W. *A Social History of Ancient Ireland*. 2 vols. Dublin: M. H. Gill & Son, 1920.

Korson, George. *Black Rock: Mining Folklore of the Pennsylvania Dutch*. Baltimore: Johns Hopkins Press, 1960.

———. *Coal Dust on the Fiddle*. Philadelphia: University of Pennsylvania Press, 1938.

———. *Minstrels of the Mine Patch*. Philadelphia: University of Pennsylvania Press, 1938.

Laws, George Malcolm. *American Balladry from British Broadsides*. Publications of the American Folklore Society Bibliographical and Special Series, 8. Philadelphia: American Folklore Society, 1957.

"Linen Workers of Long Ago Are Still Earning Praise," *Linen Trade Circular*, 29 June 1957, p. 14.

Lloyd, A. L. *Folk Song in England*. London: Lawrence and Wishart, 1967.

McCaughan, M. "Flax Scutching in Ulster: Techniques and Terminology." *Ulster Folklife* 14 (1968): 6–13.

McNeilly, Norman. *Exactly Fifty Years: The Belfast Education Authority and Its Work (1923–73)*. Belfast: Blackstaff Press, 1974.

Marshall, Leslie C. *The Practical Flax Spinner*. London: Emmot and Company, 1885.

Mercier, Vivian. *The Irish Comic Tradition*. Oxford: Clarendon Press, 1962.

Monaghan, J. J. "The Rise and Fall of the Belfast Cotton Industry." *Irish Historical Studies* 3 (1942): 1–17.

Moody, T. W., and J. C. Beckett, eds. *Ulster since 1800: A Political and Economic Survey*. London: British Broadcasting Corporation, 1954.

———. *Ulster since 1800: A Social Survey*. 2d ser. London: British Broadcasting Corporation, 1957, 1958.

Moore, Alfred S. *Linen*. London: Constable and Company, 1922.

———. *Linen from the Raw Material to the Finished Product*. London: Sir Isaac Pitnam & Sons, 1914.

Mourne Observer, 1968–1970.

O'Brien, Nora Connolly. *Portrait of a Rebel Father*. Dublin: Talbot Press, 1935.

Opie, Peter. "England, the Great Undiscovered." *Folk-Lore* 65 (1954): 149–164.

Pinchbeck, Ivy. *Women Workers and the Industrial Revolution, 1750–1850*. New York: F. S. Crofts & Co., 1930.

Purdon, C. D. *The Mortality of Flax Mill and Factory Workers and the Diseases They Labour Under*. Belfast: Adair's Steam Printing Works, 1873.

———. *The Sanitary State of the Belfast Factory District during Ten*

Years (1864–1873). Belfast: H. Adair, 1877.

Purdon, Henry S. "Flax and Linen." In *Dangerous Trades*, edited by Thomas Oliver, pp. 691–701. London: John Murray, 1902.

Quinn, Hugh. "Notes to Children's Street Tunes and Games of Old Belfast." Typescript at the British Broadcasting Corporation in Belfast.

"Sale of What Is Probably Belfast's Oldest Mill." *Linen Trade Circular*, 11 January 1947, p. 3.

"'Shuttle Kissing' Doomed." *Linen Trade Circular*, 23 August 1952, p. 17.

Smelser, Neil J. *Social Change in the Industrial Revolution*. London: Routledge & Kegan Paul, 1959.

Smiley, James A. "Background to Byssinosis in Ulster." *British Journal of Industrial Medicine* 18 (1961): 1–9.

Smith, Alan. *Discovering Folklore in Industry*. Tring, Herts.: Shire Publications, 1969.

The Textile Quarterly. Belfast: H. R. Carter Publications.

Thompson, E. P. *The Making of the English Working Class*. New York: Pantheon Books, 1963.

Thompson, Paul. *The Edwardians: The Remaking of British Society*. London: Weidenfeld and Nicolson, 1975.

Thompson, Stith. *Motif-Index of Folk Literature: A Classification of Narrative Elements in Folktales, Ballads, Myths, Fables, Medieval Romances, Exempla, Jest Books, and Local Legends*. 2d ed. 6 vols. Bloomington, Ind., 1955–1957.

Thom's Official Directory of the United Kingdom of Great Britain and Ireland for the Year 1925. Dublin: Alexander Thom & Co., 1925.

Truck Act, 1896. *The Public General Acts*, 59 & 60 Vict., ch. 44. London: H. M. Stationery Office, 1896.

"Ulster Linen Lore." *Linen Trade Circular*, 3 January 1936, p. 1.

Usitat, Lynn (pseud.). "As I Walked Down Bedford Street." *Linen Trade Circular*, 13 November 1965, p. 8.

Whitford, F. J. "Joseph Devlin." *Threshold* 1, no. 2 (1957): 24–33.

Wilson, Colin, and Patricia Pitman. *Encyclopedia of Murder*. London: Arthur Barker, 1961.

Wright, Thomas. *The Great Unwashed*. London: Tinsley Brothers, 1868.

Index

"A foolish young girl was I," 106–107, 248n.12
"A for Barney," 43, 196; variants 43, 45
American Folksongs of Protest (Greenway), 5
"Annie thought she had it," 198; variant, 199
Anthropology, xx, 7–8
Apron: in Hackling Shop, 90, 102; in song, 90; in Spinning Room, 41, 42, 59, 192; in Weaving Shed, 135, 136–137. *See also* Glazer; Rubber
"At half-past five, the horn will blow," 58; variant, 58
Attitudes toward job
—favorable: of doffers, 34, 37, 40, 47; in general, xviii, xix, 33–34; of hacklers, 94, 108; of reelers, 72–73; of spinners, xv, xix, 27, 61, 62, 66, 69, 73, 76, 158, 205, 227; of weavers, 133, 137, 145, 148, 158, 160, 168. *See also* Coping with the job; Work conditions: favorable
—unfavorable: of doffers, 34, 46–47, 48; of factory males, 131, 144, 158, 160, 161; in general, 57–58; of hacklers, 106, 111; of spinners, 66–68. *See also* Industrial hazards; Work conditions: unfavorable
Attitudes toward workers. *See also* Social relationships; Status
—in factory: cloth passer, 140–141; male weavers, 158, 160; tenter, 142; weavers, 160
—gateman, 58
—in mill: band-tiers, 44; doffers, 136; doffing mistress, 49–51, 55; in

general, 33; hacklers, 94; hackling master, 100–101; in Machine Room, 177; reelers, 72; rovers, 76, 176; spinners, 51, 62–63, 78, 79, 81, 166, 176, 177; spinning master, 52, 55–56; tramp hacklers, 102

Ballysillan Mill, 223
Band-tier, 43–45, 47, 197, 206, 239; in song, 43, 44–45
"Band-Tier Song." *See* "A for Barney"
Bath Mill, 223, 251–252n.23
BBC, 46, 245n.8, 245n.17
Beetling, 23, 100
"Be in time," 58–59
Belfast, 17, 158, 190, 192, 193–194, 201
Belfast Trades' Council, 208
Bell, Sam Hanna, 120
Berth, of hackler, 86, 88, 90, 94, 99, 101, 102, 108, 119
Bessbrook (Mill), 223
"Billy Gillespie goes down the pass," 56; variant, 56
Blacksmith Shop, 170
Bleacher, 198
Bleaching, 10, 14, 21, 23
Boatright, Mody, 4
Braid (Mill), 103
Bundler, 22
Bundling, 21

Cager, 239
Cages, 37, 43, 69, 71
Caging, 37
Calendar holidays, 235–236; Christmas, 65, 176, 184, 201,